THE FRUITS OF CONTROVERSY

Other works by the same Author:

THE MINISTRIES OF THE ANGELIC POWERS: *According to the Old Testament and later Jewish literature*

THE ANGEL TEACHING OF THE NEW TESTAMENT

SUPERNATURAL: *The Doctrine of Spirits, Angels and Demons from the Middle Ages until the Present Time*

GOOD AND EVIL SPIRITS: *A study of the Jewish and Christian Doctrine, its Origin and Development*

SATAN: A PORTRAIT, *A study of the character of Satan through all the Ages*

ESSENTIALS OF DEMONOLOGY: *A study of Jewish and Christian Doctrine, its Origin and Development*

THE PILGRIM FATHERS

by Bernard F. Gribble

THE FRUITS OF CONTROVERSY

by

EDWARD LANGTON
D.D.(Lond.), F.R.Hist.S., F.R.A.S.

LUTTERWORTH PRESS
LONDON

Printed in Great Britain by
The Camelot Press Ltd., London and Southampton

TO ALL LOVERS OF
CIVIL AND RELIGIOUS
LIBERTY

ACKNOWLEDGMENTS

I DESIRE to express sincere acknowledgments to the many writers whose works I have consulted in the preparation of the following account of the struggle for life and liberty in England and Scotland. Direct citations have been acknowledged in the appropriate places. I have aimed, however, at avoiding numerous references to a large number of works, and to present a continuous narrative in my own words. This, I believe, will suit better the class of readers for whom I have specially written. But my sense of indebtedness to other workers is vast.

Preface

THE story of the winning of civil and religious liberty in these islands has often been told, and from many different points of view; but no apology is needed for offering a further account of events which have contributed so largely to produce the present situation in our social and national life. The subject is one of perennial, inexhaustible interest to all those who wish to conserve the gains of the past, and to extend still further the bounds of freedom.

Famous historians have frequently related the events in question in great detail, and in large volumes or series of volumes. There are many people, however, who have neither the time nor the inclination to read such extensive works, valuable as they are to the student who wishes to master a particular period. In the following pages I have kept the general reader in view. It has seemed to me that there is value in a straightforward, continuous narrative which avoids numerous references to works which are seldom available to the general reader. In the composition of this brief sketch of events, however, many source-books have been consulted; and chapter and verse could have been cited in support of all the main positions taken up, had this been thought to be desirable. For the purpose in view, it has seemed to me a better plan to indicate, at the end of the book, a small number of volumes which might well be consulted by those whose interest is aroused sufficiently to make them desire to delve more deeply into the subjects treated. The list is not a bibliography in the usual sense; nor is it claimed that the volumes indicated are the best books upon the subject.

They are simply a few books which have interested me and which I think may well prove to be interesting and instructive to others.

In writing of events which have provoked so much controversy I do not claim to have attained the virtue of complete impartiality, a quality which some people regard as being so very desirable in an historian. There are times when lovers of truth, freedom and righteousness must take sides. In present-day events, where one cannot be a mere spectator, this involves active participation. In treating of the events of the past, which yet have a meaning for the present and the future, it is reasonable and justifiable to indicate the rights and the wrongs of any given situation. At the same time, I have tried to avoid the partisan spirit, and to recognize the truth and value of whatever could be said on the other side. As it seems to me, it is not sufficient to say, with reference to any given controversy, that there was truth and good on both sides. For it has often happened that there was more of good and truth on the one side than on the other; and it is at least part of the duty of a student of history to weigh attitudes and events in the balance of judgment, and to draw his conclusions accordingly. I have endeavoured to do this in presenting a brief account of epoch-making movements which resulted in a great increase of liberty, both civil and religious, in these islands and far beyond.

E. L.

Contents

PART ONE

THE CONTROVERSY IN ENGLAND

PART TWO

THE CONTROVERSY IN SCOTLAND

PART THREE

THE FRUITS OF CONTROVERSY

Part One

THE CONTROVERSY IN ENGLAND

Chapter One

THE BACKGROUND OF THE PILGRIM MOVEMENT

FEW people travelling along the Great North Road southward from Doncaster and Bawtry, in Yorkshire, would gain the impression that they were approaching the birthplace of one of the great epoch-making movements of the world. The country is rather flat, and without any landmarks of striking interest. The population is very small, and almost entirely devoted to agricultural pursuits. Anything more placid could scarcely be imagined were it not for the swiftly-moving traffic on the great road which leads from London to Edinburgh. One can hardly imagine a district more unlikely to become the source of a great spiritual movement which would have world-wide effects.

Nevertheless, a mile or so beyond Bawtry we come to Scrooby, and in the Manor House of this tiny Nottinghamshire hamlet, with a population of some 200 people, events took place early in the seventeenth century which have had a permanent influence on the whole course of American history. Spiritual influences were there generated which are still operative in the life of the great continent, and to a great extent account for some of the noblest qualities in the life of a people destined increasingly to play an important part in the preservation of freedom throughout the world.

This story of a small group of country folk who sailed to lands beyond the seas is one that cannot be too well known. It has the power to warm the hearts of all lovers of religious and political liberty. It reminds us how costly has been the winning of the heritage of the free; and, in particular, with how great a struggle of brave men British and American freedom has been achieved.

To understand this movement aright we must see it in relation to its background in the history of our land. For several centuries the freedom-loving spirit of man had been restless under the despotic sway of the medieval Roman Catholic Church. On numerous occasions individuals or small companies of people, who had observed the contrast between the life and teaching of Jesus and that of the Church of their own day, were driven to criticism and revolt. One of the most powerful of these spiritual movements took place in the fourteenth century. Its leader was John Wycliffe of Lutterworth (1325-84). He was famous alike as scholar and evangelist. At first he was content to protest against the clerical abuses which were rampant throughout the land. Further inquiry and study of the Bible convinced him that the whole basis of the Church of his time was false, and that the teaching of the Bible had been perverted to enable the clerics to gain an absolute control over the lives of men.

The central doctrine of the papal system was that of transubstantiation, which affirmed that the most corrupt and ignorant priest had the power to transform the bread and wine used in the Lord's Supper or Mass into the veritable body and blood of Jesus. To partake of the Mass at the hands of the priest was the only way to obtain salvation. Wycliffe's study of the New Testament convinced him that the doctrine of the Mass as taught by Rome was a pure superstition; it was based upon a false interpretation of the words of Jesus. Anyone who reads the records of the trials for heresy which took place during the fifteenth and sixteenth centuries will see how frequently disbelief in this Romish superstition was urged as the ground of conviction and execution.

Many other false teachings and corrupt practices in the Church came to light as Wycliffe continued his investigations. He found, for example, that pilgrimages to the shrine of some departed saint were used by the clergy as a means of extorting large sums from the poor and ignorant people. Prayers for the dead, pardons and indulgences as well as auricular confessions, were used in the same way.

Wycliffe came to the conclusion that the only real remedy for this sorry state of things was that the people must be enabled to read the Scriptures in their own language. He therefore set to work to translate the Bible into the English language, and, with the help of others, he at last succeeded in his design. As the art of printing was yet unknown, each copy had to be made by hand, and the task was stupendous.

Wycliffe also wrote many treatises setting forth the falsity of the teaching of the clerics. His translation of the Scriptures and his other works were widely distributed by bands of his followers, known as the lollards, who travelled far and wide as evangelists and missionaries.

The ecclesiastics endeavoured with all their might to destroy this work of Wycliffe and his followers. It has sometimes been supposed that they achieved their object. There is, however, good reason to believe that, though driven underground, it still lived, and that there is a direct connection between Wycliffism and the Puritanism of the Pilgrim Fathers.

Opposition to the teaching of the Romish Church continued throughout the fifteenth century, and from well-authenticated trials for heresy it appears that between the death of Wycliffe in 1384 and 1470 at least a hundred-and-twenty persons were tried for heresy;

and probably there were many more. By the end of the fifteenth century there is evidence that groups of people were in existence who separated themselves from the Romish Church, and regularly met together in secret to hear the Word of God read and expounded by their own teachers. This was many years before the Act of Supremacy of 1534, which severed the Church of England from the See of Rome. Spiritually-minded people all over the Kingdom were longing for reform, and for the pure word of the Gospel. The answer of the Roman Church to the cry for the most moderate reforms was suppression and burning. The methods of the Inquisition, which had long been in use in Spain and the Netherlands, were put into operation in England, in order to bludgeon the hearts and minds of men and women into obedience to the rule of the Church.

It will be seen from the above that the desire of Henry VIII to secure a divorce from his wife, Catharine of Aragon, was not the sole or even the chief operating factor in bringing about the Reformation. It served as the occasion, and to some extent shaped the course of events. But profounder causes had already begun to operate, and without these no real reformation would have been possible.

We must pass quickly over the controversies which so greatly agitated the nation at this time, and the successive steps which at last led up to the claim of Henry to be "Supreme Head on earth of the Church of England". In making this claim he displaced the pope, and rendered necessary a violent change of attitude on the part of the clergy towards the pope, if they were to retain their benefices, and escape punishment. No longer must large sums of money ("first-fruits") be sent abroad to support the See of Rome. Nor must appeals, another source of gain to the papacy, be carried to Rome.

It is quite true that Henry was only a half-hearted reformer so far as belief and doctrine was concerned; and this fact counted for much in the years that followed. He had little sympathy with the spiritually-minded men whose souls were in revolt against the superstitions and corruptions of Rome, and were crying out for spiritual food and simpler forms of worship. The Ten Articles of Religion, published in 1536, show that doctrinally Henry remained very much what he was before the severance with Rome took place. Monasteries, however, were suppressed on a great scale; an event which involved much interference with the lives of a large number of people.

During the short reign of Edward VI the Reformation was carried many stages further. Had his reign been even of moderate duration, the course of events would have been widely different, and England might have been spared its most shameful hours. He was but nine years of age when he began to reign, and naturally he was largely influenced by his advisers. Some of these, however, were men of ability and great reforming zeal, and their ideas harmonized with the King's own religious views, which were far more advanced than those of his father.

On the death of Edward, his half-sister Mary succeeded to the throne. Daughter of Henry VIII and his divorced wife, Catharine of Aragon, it was natural that she should espouse the religion of her mother. She proved to be implacably opposed to the principles of the Reformation. Reaction immediately followed. Mary was married to Philip II of Spain. All statutes of Church reform passed since 1529 were repealed. Cardinal Pole received the kingdom back into the Roman jurisdiction. On bended knee the two houses of Parliament received absolution from its errors and schisms. It was the most humiliating hour the kingdom had ever known.

During the years that followed many of the noblest reformers were put to death, including Rogers, Hooper, Sanders, Latimer, Ridley, and Cranmer. The land was deluged in the blood of the martyrs. Within three or four years three hundred people were burned to death for expressing a desire to see the Church purged of its corruptions, corruptions which had been acknowledged by some of its most loyal adherents. The leading motive of Mary's life during the short reign of five years was to obey the dictates of Rome, and to please the dignitaries of the Church. The primary responsibility, therefore, for the baptism of blood by which Mary thought to extirpate heresy, as the teaching of the reformers was called, was that of the pope and his tools, the bishops and other ecclesiastical officials. The policy was cruel, and was carried out by ruthless men who appear to have lacked even the most rudimentary qualities of Christian kindness and love. When Mary's reign came to an end, many even of those who viewed the Roman religion with favour heaved a sigh of genuine relief.

On the death of Mary, Elizabeth, a daughter of Henry VIII and Anne Boleyn, came to the throne. Burnings, imprisonments and persecutions in favour of Roman Catholicism were immediately brought to an end. The Queen resumed control of the Church, which had been given up by Mary to the pope. She claimed to be not indeed the "Supreme Head of the Church on Earth", but the "Supreme Governor". Religiously, her attitude was that of a mild Protestantism. Rather than take the oath of supremacy which was required, affirming the Queen to be the Supreme Governor of the Church, all the bishops, with one exception, resigned their positions.

Very different, however, was the attitude of the clergy. The majority of these took the oath and kept their places, as they had done through all the changes of the last three reigns. It is calculated that of nine thousand four hundred clergy, less than one hundred and eighty refused to take the oath, and more than half of these were dignitaries. This fact has an important bearing on the later history of the puritans; it means that most of the clergy remained Roman Catholic at heart. The result was that over a large part of the country Romish ideas and practices continued to prevail. Many parts of England, particularly in the north, were scarcely touched by the ideas of the Reformation. When Grindal was transferred from London to York (1570), he tells us that he hardly seemed to be in the same country. The Romish fasts and festivals continued, old ideas of purgatory led the people to bring their offerings of money and eggs to the burial of the dead. He was compelled to issue injunctions against crossing, breathing over the sacramental bread and wine, the elevation of the elements for adoration, and also against the use of oil, chrism, tapers, spittle, and other Romish ceremonies at baptism.

Elizabeth's own personal tastes were in favour of retaining much that had been associated with the Roman religion. Whilst breaking the connection with Rome, she was loth to give up forms and ceremonies which, in the eyes of reformers, were an essential part of the papal system. She was fond of pomp and magnificence in worship. In her own private chapel she retained the altar and the crucifix, and many ceremonies remained unchanged. She appointed a committee of divines to revise Edward's liturgy, and instructed them to strike out all offensive passages against the pope, and to relieve the minds of the people about the corporal presence of Christ in the Sacrament. But nothing was to be said in favour of the views of the stricter Protestants.

On the accession of Elizabeth many of the exiles, who had sought refuge on the Continent from the persecuting fury of Mary, returned home. From now on we begin to notice the trend of things which resulted in the movement known as "Puritanism". Whilst on the Continent, mainly at Geneva, these returned exiles had become imbued with reforming ideas which in those places had found a hospitable home. The ideas of Luther and Calvin had there become established. We have seen that the consciousness of the need for reformation in the Church had been felt in England long before the time of Luther and Calvin. Many of the ideas which these later reformers cherished had already been propagated. The pace of the movement, however, was now much quickened, and new ideas in reference especially to Church government were advocated.

Another question which now came under discussion was the nature and number of vestments and ceremonies which were suitable for ministers who were called and appointed to advocate the religion of the lowly Nazarene. This was not merely "Much ado about Nothing", as has often been suggested. It was quite impossible at that time that these things should be viewed as matters of no significance. They had a profound meaning for the people generally. They were closely interwoven with the old corrupt and cruel Romish religion. They were referred to as "rags of popery" or as "dregs of popery". Even in the view of some of the milder reformers they tended to idolatry and superstition. Jewell, afterwards Bishop of Salisbury, said that whilst the doctrine of the Reformed Church was pure, "as to ceremonies and maskings there is a little too much foolery". Another dignitary, writing to a friend, asks: "Should we not rather quit the ministry of the Word and Sacraments, than that these relics of the Amorites should be admitted?"

In view of the association of the rites and ceremonies with the papal system, many clergy, including a considerable number of influential dignitaries, urged that the rites and ceremonies should be simplified. They held that the clergy should be distinguished from the people by their doctrine rather than by their garments, and by their purity of mind rather than by the adornment of their person. The use of a seemly preaching gown was suggested. It was also requested that at the celebration of the Lord's Supper the posture of kneeling, as suggesting the adoration of the elements, should be left optional: also that the sign of the cross in baptism should be omitted.

The Queen, however, had other ideas, and she was the "Governor of the Church". She was determined that Church rites and ceremonies should be of one pattern. Uniformity must be the leading characteristic of the Church. On March 26, 1566, the London clergy were summoned to Lambeth, and in the presence of Archbishop Parker, Grindal, Bishop of London, and certain others, the Bishop's Chancellor, pointing to Robert Cole, Rector of St. Mary-le-Bow, who was habited in a square cap, a scholar's gown, and tippet, said: "The Council's pleasure is, that strictly ye keep the unity of apparel like to this man . . . as you see him . . . and in the Church a linen surplice: and inviolably observe the rubric of the Book of Common Prayer, and the Queen's Majesty's Injunctions: and the Book of Convocation (i.e., the Thirty-nine Articles). Ye that will presently subscribe, write *volo*; ye that will not subscribe, write *nolo*. Be brief: make no words."

The roll of the churches was then called, and of the ninety-eight clergy present sixty-one submitted. Those who refused, numbering thirty-seven, were suspended, and notified that unless they yielded within three months they would be deprived. A few conformed; some entered secular callings, and others were imprisoned.

The Queen sent a letter to the two archbishops directing them to investigate the practices of the clergy in respect of rites and ceremonies, and to employ such methods as would secure exact uniformity.

Thus was the idol of uniformity set up. Many decrees were passed, and proclamations issued to force the people into an absolute uniformity. A first offence against the Acts of Supremacy and Uniformity was punished by forfeiture of lands and goods; a second offence by forfeiture, excommunication and outlawry; whilst a third offence was declared to be high treason. Every clergyman was obliged to use the Book of Common Prayer under a penalty of a fine of a whole year's income of his living, and a term of imprisonment. For a second offence he was deprived of his living. Severe penalties were also imposed upon offending laymen. Every person who failed to attend the parish church, or some recognized place of worship, on Sunday and holy days was fined a shilling for each case of absence, unless he could prove a valid reason. The fines were collected by the churchwardens.

The Archbishop, Matthew Parker, was compelled to be the tool of Elizabeth, and to see that her ideas of uniformity were meticulously carried out. He was ordered to make visitations in various parts of the country, and to send up the names of *recusants*, as these early objectors to conformity were called. On these occasions diligent inquiry was made as to anyone who privily used or frequented any kind of divine service, or common prayer other than that enjoined by law. Any one who attended secret conventicles, preachings, lectures, or readings was suspected of heresy, and duly reported to the Queen's Council. In 1571 the Archbishop of York sent out injunctions which required all persons above fourteen years of age to receive the Communion in their own churches three times at least in the year. Notwithstanding these savage regulations to enforce uniformity, however, the situation, from the Queen's point of view, grew worse rather than better. In 1573 therefore she sternly ordered the prelates, justices, and other responsible officers to see that the Act was more rigidly enforced.

When the comparatively mild Grindal became archbishop (1576), still further efforts were made to suppress conventicles and secret worship of every kind. Deprived ministers and laymen were forbidden to speak publicly on religion. The Queen threatened to make examples of such bishops as failed to imprison all who attended "unlawful assemblies". Any criticism of the Queen's religious intolerance was construed as defamation and dealt with accordingly. When Whitgift became archbishop (1583) he issued an order to every priest in his jurisdiction to warn all Nonconformists as to the error of their ways, and to threaten them with excommunication and arrest.

Whitgift was a man after the Queen's own heart, delighting to "tithe mint, anise and cummin". He prohibited all private catechizing, and the holding of any religious service shared by non-members of a household. No man was to be allowed to preach who did not wear the prescribed apparel, who would not affirm the Queen's supremacy over the Church, who had not a bishop's licence, and was not prepared to express his willingness to affirm that the Prayer Book and the Thirty-nine Articles were agreeable in every part to the Word of God.

A new Parliament, summoned in 1593, condemned persistent Nonconformists to banishment and death; whilst at the same time the Queen's popish preferences found expression in the proviso "that no Popish recusant shall be compelled or bound to abjure, by virtue of this Act."

Such was the régime under which the Pilgrim Fathers lived their early days. It remains for us to glance at the moral and spiritual condition of the country after so many attempts to compel the people to walk in the strait way of uniformity. In many ways the condition of things was truly lamentable. A large part of the population was sunk in the crassest ignorance and superstition. Even those who yielded to the pressure placed upon them and entered the churches were often fed with mere external forms and ceremonies. Seldom did they hear the Gospel proclaimed. Many of the clergy indeed were quite incapable of preaching the Gospel. And in numerous churches the Gospel was not preached for many years in succession. This was in some cases due to the fact that a considerable number of clergy were appointed to a plurality of parishes. For example, one clergyman was the Vicar of St. Dunstan's, London, who at the same time held livings in Yorkshire, Warwickshire and Middlesex. But this was not the only cause of the non-existence of preaching in the days of which we speak. More often the cause was sheer incapacity to preach. Soon after Edward VI came to the throne, a Book of Homilies, or sermons in English, was prepared, to help the clergy who were largely incapable of making sermons, even of the rudest type. But some of the clergy were even too ignorant to read the Homilies intelligently: so it was stated in a sermon preached before the King in the year 1550. Many parishes were without any pretence of a preaching ministry. In some parishes no sermon had been preached since the suppression of the Black Preaching Friars some fifteen years before. In many parishes there had been little, if any, religious teaching for generations. During the reign of Queen Elizabeth the President and Council of the North of England informed the Privy

Council that in several of the churches there had literally never been a sermon for years, and that many of the ministers were utterly unable to teach. In a report of the Diocese of Chichester in 1569 it was stated that there were churches where there had not been a sermon once in seven years, or even once in twelve. There were beneficed men who had preached in Queen Mary's days, but who would not preach in Queen Elizabeth's time, and who yet had held their livings during all the ten years since Mary died.

Even Archbishop Grindal was shocked at the spiritual destitution which was revealed on inquiry. When Elizabeth urged him to put down the preachings, or "prophesyings", as they were called, of those who wished to supply this great lack, he urged that the public and continual preaching of God's Word is the ordinary means and instrument of the salvation of mankind. By this means the glory of God is enlarged, faith is nourished, and charity is increased. He reminded the Queen that he had been careful to admit to this office only competent men, belonging neither to the papistical nor puritanic parties, and generally only such as were graduates of the University. He also urged the fact that he had consulted other bishops who agreed with him that the prophesyings were profitable to the Church. Therefore he could not suppress these exercises without violating his conscience.

We do well to keep these facts in mind when considering the emphasis laid by the puritans upon preaching. As Dr. Paget, a former Bishop of Oxford, remarked: "It is easy to laugh at the puritan exaltation of sermons, at their vehement denunciation of an unpreaching ministry; but it is unjust to forget the greatness and the persistence of the neglect which they denounced."

So devoted, however, was Elizabeth to the worship of her idol of uniformity that she was greatly offended at the archbishop's representations, and resolved that he should be suspended and sequestered. Ignoring his authority, she sent her own commandment to the bishops to put down the preachings. Until his death seven years later, so far as his office was concerned, the archbishop was practically a dead man.

Chapter Two

SUCH is the background against which we must see the early Puritan or Nonconformist movement. To give a full account of this movement would take us much too far afield. The reformers were not all of one mind as to the best way of rescuing the Church from its long imprisonment, and of cleansing it from its manifold corruptions. It was to be expected that after the repression of centuries there would be a reaction towards an extreme individualism. The evils were many and various, and it is not surprising that even the most sincere and serious-minded men should differ as to the remedies that should be applied. That various parties should spring up, each urging its own proposals, was inevitable from the circumstances of the time.

There were, however, certain guiding principles which all parties agreed should determine their course of action.

First, they were agreed that the Bible, and particularly the New Testament, should be the standard of doctrine. We have seen that Wycliffe in the fourteenth century made this the touchstone by which he tested the claims and the practices of the Roman Church. What Jesus said and did must be held to be of infinitely more worth than any number of ideas and practices which had gradually come into vogue through the centuries by absorption from many different sources. To end the long night of darkness, Jesus, "the light of the world", must be known as He is portrayed in the New Testament. And it is chiefly because Wycliffe gave the benighted people the

Scriptures in their own language that he is fitly called the "Morning Star of the Reformation". The invention of printing in the fifteenth century and the publication of Tyndale's translation of the New Testament (1525) did more than anything else to make the reformation of the Church inevitable. Now for the first time it was possible for Christian people in general to approach the fountain-head of Christian truth, and to discover the nature of Christianity by a study of the primitive documents.

It is difficult for those of us who have been accustomed all our lives to the enjoyment of the freedom to read the Scriptures, to think ourselves back into the mental and spiritual atmosphere of the times of which we are speaking. It seems so natural and reasonable a thing that Christians should be heartily encouraged to read about the founder of their religion, and the early days of the movement of which they now form part, that we can hardly imagine any objection being made to such a reasonable exercise of liberty. But facts are stubborn things. And the fact is that the last thing the authorities of the Roman Church wanted at this time was that the Bible should be read by the common people. All kinds of arguments were raised against bestowing this privilege upon the people, and the sternest measures were adopted to prevent it. Fuller, who was an Anglican clergyman, and no Separatist, writing towards the middle of the seventeenth century, vividly describes the alarm felt by the Romanists when copies of the Bible in the vernacular began to appear. He says: "When the Testament of Tyndale's translation came over into England, O how were the Popish clergy cut to the hearts! How did their blear eyes smart at the shining of the Gospel in the vulgar tongue! Down must be their Dagon, if this ark be set up; down must be their Diana, if Paul be permitted to preach to the people. Some said the Bible ought not to be translated; some said that it could not be, that it was impossible; others, that it would make men rebel against the king." So full of wrath, he says, were they that they procured his book to be publicly burned in St. Paul's Churchyard, and effected the strangling and the burning of Tyndale in Flanders in the year 1536.

When Tyndale was brought out for execution, he prayed: "Lord, open the King of England's eyes." His prayer was more abundantly fulfilled than ever he imagined. More important even than the opening of the eyes of the King was the opening of the eyes of the people of England. That was the fruitful result of the translation of the Bible and its reading by the English people. They were now able to compare the beliefs and practices of the Church with the teaching of Jesus as recorded in the New Testament. They were able to study the principles of Church government for themselves. In these matters the contrast was so great that it could not fail to make a profound impression upon even the most simple-minded reader.

Another thing about which the great majority of the puritans were agreed was that, under the circumstances, separation from the Church was absolutely necessary. It was quite impossible for them to nourish their souls upon the superstitions that were often the only things that were offered to them in the churches. We have seen that even the simplest preaching of the Gospel was almost non-existent. Colet, Dean of St. Paul's, was hated by the clergy because he boldly denounced their failure in moral character and religious duty. Instead of preaching Christian truth, they urged the people to go on pilgrimage, to observe fasts, to invoke the saints, and to use other unscriptural practices. They actually encouraged them to carry wax candles round the cornfields in seedtime, assuring them that they would work so effectively that weeds would be destroyed. They exhibited drops of the blood of

the martyr Stephen, and some of the coals on which St.
Lawrence had been roasted. The boots of St. Thomas of
Canterbury and the bones of St. Botolph, if carried in
procession, it was said, would assuredly bring rain in time
of drought.

Colet told the people that the saints could not save
them. "Does heresy exist in England?" he exclaimed. "Of
course it does. The greatest heresy in England is the lives
of the clergy. They are in many cases vicious and depraved
from the bishop downward."

Is it any wonder that people who read the New
Testament came to the conclusion that clergy who lived
licentious lives, or who enjoined such superstitious
practices, were no worthy representatives of the religion of
Jesus? The Church which sanctioned such a condition of
things was not the Church which existed in the minds of
Jesus and Paul. Yet the people were compelled by law to
attend the services of the Church, and to receive the Sacrament of the Lord's Supper at the hands of the mis-
representatives of Jesus. Even simple abstention from
the services was sternly punished. To read the Bible
was a crime. To gather together in order to listen to a
devout layman expounding the Gospel was punishable by
death.

At first the puritans had no idea of separating from the
Church. They were only concerned to feed their souls, and
to practise the precepts of Christianity. But when the
Church turned upon them and savagely rent them, they
naturally began to ask questions about the nature and
constitution of the Church. Was this despotic, tyrannical
Church the true Church of Christ, or had it become
apostate? As they searched the Scriptures, it seemed to the
puritans that the hierarchical system which then existed
was foreign to New Testament teaching. Here they
read nothing about archbishops, monarchical bishops,

chancellors, and archdeacons, or many other things which existed in the Church of their own day. They found that the Church was a living fellowship under the benign rule of pastors and elders. From St. Paul they learned that God had set in the Church prophets, evangelists, pastors, and teachers, "for the perfecting of the saints, unto the work of ministering, unto the building up of the body of Christ" (Eph. 4: 11f.). Here was nothing about the King or Queen being Head or Governor of the Church; nothing about the divine right of bishops to hold despotic sway over the Church. There was no warrant here for the division of any country into parishes, or for the idea that everyone in the parish was a member of the Church, and must attend the services or suffer severe penalties.

These facts came home to the hearts and minds of these truth-seekers with the force of a new discovery. One of the first men to think along these lines was Robert Browne, a graduate of Cambridge University (1572), and afterwards an active leader in the puritan movement in East Anglia. At Cambridge he came under the influence of Thomas Cartwright, a famous theological scholar, who lectured on the constitution of the Church. Cartwright eventually reached the position that nothing should be established in · the Church but what was enjoined in Scripture. Each church should be governed by its own ministers and presbyters, and no man ought to be admitted to the ministry unless he was able to preach. These, and many other points, urged by this noted scholar and eloquent preacher, made a great stir in the University. Simple matters as they seem to us, who are familiar with the New Testament teaching and the practice of the Free Churches, they were at that time regarded as revolutionary and exceedingly dangerous. As a result, Cartwright lost his professorship and fellowship, and was expelled the University. In 1573 he went abroad, and became the minister of a congregation of English people at Antwerp, and later at Middleberg in Zeeland.

Among those influenced by Cartwright was Robert Browne. He was a man of serious mind and considerable ability. After leaving Cambridge, we are told that "he fell into great care, and was sore grieved while he long considered many things amiss, and the cause of all to be the woeful and lamentable state of the Church." After much thought, he took the view of the Church which afterwards became embodied in Congregationalism. He asserted that it is not in harmony with the teaching of the New Testament that the entire baptized population of a given parish should be regarded as the Church of Christ. The kingdom of God, he said, is not to be begun by whole parishes, but rather by the gathering of individuals into a fellowship of which Christ is the Head and Centre of attraction and union. Working on these simple principles, which are surely in accord with the New Testament teaching, he, and a friend, Richard Harrison, another Cambridge man, organized a Free Church in Norwich in 1581. In other places in East Anglia, especially in Bury St. Edmunds, assemblies of the common people gathered together, sometimes a hundred at a time, in private houses and conventicles. For this simple obedience to New Testament teaching, Browne was imprisoned. On his release, he went to Middleberg, in Zeeland, where, in 1582, he published three books in which he gave expression to his principles. One of these, entitled *A Treatise of Reformation without Tarrying for anie*, became famous, and exerted much influence in the direction of Separatism. These works of Browne were conveyed secretly to England, and in June, 1583, a royal proclamation was issued against them: all copies of these and any such books must be destroyed. At the Assizes held at Bury St. Edmunds, John Copping and Elias Thacker were convicted of sedition for spreading such books and hanged immediately. It was ruled that criticism of the Church, of which the Queen was mistress, was sedition against the Queen's person.

Robert Browne was, however, not the originator of the Congregationalist Separatist movement, as is sometimes erroneously supposed, though he is the best-known leader. A movement, inspired by similar principles, had previously arisen in London some time before 1571. In a State Paper of this period we find a reference to what was probably the earliest organized Congregational Church after the Reformation. From this we learn that a petition, signed by twenty-seven persons, was presented to the Queen. The object of the petitioners was to urge the necessity of ecclesiastical reform. They speak of themselves as being "a congregation whom God hath separated from the Church of England and from the mingled false worshipping therein". They tell how, Sabbath by Sabbath, they meet in houses, and on the fourth day of the week come together to use prayer and to exercise discipline on them that deserve it, "by the strength and true warrant of the Lord God's Word". Their minister, Richard Fitz, they say, has been imprisoned and killed, and a great multitude of others.

Along with this petition there is a printed sheet entitled *The trewe marks of Christ's Church, etc.* These are said to be three: (1) the glorious Word and evangel are preached freely and purely; (2) the Sacraments are administered according to the institution and good word of the Lord Jesus; and (3) discipline is administered agreeably to the same heavenly and almighty Word. Another document along with these sets forth reasons for separation from the Anglican Church.

What became of this little community, practising the religion of Jesus on the primitive model, we do not know. Probably they were scattered by persecution, after the leaders had been imprisoned. This was a frequent happening in those days. In 1586, for example, twenty-one persons were met together one Sunday in the house of Henry Martin in the city. As they were listening to the reading of the Scriptures by John Greenwood, they were arrested by the officers of the Bishop of London, and taken as prisoners to his palace at Fulham for examination. Eleven of the number were kept close prisoners. One of these died of the infection of the prison; two others died in the prison.

John Greenwood, who is referred to above as reading the Scriptures on the occasion mentioned, was also an influential leader of these times. Graduating at Cambridge in 1581, he was ordained by the Bishop. Soon, however, Browne's *Treatise of Reformation without Tarrying for anie* came into his hands. His mind was greatly perturbed as he thought upon the questions then being hotly debated. Four years later he was deprived of his benefice by the bishop, "for the disliking he had to the order of the Book of Common Prayer." A little later we find him acting as chaplain to a puritan nobleman, Lord Rich, at Rochford Hall, in the county of Essex. He and another conducted services in a room at the Hall, and the people forsook the parish church and went in large numbers to hear these Gospel preachings. Soon, however, Greenwood had to flee for his life from the wrath of the bishop, and took refuge in London. There he joined the fellowship of the secret Church, at one of the services of which we have seen him reading the Scriptures. In 1587 he was arrested, along with twenty others, "for being at private conventicles in Henry Martin's house in St. Andrew's in Wardropp." He was examined before the Bishop of London, and sent to await his doom in the Clink Prison.

We now come across another name worthy of honourable mention in this brief account of those who influenced the minds of the Pilgrim Fathers. Henry Barrowe was the son of a Norfolk squire. In early days he had been trained for the law, and lived a wanton life. One day, however, passing a London church, and hearing a preacher's voice, he turned in, and was suddenly converted. Lord Bacon, his kinsman, states that "he made a leap from a vain and libertine youth to a preciseness in the highest degree." Henry Barrowe and John Greenwood became intimate friends. On hearing that John Greenwood had been sent as a prisoner to the Clink, Barrowe went to visit him. He was at once arrested, and sent in a boat up the river to Lambeth, where he was examined by Whitgift, who was now archbishop.

At the Newgate Sessions of May, 1587, both Greenwood and Barrowe were indicted for "withdrawing from the religion now by Her Highness's authority established." Both were committed to the Fleet Prison.

From May, 1587, until his execution at Tyburn in April, 1593, Barrowe lay in prison. During his imprisonment he wrote a number of books setting forth what he held to be sound principles of Church government. The sheets were smuggled out of prison as he wrote them, and printed abroad at Dort. His main contention is that a truly Christian Church must be composed of truly spiritual men. It is a company of faithful people, separated from unbelievers, gathered in the name of Christ, whom they truly worship and readily obey. They claim the Christian liberty to practise whatever God has commanded and revealed unto them in His holy Word. The Word of God, and not tradition, is to be their guide. Such a company of spiritual men, recognizing the headship of Christ, has both the right and the power of self-government and of discipline. Barrowe is therefore opposed to all ecclesiastical hierarchies. Christ is the Head of His Church (Eph. 5: 23), and no other is necessary or desirable.

Such views find very strong support in Scripture, as is now generally recognized. They were, however, fundamentally opposed to that system of Church government which had grown up during the centuries. This now recognized the Queen as Governor or Mistress of the Church, and it was ruled as with an iron rod by the Privy Council, archbishops, bishops, and archdeacons. These persons enforced their will by means of the Star Chamber and the Court of High Commission. Scriptural authority mattered nothing to these worshippers of the idol of uniformity. Spiritual devotion to Jesus, the Head of the Church, and passionate zeal for true religion, and for the cleansing of the land from its manifold corruptions—these were as the small dust of the balance as compared with an offence against the man-made rules and ceremonies, in which the Church had become encased. Barrowe and Greenwood were convicted of publishing seditious books and condemned to death for the offence.

I shall not attempt to tell in detail the pathetic story of the martyrdom of these puritan heroes. On the morrow of their sentence (March 23, 1593) they were taken out of their dungeon. After their chains had been struck off, they were bound to the death-cart. But a reprieve arrived, and they were taken back to prison. A week later they were again taken to Tyburn, where they were tied by their necks to a tree. They were allowed to address the people. They prayed for the Queen, the magistrates, and the people, and also for their enemies. Again a reprieve arrived, and they were escorted back to the prison amidst the rejoicing of the people. Finally, on April 6, 1593, they went forth once again to Tyburn and were executed, true martyrs in the cause of religious freedom.

I have already pointed out that all the puritan reformers were not of one mind as to the best way of carrying out

the much-needed reformation of the Church. In addition
to the Congregationalists (or Independents), whose views
have been given above, there were those who maintained
that each community of Christians should be ruled by a
session of *elders*, making use of a term to which there are
many references in the New Testament (Greek *presbuteroi*).
These were known as Presbyterians, by a simple trans-
literation of the Greek word. This party made a notable
contribution to the religious controversies of the seventeenth century. Without some knowledge of their point of
view, we cannot understand the many-sided puritan
movement. A fuller account of the working out of the
principles of Presbyterianism will be given in Part Two of
this work, when we come to treat of the Reformation in
Scotland.[1] It is admitted that in the New Testament
period the Christian communities or churches were very
largely governed by presbyters. The bishops were simply
presbyters elected to discharge particular functions, much
as a chairman is elected to preside at a meeting, or a
person may be delegated to discharge a commission, while
still maintaining the same character or rank as those who
have selected him. So, in the earliest days, the bishop was
only "first among equals". It was only later that the
bishop was recognized as belonging to a class different
from the presbyter. The word *episkopein*, from which
bishop is derived, has a very simple meaning. It means
simply "to oversee" or "to superintend", that is, the
affairs of the Church; and at first the functions of the
bishops were limited to a single community. These
functions corresponded very closely to those of the pastor
or minister of any Free Church to-day. If this fact is kept
in mind it will be seen how vast are the accretions which
have gathered round the term *bishop* during the succeeding
centuries.

[1] See especially pp. 129ff.

The Presbyterians repeated the mistake of the Episcopalians. They espoused the false ideal of uniformity. As a
matter of fact, no one form of Church government is
precisely defined in the New Testament; hence the many
different forms of Church constitution which can reason-
ably claim the sanction of the New Testament. Certainly
there is much in the New Testament which can be cited
in support of the Presbyterian constitution; but there is
much also that makes it difficult or impossible to suppose
that this is the one and only basis of Church organization.
In their passion for uniformity, the Presbyterians were as
foolish as the Episcopalians; and their attempts to force
all Christian people, and, indeed, all the nation, whether
Christian or not, to accept this one form of ecclesiastical
policy was a criminal bludgeoning of the rights of reason
and conscience. Despite the many references in the New
Testament to presbyters, there is far more to be said for
the principle of free association of Christian people embodied in Congregationalism or Methodism than there is
for an enforced uniformity such as was attempted in
Presbyterianism or Episcopalianism at that time. In any
case, any attempt to enforce a uniformity in religious
thought and usage by the use of the secular power is a
gross infringement of the liberty of the Christian man. It
offends against any reasonable interpretation of the
teaching of Jesus.

We have seen that during the last half of the sixteenth
century there sprang up, in various parts of the country,
but particularly in London and East Anglia, small groups
of serious-minded people who themselves wished to find,
and then to show to others, the way of salvation. At first
they were not agitators or contentious people, resolved to
overturn the system of Church government. They were
rather people in deep concern for their soul's well-being.
They found that the ministries of the Church did not

satisfy them. They longed to hear the Gospel message—
the good news of God in Jesus Christ—and preachers at
that time were almost non-existent. They desired to feed
on the bread of life, and were offered the mere chaff of
superstitious usages by priests, "teaching", as Jesus said
of the Scribes and Pharisees, "as their doctrines the
precepts of men" (Matt. 15: 9). They transgressed the
commandment of God because of their traditions (Matt.
15: 3). Truly, "the sheep looked up, and were not
fed".

No one who has any regard for the New Testament
teaching can deny the right of the hungry sheep to be fed
with the food which God Himself has provided in His
Word. Nor can it be said that, when the pastors of the
Church failed in their most elementary duty, those pastors
had any sound reason for preventing the followers of
Jesus from seeking food elsewhere. Yet when those hungry
people sought to do this, all the machinery of the ecclesia-
tical and civil powers was set in motion to harry, torment,
and destroy them. It was decreed that they must attend
the services of the Church, however spiritually worthless
those services had proved themselves to be—and we must
remember that the most impartial writers have testified to
the corruption and shameful failure of the Church at this
time—or else suffer the penalties of fine, imprisonment,
and cruel death. On the other hand, they must *not* read
the Bible in their own homes, or meet together to hear
it expounded by pious and learned men, for this was
regarded as an aggravation of their crime.

Was it not inevitable, in view of this gross dereliction
of duty on the part of the ecclesiastical authorities, and
in view of this almost complete denial of the spirit and
teaching of Jesus, that deeper questions should be started
as to the right of this Church to claim to represent Jesus of
Nazareth? It was under these circumstances that the

Separatist or Nonconformist Churches took their rise. And it can be truly said that, in a vast number of ways, the puritan movement has proved itself to have been born of the Spirit of God to promote the salvation of the world.

Chapter Three

THE SOCIETIES AT SCROOBY AND GAINSBOROUGH

"THE wind bloweth where it listeth, and thou hearest the voice thereof, but knowest not whence it cometh, and whither it goeth: so is every one that is born of the spirit" (John 3: 8). This saying of Jesus comes readily to mind as we visit Scrooby and strive to realize that it was the birthplace of one of the great epoch-making movements in the history of the world. It is quiet, pleasant, and unpretentious. There is nothing to suggest that here, not so very long ago, the freedom-loving spirit of man revolted against an ancient tyranny, and, rather than allow itself to be deprived of its birthright, bade farewell to home and kindred and went forth to a strange land, sacrificing all for the sake of freedom of worship and of life.

In the days of which we are speaking, Scrooby was, in a number of ways, a much more notable place than it is to-day. It was an important posting-station on the Great North Road, which runs from London to Berwick and then on to Edinburgh. The road has now been taken some little distance from the village. The goings to and fro on this old Roman highway had not a little to do with the story of the Pilgrim Fathers. Bawtry, about a mile and a half away, was a notable centre of Roman Catholic influence. Robert Morton, of Bawtry, in 1390, founded the Hospital of St. Mary Magdalen, which still remains. Long after the Reformation, the family of Mortons were firm supporters of Roman Catholicism. In the early days of Queen Elizabeth, Nicholas Morton sought refuge in Rome, but during the next thirty years, whilst some of the

43

leading members of the pilgrim movement were growing into youth and manhood, he might have been seen passing to and fro along this highway on his secret missions between Rome and England. He was involved in the Romanist rising of 1569. This was also the man who, in 1570, brought over the papal bull by which Pope Pius V declared Queen Elizabeth a heretic, and proclaimed that she had forfeited her crown. The fact that the corruptions of the Roman Church still largely prevailed here, and that the principles of the Reformation had only slightly changed the face of things, had an influence in shaping the movement with which we are concerned.

The *Domesday Book* shows that the Manor of Scrooby belonged to the archbishops of York. For centuries later it was the centre of important events upon which we can touch but slightly here. Judging from the notable people who stayed there, often bringing with them numerous companies, a large residence or palace must have been established there primarily for the use of the archbishop and his retinue when travelling in this part of his large province. Seven or eight archiepiscopal residences belonged to the See of York, and the prelate was continually itinerating among them. Early in the sixteenth century Archbishop Savage, who was fond of hunting, is said to have considerably extended the place. Hawks and hounds, we are told, in the early days, frequently attended the archbishops in their travels. Behind the archbishop there rode a long train of domestics.

Wolsey, next but one in succession to Archbishop Savage, who was promoted to the See in 1514, spent but little time in his northern province. It was not until 1529, when he had fallen from royal favour, that he came northward. After spending some time at his manor of Southwell, he came to Scrooby. The notorious Bonner, afterwards Bishop of London, in the reign of Queen Mary, was a member of his train, and a letter from him to Thomas Cromwell is dated "At Scrooby with my Lord's grace" in 1530. The fallen minister spent three months at Scrooby. Thence he travelled to York, and two months later he died at Leicester Abbey. Ere he died he sent a message to the King urging him to put down the new pernicious sect of the Lutherans. Little did he dream that within the short period of eleven years, in 1541, when the King himself slept a night at Scrooby on his way north, the sect of the Lutherans would be supreme in the State. The King himself would be, in some measure, a Lutheran, the link with Rome would be broken, and the nation would have passed over to the Protestant faith. Still less could it be foreseen that at the beginning of the next century a movement would originate at Scrooby, among a small band of serious-minded men, which in a very few years would establish, in a land beyond the seas, the principles of freedom and self-government that are rooted in the truths of the Reformation.

In course of time great changes took place at Scrooby. It became customary for the archbishops of York to grant a lease of the Manor House at Scrooby, with its park and lands, to a tenant. And in 1575–76 Archbishop Sandys appointed William Brewster as his receiver at Scrooby, and as the bailiff of the Manor House. This William Brewster was the father of the Elder Brewster who was destined to be one of the Pilgrim Fathers. The latter was probably born somewhere about the year 1566. Not much is known about his early years, but doubtless he received his early education at a village school. Thence he went to Cambridge University, where he matriculated at Peterhouse in 1580, when only fourteen years of age. He does not seem to have remained at the University long enough to take a degree.

When next we hear of Brewster he had entered the

service of William Davison, the Queen's representative in the Netherlands and at one time Secretary of State and Clerk to the Privy Council. Davison was a man of high Christian character and considerable ability, and was employed by his sovereign in the carrying through of delicate negotiations and in the discharge of much important business. Just how he came to engage the services of Brewster is not clear. Quite probably Davison first came to know the young man when he stayed at Scrooby on his various journeyings to Scotland. The important fact is that, in the service of Davison, from 1583 onwards, Brewster would for several years be in contact with refined and well-educated people. Bradford, later Governor of the colony founded in America by the Pilgrim Fathers, who knew him well, tells us that Davison found young Brewster so discreet and faithful that he trusted him above all others who were employed in his service, and that he treated him rather as a son than as a servant.

A swift reversal of fortune, however, awaited both Davison and Brewster, and our story now touches the tragic history of Mary Queen of Scots. Owing to events which we shall not attempt to relate here,[1] in 1568 Mary, Queen of Scots, came into the hands of Queen Elizabeth, who kept her a prisoner for eighteen years. Mary was an ardent Roman Catholic, and during all this time she was the centre of Romanist plots to secure her own release, and for the assassination of Elizabeth. Mary was entrapped into a secret correspondence with Romanists at home and abroad. At the same time, the Babington conspiracy was hatched. With the blessing of the pope, nearly a dozen young papists bound themselves together to kill Elizabeth and a number of her advisers. A revolution was to be set on foot, Philip of Spain was to invade England, and the

[1] An account of these dramatic events in English and Scottish history will be found in Part Two of this work, pp. 166ff.

country was to be made once more a Roman Catholic country, with Mary upon the throne.

Mary was clearly implicated in these plots against the Queen's life and the State of England. The Queen's advisers were naturally alarmed both as to the safety of the Queen and of the State. After much hesitation and discussion, it was decided that the only way to secure the safety of the Queen and of the State was by the death of Mary. Elizabeth was manifestly reluctant to proceed to this extreme. She knew that in many quarters the penalty, however just, would be misconstrued, and she would be represented as a monster of inhumanity. Eventually, however, the decision was taken. Parliament, after much debate, petitioned Elizabeth that "a just condemnation might be followed by as just an execution". The death-warrant was prepared, and, after considerable delay, was signed by the Queen. Mary was executed in Fotheringay Castle, Northamptonshire, on February 8, 1587.

When the deed was done, Elizabeth sought to place the responsibility on other shoulders than her own. Davison, who actually presented the warrant to the Queen for signature, was made the scapegoat. He was ordered to the Tower. Some time later he was tried and a heavy fine was imposed upon him. He was likewise dismissed from public service, and ordered to be imprisoned at the Queen's pleasure. His imprisonment lasted for about two years.

Brewster was perforce involved in the fall of his master, to whose needs he seems to have ministered during the greater part of his imprisonment. Probably he left Davison's employment on his release: perhaps because his master was no longer able to keep such a servant on account of the heavy fine and the many expenses of his imprisonment. Somewhere about the year 1587 or 1588 Brewster returned to Scrooby and helped his father, who was in failing health, and who for a considerable time had performed the duties of postmaster. Brewster was appointed to succeed his father in this office on the latter's death in 1590.

The office of postmaster at such an important posting-station was one of considerable importance. Posts at that time were few, and were used only by persons of note, and, particularly, by those engaged in the business of the State. They were often the means of transmitting the sovereign's letters and other valuable documents. Further, relays of horses had to be in constant readiness so that persons travelling on important and urgent business might quickly pass from place to place. We see therefore that the office of postmaster at this time was of such importance that only a man of proved integrity would be likely to secure the appointment. The emoluments of the office were from £275 to £325 per year in present value.

We may now pass from Brewster, and consider briefly the character of another person who was destined to play a notable part in the history of the Pilgrim Fathers. About two miles from Scrooby lies the little hamlet of Austerfield; and here, in a cottage which still stands, was born, in 1590, William Bradford, later to become the Governor of Plymouth Colony, U.S.A., and the first historian of the Plymouth Plantation. He was the junior of Brewster by about twenty-three years. His father was a yeoman of fairly good standing. He died, however, when the boy was only about a year old, and the future Governor was left in the care of his grandfather, and later of his uncles, by whom he was trained for the farming industry. The virile character of the lad so brought up will appear in the course of our study.

We have already noticed that the earlier reforming movements in the Church owed much to spiritually-minded clergy and well-educated laymen, who failed to find satisfaction in the services of the Church, and in many

cases came to the conclusion that they must either find
what they needed in secret societies within the Church or
in entire separation from it. Some of the earliest martyrs
were members of the Universities of Oxford and Cambridge. They were therefore mentally capable of studying
the questions at issue, and coming to a reasoned conclusion.
It is a noteworthy fact that the most outstanding Nonconformists and reformers in the Church have been men
of high intellectual attainments, capable of holding their
own with any who have preferred to maintain the
traditional position.

So it was now in the district of which Scrooby may be
regarded as the centre. We have already remarked upon
the strong Roman Catholic leaven still remaining in the
district. But here also, as in London and East Anglia,
there were not lacking earnest men whose souls cried out
for the bread of life, and refused to be satisfied with the
beggarly ceremonies which were all that, in many cases,
the Churches at that time offered to them. Bradford, in
his *History of the Plymouth Plantation,* tells us that it was
"by the travail and diligence of some godly and zealous
preachers, and God's blessing on their labours" that many
became enlightened by the Word of God, and by His
grace began to reform their lives.

One of these puritan-minded clergy was Richard
Bernard, Vicar of Worksop, a small town some eight miles
south-east of Scrooby. He graduated at Cambridge
University, and in 1598 was presented to the living of
Epworth, later to be the birthplace of John Wesley. About
the time of which we are now speaking, i.e., in 1601, he
became Vicar of Worksop. He was a man of considerable
ability, and shared many of the views of the puritans. So
much indeed that his near neighbours at Scrooby, to whom
he was well known, at one time thought he would throw in
his lot with them. He even took the step of setting up a

Congregational Church within the area of his parish. We read that he separated from the rest of his parishioners "a hundred voluntary professors into a covenant with the Lord, sealed with the Lord's Supper, to forsake all known sin, to hear no wicked or dumb ministers".

Bernard, however, having put his hand to the plough, turned back. After the passing of the Canons of 1603, for a time he refused subscription; but, after being silenced by the Archbishop of York, he amended his puritan ideas, and kept his place in the Church. As if to justify his action, he became one of the principal writers against the Pilgrims. In controversy with him, John Robinson, the most notable of the Pilgrim Fathers, wrote his greatest work.

More stalwart and thoroughgoing in his puritanism was Richard Clyfton, Rector of Babworth, which lay some seven miles south of Scrooby. He was instituted to the living in 1586, and soon began to preach puritan doctrine, probably soon after Brewster returned to live in the old Manor House. There is evidence that he was an able and good man, and that his labours overflowed the boundaries of his parish. He was probably one of the first of the clergy of that district who sought to inculcate those truer conceptions of religion which led to Separatism. In later days Bradford recalled the fact that in his youth he walked some nine miles from Austerfield on Sunday mornings to hear this earnest preacher. He speaks of him as a "grave and fatherly old man", and declares that it was a pity that such a reverend old man should be forced to leave his country and at those years go into exile: "but it was his lot, and he bore it patiently. Much good had he done in the country where he lived, and converted many to God by his faithful and painful ministry both in preaching and catechizing." Unlike Bernard, Clyfton decided to go all the way with the Pilgrims. He appears to have been the spiritual father of many of those who later formed the

Scrooby Church. He was probably expelled from his cure about the time of Bancroft's enforcement of the Canons of 1603. He became the first pastor of the Scrooby Separatist Church, and in 1608 went with them into exile in Amsterdam, though he did not accompany them to New England.

Yet another of the puritan clergy was John Smyth, M.A. Leaving his Fellowship at Christ's College, Cambridge, he became a preacher in Lincoln. Thence he passed to Gainsborough. It is uncertain whether he was beneficed there or not; but it is known that, after passing through months of anxious doubt and inquiry, he became the pastor of the Separatist Church in Gainsborough in 1602, and remained there until 1606. He was a man fervent in spirit, devoted to the search for truth, though events proved that he was unstable. Through a wide area serious-minded people gathered to his church in Gainsborough, and among them men from Austerfield and Scrooby, who walked the ten or twelve miles between the two places. This went on for three or four years until about 1604, at which time those around Scrooby formed a separate Church, meeting in the old Manor House.

We have noticed that the leaders of this Separatist movement were well educated and refined men. The people who formed the Church, however, were mostly drawn from the common walks of life, as is natural from the character of the district. For the most part they were plain farmers, and men of inborn intelligence, industrious habits and self-reliance. Without these qualities they could never have made that venture into the unknown, involving many risks and great hardships, which has had such stupendous results.

Usually they met at Brewster's house, and this noble-hearted man entertained them at considerable expense to himself. Bradford says of him: "He did much good in the country where he lived in promoting and furthering religion, not only by his practice and example and provoking and encouraging others, but by procuring good preachers to the places thereabout, and drawing on others to assist and help forward in such a work, he himself most commonly deepest in the charge, and sometimes above his ability."

We must now say something of John Robinson, perhaps the most justly famous of all the Pilgrim Fathers. He seems to have been born in Lincolnshire, and perhaps at Gainsborough, about 1576. Nothing is known of his parentage or early training; but we find him at Cambridge University in 1592. In 1598 he became a Fellow of Corpus Christi, and presumably took orders at the same time. He appears to have held a benefice near Norwich between the years 1600 and 1604, and to have been suspended on account of his Nonconformity. From the first he appears to have had doubts about the vestments and ceremonies which were enforced in the Church. But he did not easily bring himself to break his connection with the Church. He tells us how he entered into a more serious consideration of these things, and searched the Scriptures to find out whether these things were so. He says: "Had not the truth been in my heart as a burning fire shut up in my bones (Jer. 20: 9), I had never broken those bonds of flesh and blood wherein I was so straitly tied, but had suffered the light of God to have been put out in mine own unthankful heart by other men's darkness."

Robinson, and the other men who formed the Church at Scrooby, were not Separatists merely for the sake of Separatism. If they could have remained in the Church with a clear conscience, and have found there that which nourished their souls, they would certainly have done so. It was only when they were impelled by an inner necessity—by the fire burning in their bones—that they responded to the call of God: "Come ye out from among them."

For a short time Robinson became pastor of a Separatist or Congregational Church in Norwich. After the fashion of that time, these seekers after their soul's salvation were harassed by fines and imprisonments, and were driven to seek refuge elsewhere. No doubt they were aware of the growth of the Separatist communities at Gainsborough and Scrooby, and thither Robinson made his way. Even there things were but little better. Bradford says that the members of the Scrooby community could not continue long in any peaceable condition. They were hunted and persecuted on every side with a growing malignity. Some were clapped in prison. Night and day these puritans were watched and beset on every side. Many of them were fain to fly and leave their houses and habitations and their means of livelihood. Eventually, about the year 1607–08, Brewster was forced to resign his position as postmaster and leave the Manor House. Very shortly after his resignation he was cited before the infamous Court of High Commission, and was fined the sum of £20. Many of his friends shared the same fate.

It is surely not surprising that under such circumstances the puritans began to wonder whether there was not, in a land beyond the seas, some place where they might settle in peace, and be allowed to worship God according to the light which He Himself had given them. John Penry, the Welsh martyr, a few days before his death in 1593, sent a farewell address to his brethren of the Separatist Church in London, in which he advised them to go into exile, since there was no hope of religious freedom at home. Already, before the date at which we have now arrived, certain Separatists had taken his advice. Before the Pilgrim Fathers ventured forth, two Separatist communities had been established in Amsterdam. Of the one from London, Francis Johnson was the pastor; whilst John Smyth was the leader of the party from Gainsborough. These had an interesting if chequered career, which I shall not attempt to relate, since they do not belong to the Pilgrim Fathers proper.

Chapter Four

PREPARATIONS FOR DEPARTURE AND THE ESCAPE TO
HOLLAND

THE resolution to go into exile was not taken without a good deal of anxious thought. Such a venture was well known to be fraught with much peril. It would involve turning their backs upon their kith and kindred, leaving their homes, and living among strangers whose language was unknown to them. In all probability they would have to learn a new profession or trade. Hard work would certainly be their lot, probably poverty would await them. Never again, it might well be, would they see the land they loved so well, though she had treated them as a cruel stepmother.

But what was the alternative except heavy fines, cruel persecutions of many kinds, and long imprisonments? When James I (James VI of Scotland) succeeded Elizabeth in 1603, the puritans cherished the hope of better treatment. For the new King had lived in Scotland, where the principles of the Reformation had taken deep root since 1560. James, however, was no Presbyterian at heart. He had considerable learning, but so little commonsense that he was dubbed by Henry IV of France "the wisest fool in Christendom"; and many of his acts justify the appellation. He was inflated with an enormous self-conceit, and had adopted the strange notion of the divine right of kings. The democratic element in Presbyterianism and Congregationalism was abhorrent to him. His favourite saying was "No Bishop, no King"; and he affirmed that "A Scottish Presbytery as well agreeth with a Monarchy

55

as God and the Devil". He wished, like Elizabeth, to be the Governor of the Church, with absolute power, and to rule by means of the bishops as his willing instruments. The real temper of his mind was clearly shown at the Hampton Court Conference (1604). On this occasion the four puritan leaders present humbly urged the following reforms: (1) That the doctrine of the Church might be preserved in purity, according to God's Word. (2) That good pastors might be planted in all the Churches to preach the same. (3) That the government of the Church might be sincerely administered according to God's Word. (4) That the Book of Common Prayer might be fitted to more increase of piety.

There was nothing here very revolutionary. But the bishops were in the most unbending humour and sneered at the petitioners. "A Puritan", one said, "is a Protestant frayed out of his wits." The King, angry and excited, frequently remarked: "No Bishop, no King." Speaking of Christian liberty, he declared: "I will none of that: I will have one doctrine and one discipline, one religion in substance, and in ceremony." As James withdrew from the Conference, he remarked: "If this be all that they have to say, I shall make them conform themselves, or I will harry them out of the land." It was thus made perfectly clear to the puritans that there was not much hope of liberty of worship under this royal devotee of the idol of uniformity.

The situation was made the more hopeless by the flattery and adulation of the bishops, who had found another monarch after their own hearts. After another meeting, so impartial a witness as Sir John Harrington, of the Privy Council, wrote that the King used upbraidings rather than arguments, and bid them "away with their snivellings". The bishops seemed much pleased, and said his Majesty spake "by the power of inspiration". "I wist not what they mean," says the chronicler, "but the [inspiring] spirit was rather foul-mouthed." Barlow relates that, following the King's speech, "the Archbishop of Canterbury said, that undoubtedly his Majesty spake by the special assistance of God's spirit. The Bishop of London upon his knees protested that his heart melted within him (and so, he doubted not, did the hearts of the whole company) with joy, and made haste to acknowledge unto Almighty God, the singular mercy we have received at His hands, in giving us such a King, as since Christ's time, the like he thought had not been; whereunto the Lords, with one voice, did yield a very affectionate acclamation."

Thus it was determined that a policy of brute force, of cast-iron, rigid uniformity at all costs, should prevail alike over reason and Scripture. The divine right of kings, and the divine right of bishops, displaced the crown rights of the Redeemer. It was in vain that so eminent a man as Lord Bacon urged that reforms were doubtless needed: that Church government ought to be varied to suit "time and place, and accidents"; and that while the substance of doctrine was immutable, rites, ceremonies, and particular hierarchies, policies and discipline of the Churches might be varied according to circumstances. There was no hope of even the most moderate reforms or toleration from this blend of royal bigotry and ecclesiastical intolerance. Even for the most reasonable of the puritan reformers there was no alternative to exile except fierce persecution, long-continued or frequent imprisonment, or even death at the stake. So cruel a Moloch is the idol of uniformity.

A few years of bitter experience drove home the conviction that even the most devoted life of piety and service to the community would not be permitted outside the established system. Canons issued by Convocation in 1603 attacked the puritans. They bitterly denounced all who separated themselves from the State Church and combined to form a new brotherhood. All such persons were excommunicated. Licences previously issued to Nonconformist ministers were declared to be void. No religious meetings were to be held in private houses on pain of excommunication. All whom the churchwardens and their assistants regarded as schismatics were to be presented to the bishop's court. And, to crown all, these rigid statutes were to be read by every minister to his congregation once a year. In consequence, three hundred ministers are said to have been deprived of their livings at once.

King James had said that he would either make the Separatists conform or he would harry them out of the land. From this language it would seem as if the King was willing that these stiff-necked puritans should at least have the option of going beyond the seas without let or hindrance. But such in fact was not the case. The bishops were bent upon quenching the light of freedom, rather than allowing it to pass into and to illumine other parts of this dark world. Every effort was made to prevent the would-be fugitives from finding an asylum in a distant land. Bradford says: "Though they could not stay, yet were they not suffered to go, but the ports and havens were shut against them, so that they were fain to seek secret means of conveyance, and to bribe and fee the mariners, and give extraordinary rates for their passages. And yet they were oftentimes betrayed (many of them), and both they and their goods intercepted and surprised, and thereby put to great trouble and charge, of which I will give an instance or two and omit the rest."

By the autumn of 1607 the Scrooby Separatists had firmly resolved to go over to the Low Countries as soon as opportunity offered. But how were they to reach the friendly shelter of Holland? It was as unlawful to flee from

England as it was painful to remain. Emigration was prohibited under an ancient statute of Richard II. The ports of the country would therefore be closed against them. If they were to get away, it must be by stealth. They must somehow gain a passage in secret on one of the boats passing between the two countries. Several such attempts were made by separate parties; but they were betrayed and prevented. A very brief description of two attempts ought to find a place in our account.

Bradford relates how a large company purposed to get a passage at Boston in Lincolnshire, some fifty miles as the crow flies from Scrooby, but much further by road or waterway. In this case the means adopted was to hire a vessel for themselves. They agreed with the master of the ship to be ready on a certain day, and to take them and their goods on board at a place defined. After much waiting and many expenses incurred, he at length came and took them aboard during the night. But when he had got them safely on board, he betrayed them. He had plotted with the officers of the law, who arrested them, put them into open boats, searched them to their shirts for money, even the women further than became their modesty. They then carried them back to town and exhibited them to the multitude, who came flocking round to see these fugitives who were willing to forsake all for freedom's sake.

Having been robbed of their money, books, and many other things, they were presented to the magistrates, who committed them to prison. Eventually, after a month's imprisonment, the greater part were dismissed, and taken back to the places whence they came. Seven of the leaders, including Brewster, were kept in prison, and bound over to the Assizes. Somehow or other, a portion of the Scrooby society managed to reach Holland during the year 1607.

The following spring (1608) a further attempt to escape

was made by another party. This time they made an agreement with a Dutchman at Hull to carry them over. They hoped to find him more faithful than the last wretch who had betrayed them. It was arranged that he should take them on board at a point between Grimsby and Hull, where there was a large common at a considerable distance from any town. At the time appointed, the women and children, with the goods, were sent by boat, by way of Gainsborough and the Trent, to the place agreed upon. The men travelled across country some forty miles. Both parties arrived a day before the ship came. As the sea was rough, and the women sick, they prevailed upon the men in charge of the boat to run it into a creek near by, where it lay on the ground at low water. The next morning, when the ship came, they were fast and could not stir until about noon. The master of the ship decided that the best thing to do was to send his boat to fetch the men, whom he saw ready and walking about the shore, aboard. But after the first full boat had got aboard, and she was ready to go for more, to his great alarm he saw a large company of men, both horse and foot, equipped with a variety of weapons, who were coming to capture these fugitives from persecution. The Dutchman, thinking his first business was to look after himself, weighed anchor, hoisted sails, and fled.

Those aboard, and those still on shore, were alike in a lamentable situation. The men aboard were in great distress for their wives and children. They had nothing with them save the clothes in which they were dressed. Their money and their goods were in the boat which was stuck fast in the creek. Tears sprang to their eyes, and they would have given anything to have been set ashore again to share the fate of wives and children. The women too were in no less evil case. There was weeping and crying out on every side, some for their husbands, thus torn away from them; others for their children, who were crying out with terror. And all alike knew that they were in the hands of rude and callous men from whom nothing but torment could be expected.

They were hurried from place to place, and from one Justice to another. These magistrates seem to have had some sense of shame which made them unwilling to incur the odium that would result from sending women and children to prison for the natural desire to go with their husbands and fathers. On the other hand, they could not send them back to their homes, for the simple reason that they had no homes to go to. At last the constables and magistrates were glad to get rid of them upon any terms. What became of them between the time of their arrest and their final departure to the land of exile is unknown. Probably they found shelter in the homes of kindly country folk.

Meantime, the menfolk were enduring the full fury of a storm at sea. They were driven out of their course until they found themselves near the coast of Norway. It took them fourteen days to reach port, and during seven of these they saw neither sun, moon, nor stars. The mariners themselves often despaired of life, and once uttered shrieks and cries, thinking the ship was foundering. In despite of all, however, they eventually reached the harbour, and there they were warmly welcomed by those who had given them up for lost.

In the end, at different times, and by many means, the Pilgrim Fathers reached their desired haven. As the last detachment arrived, and were welcomed at Amsterdam by those who had preceded them, their beloved pastors, Clyfton and Robinson, led their praises and their prayers.

The question naturally arises in our minds as to why these fugitives from the violence of ecclesiastical tyranny made their way to Holland rather than to some other place. When we seek to find an answer to the question, we discover that the reason lay not so much in the close proximity of that country to England as in the character of the Dutch people, which character had been largely moulded by forces not unlike those which had made England an impossible place for a devout people who had a passion for liberty. Long conflict with the encroaching sea had helped to make the Dutch a vigorous and independent people. It is equally true to say that their experience of the pitiless priestcraft of the corrupt Romish Church made them kindly and hospitable to those beyond the sea who were engaged in the same bitter warfare. It will be worth while to glance at the history of this noble people, and think of the price which they themselves had already paid to achieve religious freedom.

When the Reformation broke out in Germany, its influence was felt throughout all the countries of Europe. The Dutch were a venturesome people, and had promptly taken advantage of the geographical discoveries of the sixteenth century. They had become a great trading people. In 1601 the Netherlands led the commerce of the world. It was natural, therefore, that during the great ferment of thought associated with the Renaissance and the Reformation traders should have traded in more than material merchandise. Men whose minds had become imbued with new thoughts of God and man, of Christ and salvation, carried their new knowledge and experience wherever they went on their trading missions. It was inevitable that the Netherlands, and Amsterdam in particular, should be infected with the passion for reform.

At the middle of the sixteenth century the Netherlands comprised some seventeen provinces, which were roughly coextensive with the present countries of Holland and Belgium. Each province had a ruler of its own, and jealously preserved its independence. There was, however, a central and confederate Assembly, known as the States-General. Despite their independence, these Netherland provinces owed a certain allegiance to the Emperor Charles V.

One day, about 1520, the Emperor was greatly distressed to find that the dreadful heresy, which had begun to make such a stir in Europe, had become rooted among the Dutch people. He immediately resolved to stamp it out by brute force. He issued a series of eleven "placards", by which he endeavoured to destroy Protestantism from the Dutch provinces by destroying every person who professed it. It was decreed that everyone convicted of heresy should be burned, buried alive, or beheaded. Those who read, copied, or dealt in heretical books, or who publicly and privately expounded the Scriptures, or taught the reformed doctrines were to suffer the same fate. The courts were forbidden to show the slightest mercy. A branch of the Inquisition was established, and a member of the Council of Brabant was made Inquisitor-General. Under these horrible decrees many thousands of people lost their lives.

Philip II succeeded Charles V in 1556. Unlike his father, who had lived in the Netherlands, he had but slight sympathy with the aspirations of the Dutch people. That he would not rule over "heretics" was his guiding principle, and his policy was to burn and butcher until heresy had been extirpated. With the help of the hateful Duke of Alva, he drove the Dutch into a terrible war. A confederacy of Dutch people was formed, known by the nickname of "the Beggars", and under the leadership of these there was an outburst of iconoclasm which resulted in many churches being stripped of images and the usual accompaniments of Romanist worship. The Duke of Alva, savage and bloodthirsty, was commissioned to march a Spanish army from Italy into the Low Countries to put down the insurrection. Within three months one thousand eight hundred men were sent to the scaffold. On February 16, 1568, all the inhabitants of the Low Countries, with but few exceptions, were condemned to death, and Philip himself ordered that this sentence should be put into execution without favour or respect of persons.

These unparalleled and shameful cruelties served only to intensify the courage of the Dutchmen, and finally the Utrecht union of Holland and Zeeland, with five other provinces, became the germ of the Dutch Republic. The result was the establishment, in 1569, of the principle of toleration in religious matters on a scale unknown elsewhere. The Reformation at first did not recognize the principle of liberty of conscience. William of Orange, who now took the lead in the affairs of the Netherlands, urged that religious persecution was both barbarous and useless, and to him belongs the credit of making Holland a safe refuge for all liberty-loving people who revolted against the strange policy of a rigid uniformity of belief as well as of practice. The assassination of William in 1584, by the agents of Philip, served still further to increase the spirit of hospitality of the Netherlanders, especially towards those who, like themselves, had been the victims of tyrannous ecclesiastical authorities.

Chapter Five

WE have now seen the Pilgrim Fathers, after a very rough voyage, safely across the North Sea, and established in the hospitable city of Amsterdam. The date of this notable event was August, 1608. The exact number of these voluntary exiles is uncertain; probably there were between one hundred and twenty-five and one hundred and fifty persons. Robinson was their pastor, and Clyfton their teacher. It seems probable they they never intended to settle permanently in Amsterdam, along with those who preceded them from London and Gainsborough. But until they could choose another place of residence they must needs obtain some means of securing a livelihood. If not entirely penniless, they had few resources. It is probable that many of their goods had perished at the time of the embarkation. Bradford tells us that it was not long before they saw the grim and grisly face of poverty coming upon them like an armed man, with whom they must buckle and encounter, and from whom they could not fly.

After about a year at Amsterdam, in April or May, 1609, they made preparations for removal to Leyden, a busy city of about fifty thousand people. The staple manufactures of the city were serge, baize, bombazine, fustian, and the like. As the era of weaving by machinery had not yet arrived, weaving was done, not in large mills as now, but in private houses by handlooms and spinning wheels. Occupational particulars are given in the public records of many persons belonging to the company of the Pilgrim Fathers, and these include such occupations as weaving, baking, cabinet-making, candle-making, carpentry, glove-making, etc. In the interval between their settlement in Leyden and their voyage to take possession of the New World, we must picture them as engaged in these various manual labours. We have seen that in their own country most of them had been people of lowly station: they had earned their livelihood as farmers or farm-labourers. They were not fitted therefore to engage in the more exalted professions or businesses which find a place in city life. They had to do that which lay nearest to their capacity.

But though they might be poor, they soon won the esteem and confidence of the strangers among whom they dwelt. "Though many of them were poor," Bradford says, "yet there were none so poor but if they were known to be of that congregation, the Dutch (either bakers or others) would trust them in any reasonable matter when they wanted money. Because they found by experience how careful they were to keep their word, and saw them so painful and diligent in their calling; yea, they would strive to get their custom, and to employ them above others in their work for their honesty and diligence." The Dutch officials also held them in high regard, as we see from the fact that before the exiles left their city the magistrates said: "These English have lived among us these twelve years, and yet we never had any suit or accusation against any of them."

In Leyden they remained until July, 1620. During all these years, says Bradford, they continued in a comfortable condition, "enjoying much sweet and delightful society and spiritual comfort together in the ways of God, and under the able ministry and prudent government of Mr. John Robinson, and Mr. William Brewster who was assistant to him, in the place of an Elder, unto which he was now [that is, at Leyden] called, and chosen by the Church. So they grew in knowledge, and other gifts and graces of the Spirit of God, and lived together in peace, and love and holiness."

The picture which Bradford gives of the condition of Church life during this period is attractive. If differences arose, or offences broke out, as they naturally will, even amongst the best of men, they were generally so dealt with that love and peace and communion were continued: or when other means failed, the Church was purged of those that were incurable and incorrigible; but this seldom happened. High tribute is paid to Robinson's character and influence, a tribute which we know from many sources was fully justified. Such, Bradford says, was the mutual love and reciprocal respect that this worthy man had to his flock, and his flock to him, that it might be said of them, as it once was said of the famous Emperor Marcus Aurelius Antoninus and the people of Rome, that it was hard to judge whether he delighted more in having such a people, or they in having such a pastor. He was evidently a man of many parts and great adaptability. He loved the people and cared for their bodies as well as for their souls. He could give wise directions in civil matters: and in the affairs of daily life he gave both timely help and much encouragement, and was in all ways as a father unto them.

Such, says Bradford, was the pure piety, the humble zeal, and fervent love of this people; such was their sincere affection towards each other, that they came as near to the primitive pattern of the first churches as any other church of these later times has ever done.

The period was one of theological disputation, as was natural after the dogmatic oppressions of many centuries. Enjoying as never before the freedom of the sons of God, mind as well as heart soared into the heavenly places of divine truth. They saw Christian truths from many different angles. Their Nonconformity and Puritanism was not a mere negative matter. It did not consist essentially in ridding themselves of vestments, or in turning their backs upon ancient ceremonies, or in giving up superstitious beliefs. Much more did it consist in the positiveness of a great faith which brought them new joy and power. For the first time they could understand the words of St. Paul: "If any man is in Christ, he is a new creature: the old things are passed away; behold, they are become new." It was this richer experience of life which gave them power to endure the sting of poverty, the fierceness of persecution, and the loneliness of exile.

It will be well to see a little of what the leaders of the exiles had to say for themselves during this period. The intellectual eminence of John Robinson was honourably recognized by the authorities of Leyden University when, with the consent of the magistrates, he was received as an honorary member of the University on September 5, 1615. But his spiritual and intellectual eminence are alike plainly revealed in the many works which flowed from his pen during these years. Some of these have considerable value in that they give lucid and succinct expression to the theological and ecclesiastical position now firmly taken by the Pilgrims. We have seen that Mr. Bernard, Vicar of Worksop, had at one time gone a long way with the puritans in their ideas about the purity of the Church, though he later turned back and became one of the most prolific writers against them. Among his books was one entitled *The Separatist's Schism*; and another, *Christian Advertisements and Counsels of Peace*, published in 1608.

In these works Bernard objects to what was commonly known as "Brownism" because of its novelty, its schism, its abuse of Scripture, and on other grounds. As against this new form of Church life he maintains such points as the following: that the English Church is a true Church; that a particular Church should not be expected to be

68

free from false professors; that a popular government of the Church is unwarrantable: that the Established Ministers are true Ministers, while the Separatists are not "lawfully made"; that "stinted and set prayer" is lawful, and so on.

In reply Robinson wrote a weighty volume of four hundred and eighty pages, entitled *A Justification of Separation*, in which he answers in detail the many criticisms upon Separation raised by Bernard. Whilst firmly meeting the challenge to justify Separatism, he does so in no narrow or uncharitable spirit. He is quite persuaded, he says, that there are in many congregations of the English Church many persons who truly fear God, and he prays that the Lord may increase their number. He does not doubt that the truths taught in Rome have been effectual in the salvation of many. But he urges that the system which Bernard champions is in many ways vulnerable, as, indeed, he himself had at one time asserted. He quotes from a paper which had been composed by Bernard in the days when he was almost a Nonconformist, in which he gave eight reasons for asserting that the bishops were anti-Christian. He reminds him that in those days he had in his own parish separated from the rest of the parishioners a hundred voluntary professors and joined them in covenant with the Lord, sealed with the Lord's supper, to forsake all known sin, to hear no wicked or dumb ministers, and the like.

In criticism of the parochial system, he points out that such was the constitution of the Established Church that a man might leave Holland and come to England, where he could hire a house or farm, and by virtue of so doing he would become a member of the parish church where he dwelt, though he might have been nursed all his life long in popery or even in atheism, and though he formerly were of no church or religion. Yea, even if he professed that he did not look to Christ for salvation, but rather to his own good intentions and well-doings, yet if he would come and hear divine service he would be counted a true member of the Church.

Further, he supposes a situation not unfamiliar to persons engaged in missionary work. What if the Lord should raise up a company of faithful men and women in Barbary or America, by the reading of the Scriptures, or by the writings, conferences, or sufferings of some godly men, must they not separate themselves from the filthiness of the heathen unto the Lord? Must they not have any communion together for their mutual edification, and comfort, till some vagrant priest from Rome or England be sent unto them to begin their church matters with his service book? If it be true that church life may not be begun without officers, it would be impossible that such a people should ever enjoy officers or become a church.

As to the high quality of church life outside the enforced order of the Established Church, he is able to cite his own experience of the Church of the pilgrim Fathers. "If ever I saw the beauty of Zion, and the glory of the Lord filling His tabernacle," he says, "it hath been in the manifestation of the divers graces of God in the Church, in that heavenly harmony, and comely order, wherein by the grace of God we are set and walk: wherein, if your eyes had but seen the brethren's sober and modest carriage one toward another, their humble and willing submission unto their guides, in the Lord, their tender compassion towards the weak, their fervent zeal against scandalous offenders, and their longsuffering towards all, you would (I am persuaded) change your mind."

There is plentiful evidence that these Pilgrim Fathers were no lovers of separation for mere separation's sake. They were constrained to their course of action by the sincerest motives. They firmly believed that they were contending for the truth of the Gospel, and for the primitive, apostolical constitution of the Church, which, as they believed, had for centuries been forced into a false rigidity, which denied the freedom of the Christian man in Christ, and had been the source of innumerable evils.

Apart altogether from the material losses entailed by their Nonconformity, it was no light matter for them even to appear to be guilty of schism. On this point we have the evidence of Governor Winslow, who rebuts the accusation that the New England plantations had been based upon schism, division, or separation. He knew Robinson well, and for three years (1617–20) had followed his ministry, and he affirms that his doctrine was altogether against separation from any of the Churches of Christ. He professed and held communion with both the French and Dutch Reformed Churches, and also with the Scottish. He often remarked how wary persons ought to be in separating from a Church.

Though circumstances compelled Robinson to separate from the Church of England, it was with great reluctance that he did so, and even when it took place he recognized what was good in that Church; he allowed private communion with its members, and with all the faithful in Christ Jesus in the Kingdom of England. He honoured the puritan Anglican clergy above all other professors in the world. In his later days particularly he was all for peace and union, so far as this was consistent with faith and a good conscience. As for schism and division, there was nothing in the world more hateful to him.

Robinson had, however, strong objections to the episcopal form of government in the Church of England, to the Liturgy, and to the "stinted" prayers of the Church, to its constitution as national, and to its recognition in the one communion of the worthy and unworthy receivers of the Lord's Supper.

Despite the hospitality shown by the Dutch people to the English settlers, it was not within the providence of God that Leyden should become their permanent abode. It was not any failure to appreciate the kindness of their hosts which made them think of turning their backs upon their city of refuge. To account for their next move it might be sufficient to say that God quickened the migratory instinct within them, as in the case of the birds, and made them feel that "here we have no abiding city". But we know that God works by secondary causes; He overrules the events of history to shape the lives of men and of nations. In the present instance it is possible to discern some of the secondary causes which led the Pilgrims once again to strike their tents, brave a long and dangerous voyage, and settle in a distant land.

No one knew the facts so well as Bradford, who became the first historian of the Pilgrim movement. One reason that he gives for the failure of the Pilgrims to settle permanently in Holland is that comparatively few puritans were willing to leave England to come and join them. They were either unable or unwilling to endure the great labour and hard fare, and the many inconveniences which life in Holland involved. They rather preferred to choose prison life in England than to suffer the afflictions of exile.

Moreover, they were aware of the danger of becoming absorbed in the Dutch nation, and so of losing their English characteristics. We have already remarked upon their love of the land which had treated them so cruelly. They were English and proud of it, and they wished to retain their nationality. That there was real danger of losing it we see from what happened to some of their party who remained behind in Holland.

Another important consideration was that the twelve years' truce with Spain would shortly come to an end, and if the Pilgrims remained in Holland they might find themselves involved in war between the Spanish and the Dutch.

Again, even in Holland they were not beyond the reach of their enemies in England. Certain books printed in Holland had infuriated the King of England. Suspicion fell upon Brewster, who had turned printer. Official correspondence shows how anxious the King was that Brewster should be seized and brought to England. It was natural that the Leyden authorities should desire to avoid conflict with the English, since they would wish to have their help against Spain.

Still more powerful, however, was the missionary motive. They had a great hope and inward zeal, says Bradford, of laying some good foundation for the propagating and advancing of the Gospel of the Kingdom of Christ in a remote part of the world. They had in mind some of the vast countries of America which were without any civilized populations. Here they might establish a puritan colony in which they would have full freedom of worship, and at the same time be able to mould social and civil life in ways that were entirely impossible in a strange, if friendly, land.

These thoughts were cherished long before the migration actually took place. Various places were suggested as likely to be suitable for the establishment of a puritan colony, among them being the West Indies, Guiana, and Virginia. As early as 1606 some London merchants had received from King James a patent constituting them the Virginia Company. It consisted of two branches, known as the London and Plymouth Companies. The former had its headquarters in London, the latter in Plymouth. The first party of emigrants, to the number of one hundred and forty-three, sailed in 1607. They were of an idle, thriftless type, and not such as to make good their hold in a virgin country. The result was naturally disappointing, and not such as to encourage others to venture on a similar enterprise. Other attempts at colonization there were no great success.

There were various things to dissuade from the enterprise, so far as Virginia was concerned. For instance, under the charter granted by King James, conformity to the Church of England was insisted on as a matter of course. A regulation required that even on working days every man and woman must, when the church bell tolled, repair to the church to hear divine service. The penalty for failing to comply was the loss of a day's allowance for the first omission, whipping for the second, and six months' service in the galleys for the third. Penalties for the neglect to attend Sunday services were even more severe. In this case a third offence was punishable by death. Was it reasonable to suppose that those who had fled from England to escape the tyranny of the ecclesiastical authorities would venture into such a hornet's nest as this?

After due deliberation and discussion, it was at length decided to make inquiry whether they might not be allowed to live as a distinct body by themselves, under the general government of Virginia, and to be permitted to enjoy full freedom in the practice of religion.

For the purpose of negotiating the matter with the Virginia Company, two of their number, Robert Cushman and Deacon John Carver, were sent to London during the summer of 1617. They submitted to the Council a document, signed on behalf of the Leyden Church by Robinson, its pastor, and Brewster, its elder. It is remarkable for its conciliatory character, and for the number of concessions it makes in the direction of the forms and constitution of the Established Church. It assents to the Articles of the Church of England, acknowledges the authority of the King, and that of the bishops and other ecclesiastical officers. There are, however, careful qualifications. For example, the Articles are accepted in the sense in which they are accepted by the Reformed Churches of the continent; they acknowledge obedience to the King's authority "if the thing commanded be not against God's Word". In assenting to the authority of the King and bishops, they discriminated between civil and religious authority.

The authors evidently saw that their only hope of obtaining the permission they desired lay in minimizing as far as possible their differences with the Established Church. They wished to avoid a conflict with the King and the hierarchy at such a time. They also cherished the hope that whatever might be the letter of the law, at so great a distance it was unlikely that the King and the bishops would be able to prevent them from exercising a very large measure of religious freedom.

The agents of the Pilgrims were courteously treated by the Council. It was indeed a favourable time for securing their object. For some time things had not been going well with the colony. The company were anxious to obtain emigrants of a nobler quality and were therefore the more willing to come to terms. Some of the leading members of the Council for Virginia went so far as to give assurances that they had good reason to expect to obtain their suit with the King for liberty in religious matters.

The negotiations, however, did not altogether run smoothly. The correspondence between the parties shows that certain of the Council had taken exception to the ecclesiastical order of the Pilgrims. An interesting letter, dated December, 1617, signed by Robinson and Brewster, gives certain "instances of inducement" to prevail upon the Council to grant the desired permission. I will give a brief summary of the points mentioned.

"First," they say, "we verily believe and trust that

the Lord is with us. Secondly, we are well weaned from the delicate milk of our mother country; and are inured to the difficulties of a strange land: which yet, in great part, we have by patience overcome. Thirdly, the people are, for the body of them, industrious and frugal. Fourthly, we are knit together as a body, in a most strict and sacred Bond and Covenant of the Lord, of the violation whereof we make great conscience; and by virtue whereof we do hold ourselves straitly tied to all care of each other's good. Lastly, it is not with us as with other men whom small things can discourage, or small discontentments cause to wish themselves home again."

At last a patent was granted to them by the Company in June, 1619. This contained no formal grant of freedom of worship by the King or bishops; but the leading men of the Virginia Company encouraged the Pilgrims to go forward in the hope that if they conducted themselves peaceably they would not be troubled by the authorities in the homeland. Some of the Pilgrims were discouraged by the prospect; but the leaders were of the opinion that the King would connive at irregularities in the religious situation of the colony: though he had reasons for not explicitly stating his attitude. There were reasonable grounds, they felt, for a venture of faith. Having done the best they could, they could afford to trust themselves to God's good providence. It was resolved to seek God's direction on a day specially set apart for humiliation, thanksgiving and prayer. After a sermon by John Robinson, many of the Pilgrims offered prayer. By the end of the day it was finally decided that they should make the venture of faith and travel to the New World.

It was proposed that, to begin with, only a part of the church should go, and that these should be the youngest and the strongest, and all should be volunteers. If the majority of the Church should choose to depart now, then their pastor, John Robinson, should go with them; if only a minority, then Robinson should remain at Leyden, and Elder Brewster should go as their leader. It was further resolved that if the enterprise should be a failure, then those who remained behind should welcome them back on their return. On the other hand, if it should prove to be successful, the forerunners should do all in their power to help those who remained to get over.

The next point was to secure the ways and means of transporting so large a company of people across the Atlantic ocean; no small undertaking at that time. In this matter, however, they had the assistance of a certain Thomas Weston, of whom not much is known. Learning of their project, he went over to Leyden, and offered to find the necessary funds to enable the party to reach their destination. He associated with himself some seventy other English merchants (later known as Merchant Adventurers) who were prepared to take stock in this emigration scheme at ten pounds a share, providing that at the end of seven years there should be a division between the shareholders and the Pilgrims of all the colony's possessions and earnings. The terms were agreed to, and articles were signed by both parties. Carver and Cushman were sent over to England to receive the money from the shareholders; to secure ships, and to purchase the necessary provisions for the voyage. Meantime, those that were to go, says Bradford, prepared themselves with all speed. They sold what estates belonged to them, and put the money into the common stock.

Before we pass on, we must note that ere the voyage was begun, the Merchant Adventurers, who were now so deeply interested in the voyage, along with the Pilgrims, conceived the idea that New England with its fisheries might offer better opportunities than Virginia. They therefore abandoned the patent which they had obtained and secured another, which was granted to John Pierce, one of the Adventurers. This conferred the powers of self-government, and the right to a tract of land to be selected by the planters near the mouth of the Hudson River.

Further, an unauthorized change was made in the agreement between the Merchant Adventurers and the Pilgrims by the agents, Martin, Carver and Cushman, whom they had sent to England to arrange matters. The original agreement had provided for a seven years' partnership, during which the labour of the colonists was to be for the common benefit, *except that each colonist might reserve two days in the week for his own purposes.* The later agreement omitted this reservation, so that the whole of the labour of the colonists was to go to the common fund. The later agreement also provided that at the end of seven years everything, including houses, lands and goods, should be equally divided between the settlers and the Adventurers. The new agreement was severely criticized because it discouraged the spirit of individual enterprise. It was felt, however, that it was too late to change the agreement.

Chapter Six

TO carry the party to their new home two ships had been chartered. The one, the *Mayflower*, a vessel of one hundred and eighty tons, whose master was Thomas Jones, was to journey from London to Southampton, and would carry their English friends to meet them in that port. The other, the *Speedwell*, a vessel of sixty tons, had been purchased for the Adventurers, and fitted out in Holland. This was to take the Leyden people to Southampton, and then journey with the *Mayflower* to America, and remain at the disposal of the colony for a year.

When the latter vessel was ready to sail, a day of fasting and prayer was kept, and Robinson preached from Ezra 8: 21. It was the last time the colonists were to hear him; for it had been decided that he should remain behind with the majority of the exiles who were, for the time being, to remain in Leyden. The occasion was an historic one, and the scene must have been deeply affecting. Family ties were about to be severed by thousands of miles of ocean. It was not to be expected that all the exiles would see each other again. The voyage across the Atlantic Ocean at that time was exceedingly hazardous. What awaited them at the other side they knew not; but they had good reason to anticipate much toil, hardship and danger.

The address given by the noble-hearted pastor suited the occasion, and some of his words are worthy to rank among the most famous utterances of the leaders of peoples. According to the summary preserved by Governor Winslow, he said in the course of his address: "We are now ere long to part asunder, and the Lord knoweth whether he should live to see our faces again: but whether the Lord had appointed it or not, he charged us before God and His blessed angels, to follow him no further than he followed Christ. And if God should reveal anything to us by any other instrument of His, to be as ready to receive it, as ever we were to receive any truth by his ministry. For he was very confident that the Lord had more light yet to break forth out of His holy Word."

After their worship, Winslow says: "they that stayed at Leyden feasted us that were to go at our Pastor's house, being large, where we refreshed ourselves after our tears, with singing of Psalms, making joyful melody in our hearts, as well as with the voice."

On a July day in 1620 the emigrants left Leyden by barges for Delfshaven, the port of Delft, on the Maas, accompanied by most of the brethren who were to remain. Arrived there, the last night on shore was spent mostly in friendly entertainment and Christian discourse. After prayer by Robinson, Winslow says: "when a flood of tears was poured out, they accompanied us to the ship, but were not able to speak one to the other for the abundance of sorrow to part." As the *Speedwell* left the quay-side those on board fired a parting volley with their muskets. This was followed by the booming sound of shots from three of the ship's cannons: "and so lifting up our hands to each other, and our hearts for each other to the Lord our God, we departed, and found His presence with us; in the midst of our manifest straits He carried us through."

The voyage to Southampton was uneventful. There they were joined by the other party in accordance with the arrangement made with the Merchant Adventurers. These consisted partly of labourers employed by the Merchants, and partly of godly Englishmen who shared their religious convictions. Of the party, which numbered about one hundred and twenty, ninety were allotted to the *Mayflower* and thirty to the *Speedwell*. The two vessels set sail on August 5, 1620. Soon, however, the *Speedwell* belied her name. After covering about one hundred and fifty miles, Reynolds, her captain, reported that she had sprung a dangerous leak and declared that they must put into Dartmouth for repairs. She was speedily overhauled, and the two ships put to sea again. Hopes of now making good progress were again doomed to disappointment. While yet only three hundred miles beyond Land's End the captain pronounced his ship to be unseaworthy. She could only be kept afloat by the constant use of the pump.

There was nothing for it but for the two ships to return. This time they put into Plymouth. There it was decided to reduce the expedition to one ship's load. The *Speedwell*, with some eighteen passengers, returned to London, and the rest of her passengers, twelve in number, were added to the already overcrowded passengers in the *Mayflower*.

Fortunately, such men as the Pilgrims had shown themselves to be were not easily daunted. As their leaders had said, in a letter already quoted, it was not with them as with other men whom small things could discourage or small discontents make them wish themselves home again. They never imagined that such trials were intended to turn them back from their purpose. Nor did they make the mistake of assuming that because God had called them to this enterprise He would make a smooth way for them. They were firmly resolved to proceed. Concerning these events, Bradford remarks: "like Gideon's army this small number was divided, as if the Lord by this work of His providence thought these few too many for the great work He had to do."

How long the ship remained at Plymouth is unknown, but on September 6 they once more resumed their interrupted voyage. There were now one hundred and two passengers on board. The voyage took sixty-seven days. Until they got halfway across the Atlantic the weather was favourable, and they made good progress. Then storm after storm broke upon them. The ship was shaken from stem to stern. One of the main beams was twisted out of its place. Even the mariners became alarmed for the ship's safety. Fortunately, there were implements on board by which they were enabled to get the beam back into its place. For days together the winds were so fierce, and the seas so high, that not a sail could be spread, and the vessel drove before the gale with bare poles. The passengers were crowded below for safety, but their clothing and their bedding were drenched with sea-water. One of their number, who ventured aloft, was washed overboard, but fortunately, as he went over, he seized a rope and was hauled to safety again. Only one of the passengers died during this eventful voyage.

At last, after some nine weeks, to the great joy of all, land was sighted, and proved to be Cape Cod. For a time they were in danger from perilous shoals and roaring breakers. But the next day they got safely into the Cape harbour. Thereupon, Bradford says, they fell upon their knees, and blessed the God of heaven, who had brought them over the vast and furious ocean, and delivered them from all its dangers and miseries.

We have noticed above that before leaving England a change was made in the intended destination of the Pilgrims, from Virginia to New England. The Virginia Company had no rights in New England, nor was there any other recognized authority there. There was therefore a serious danger that when the emigrants landed it would not be long before disorders arose unless some form of government was immediately established. Not all members of the party were God-fearing men, like Brewster and Bradford. Already certain of the company, probably the

82

hired labourers, had made remarks to the effect that as there was no authority in the new land, each man might go his own way and do as he liked. The leaders of the expedition therefore felt that something must be done immediately to obviate possible disorders. Since there was no existing government, they must create one for themselves. They therefore summoned all the adult males among the emigrants into the cabin of the *Mayflower*, and there they formed a compact, which became the basis of the constitution of the colony. The compact was in the following terms, the spelling only being modernized:

In the name of God, Amen. We, whose names are underwritten, the loyal subjects of our dread sovereign Lord King James; by the grace of God, of Great Britain, France, and Ireland King; Defender of the Faith, etc.

Having undertaken for the glory of God, and advancement of the Christian faith, and honour of our King and Country, a Voyage (Expedition) to plant the first Colony in the Northern parts of Virginia: (we) do, by these presents, solemnly and mutually, in the presence of God and of one another, covenant and combine ourselves together into a civil Body Politic, for our better ordering and preservation, and furtherance of the ends aforesaid: and, by virtue hereof, to enact, constitute, and frame such just and equal laws, ordinances, acts, constitutions, offices, from time to time, as shall be thought most meet and convenient for the general good of the Colony: unto which, we promise all due submission and obedience.

In witness whereof, we have hereunto subscribed our names. Cape Cod, 11th of November, in the year of the reign of our Sovereign Lord King James, of England, France and Ireland 18; and of Scotland 54. Anno Domini 1620.

This compact was signed by forty-one of the sixty-five adult male passengers then on board the *Mayflower*. In addition to the Captain and crew one hundred and two passengers had left Plymouth, one died on the way over, and a child was born, so that there were still one hundred and two passengers on the arrival in the New World— seventy-three males and twenty-nine females. The colony proper consisted of thirty-four adult males, besides whom there were various menservants and maidservants, sailors and craftsmen, who were hired for temporary service. The great majority of the thirty-four men were from Leyden, only four of the men being known to have joined them at Southampton.

The day after the signing of the compact John Carver was chosen as the Governor for the ensuing year. The vessel remained at anchor while explorations were made before the final settlement at Plymouth. The emigrants were naturally concerned to know the nature of the country which they had reached, and its suitability or otherwise for a permanent settlement. On the afternoon of the day of their arrival, being Saturday, sixteen men, well-armed, were set ashore to explore the country, while others were sent to secure firewood. The former reported that the land consisted of sandhills, much like the downs of Holland, but much better. There were plenty of woods, but without underwood, making travelling easy either for walking or riding. They found no person or signs of habitation. The next day, being Sunday, they rested quietly, and had Sabbath worship. They gave thanks to Him who had brought them safely through so many dangers to the desired haven.

The Captain of the *Mayflower* was impatient to take his ship back to England; the Pilgrims were therefore compelled to find the most desirable site for their colony as soon as possible, so that he could put all his passengers ashore, together with their goods. A number of expeditions were therefore despatched. Some of the party explored the coast in a shallop, a little craft which they had brought with them. Sixteen others, well-armed, under the command of Captain Miles Standish, went inland.

I shall not attempt to relate in detail their experiences during these exploratory journeys. They soon came into contact with the Indians, who sometimes fled at their approach. At other times they attacked them with showers of arrows. The emigrants also found Indian huts or wigwams, and hoards of supplies, such as baskets filled with corn. Some of these they, like the men of Eshcol, carried with them and showed them to their brethren: "of which, and of their return, they were marvellously glad and their hearts encouraged." Payment for these was made to the Indians at a later date.

On the third and last exploration they eventually reached a place, twenty-five miles away from where the *Mayflower* was lying, which was to be their future home. They set foot on Plymouth Rock on December 11 (N.S. 21), 1620. On his return to the ship William Bradford learned that his wife, whom he had married only seven years before, had fallen overboard and been drowned.

Chapter Seven

THE SETTLEMENT AT PLYMOUTH

WHEN the Pilgrims left Leyden they had hoped to arrive at their destination in time to allow them to build some sort of homes before the winter set in. Their time-table, however, was greatly disarranged by the misfortunes which overtook the *Speedwell*, and the storms encountered during the voyage. It was midwinter ere they reached their destination.

No time was lost in laying the foundations of the colony. Some twenty men landed and built barricades, having decided to spend the night ashore. Others remained on board ship, and prepared to land food and other supplies the next morning. The weather suddenly changed for the worse. Those on land were drenched to the skin with torrents of rain, while it took all the anchors of the *Mayflower* to save her from being carried away. When the storm abated, building operations began in earnest. The first aim of the Pilgrims was to erect a large common house, intended for the use of all until homes could be provided for each family. As they were in danger of being attacked by the Indians, they also erected an observation post, and placed a cannon from the ship in a good position. The whole company was divided into nineteen families, the single men being assigned to different households, so as to reduce the number of houses required. Each family was expected to build its own house, and it was agreed that each should have a plot of land three rods long and half a rod broad. The choice of position was to be determined by lot, but the houses were to be built so as to form a single street.

Very soon the health of the community was severely tested. The unhealthy crowding on board the ship had seriously affected the health of the emigrants, and the harsh wintry weather immediately following upon the disembarkation caused much serious sickness. During the following January and February members of the community died, sometimes at the rate of two or three a day. At one time there were only six or seven people well enough to attend upon the sick and dying. Bradford, who was himself stricken, pays high tribute to the devoted care of William Brewster and Miles Standish. The first house built had to be used as a hospital for the sick. By the end of February thirty-one of the emigrants had died. Of the hundred and two who reached the colony three months before only about fifty survived.

By the middle of March, however, the tide began to turn. The mortality abated, and hope sprang up once again in the dark days of misfortune.

There were other anxieties which pressed upon them besides those caused by sickness and disease. They had to keep constant guard against wild animals. Still more dangerous were the possible attacks of Indians. These had frequently been seen near the camp. It was therefore decided that a military organization should be established under the direction of Miles Standish. Five cannons were brought ashore from the *Mayflower* and placed on Fort Hill, so as to guard the approaches to the village on every side.

The first contacts with the Indians proved to be friendly. Towards the end of March a solitary Indian was seen coming down the main street, He was naked except for a girdle of leather about his loins. His only weapons were a bow and arrows, one of which was headless. He came boldly on, and to their great surprise he addressed them in English, and gave them a cordial welcome. He told them that his name was Samoset, that he was the chief of an island not far away, and that he had learned what English he knew from men who came there fishing. He also informed them that the Indian name of the place where they had established themselves was Patuxet, or the "little bay", and that the original inhabitants had all been swept away by the plague nearly four years before. Therefore there was no one left to dispute the possession of the place with them. He also volunteered to give information about their nearest Indian neighbours.

Samoset stayed the night with them, and the next day departed, saying that he would soon return bringing other Indians with him. He came back the next day in the company of five tall, powerfully-built, Indians. As a sign of their peaceful disposition they left their bows and arrows a quarter of a mile from the settlement. They also brought with them a number of tools taken in the woods a month before. Their chief object in coming was to prepare the way for a visit from a great Indian chief named Massatoit.

A few days later Samoset came again, and brought with him another Indian called Tisquantum, who proved to be a great friend of the settlers, and rendered them invaluable help. He was the sole survivor of the Patuxet tribe. To their great surprise, they learned that he had spent three years in London, and knew it far better than most of the emigrants. He was an escaped slave, who had been destined for Spain. Making his way to England, he had entered the service of a London merchant. Some six months before the arrival of the Pilgrims, he had been brought back to his native country and there found himself the sole survivor of his tribe. He came now to announce that Massatoit would shortly arrive with his warriors.

Massatoit presently came and requested that one of the Pilgrims should be sent to confer with him. It was a momentous occasion. For if peaceful relations could be established with this near neighbour, the fact might greatly further peaceful contacts with other Indian tribes. Edward Winslow was sent on this errand, which proved so far successful that the chief expressed his wish to go on to the settlement, which he did, with a bodyguard of twenty warriors; Winslow being left in charge of the Indians as a hostage. Massatoit was received with every mark of respect by Governor Carver. A treaty was made, each side binding itself not to injure the other, and to render mutual aid in the event of war. Thus the little kingdom of the Pilgrim Fathers made its first alliance and foreign treaty. The treaty was honourably kept for more than fifty years.

The time had now come for the *Mayflower* to return home, and on April 5 the crew hoisted sail and prepared for the homeward voyage. Her departure would mean the severance of the one link of the Pilgrims with the home-land. After she had sailed, their nearest neighbours would be the French of Nova Scotia, some five hundred miles to the north, and the English settlers in Virginia, five hundred miles to the south. We can imagine therefore with what emotion the Pilgrims would watch the departure of the *Mayflower*.

But this was no time for useless repining. If they were to make a success of the enterprise to which they had set their hands they must buckle to the work. It was spring-time, and the ground must be cleared and cultivated, ready to receive the seed upon the fruition of which they must largely depend during the summer and the months that followed. It was somewhat of a puzzle to know what crops could be most usefully grown in this new land. The services of the Indian Tisquantum now proved exceedingly valuable. He told them that they must chiefly depend upon Indian corn and that it should be sown when the young leaves on the oak tree were as big as the ears of a mouse. He showed them also how to fertilize the land by means of decayed fish. The colony was soon a hive of industry. Some of the Pilgrims were engaged in felling trees, others in digging and planting; and yet others in securing the necessary supplies of food for their present needs by hunting and fishing. Only twenty-one men and six big lads were left to do the work; nevertheless, during the first season twenty-one acres of corn-land were tilled, and six acres sown with wheat, rye and barley. This was in addition to the cultivation of the gardens round the houses.

In the midst of this activity, the colony was bereaved of its first Governor, John Carver, and also of his wife. He had served them well, and his death brought great sorrow to the infant community. William Bradford was chosen as his successor; and Isaac Allerton as his assistant. The choice proved to be a wise one. Not only did Bradford possess qualities of leadership, and reveal in all his dealings with his fellows real integrity and Christian character, but we owe to him also most of the information we possess concerning the affairs of the colony during the earlier period. Many of the facts mentioned above have been drawn from his historical account of the Pilgrim movement. It has been pointed out that special interest attaches to this election of Bradford as that of the first American citizen of the English race who was called by the free choice of his brethren to rule over what has now become the great Federal Republic of the United States of America.

When the spring sowing was completed a number of expeditions were undertaken to establish, if possible, friendly relations with the various native tribes in the

district. It was the earnest desire of the Pilgrims to establish themselves in their new home by friendliness rather
than by force. But when they, or their friends and allies
among the tribes, were in danger of treacherous assaults,
they did not hesitate to threaten or even to use military
force.

Towards the end of their first year in the colony they
were able to take stock of their situation with a certain
amount of satisfaction. They had suffered great sorrows;
many of their friends had fallen. But they could feel that
they had made a real beginning of colonial life. Seven
dwelling-houses had been erected, and also four main
buildings. One of these served as a place of worship and
for the holding of town meetings. The others were used
as storehouses for provisions and supplies. Friendly
relations had been established with many neighbours. It
was therefore decided to hold a Day of Thanksgiving.
Thus began the New England Festival of Thanksgiving
Day.

During the month of December this year (1621)
Governor Winslow (as he became later) wrote a letter to
a friend in England in which he gives an interesting account
of these matters. He tells how on this festival occasion they
entertained the native king Massatoit, and some ninety
of his men. He pays a tribute to the general friendliness
of the Indians and to their faithfulness to the covenant
they had made. The air of the colony, he reports, is similar
to that of England, though somewhat warmer in summer.
They have enjoyed a most seasonable year, and he avows
that when once they have kine, horses and sheep, they
will live there as contented as in any part of the world.
They have fish and fowl in abundance. The earth yields
naturally many kinds of herbs, and there are grapes,
strawberries, gooseberries and raspberries. The country
only wants industrious men to cultivate it. It is grieving

to think of England being so greatly burdened with a large population, whilst such vast spaces are uninhabited.

The writer then gives instructions with reference to the things which any new-comers to the colony would find most useful.

About this time the Pilgrims were surprised at the appearance of an English vessel in the harbour. It proved to be the ship *Fortune*, bringing thirty-five new colonists. Among them were William Brewster's eldest son, Robert Cushman, and John Winslow, a brother of Edward. These were a welcome addition to the strength of the colony. For a time, however, they were an additional burden, as they brought few provisions with them. The *Fortune* also brought a patent of their land from the Council of New England, drawn up in the name of John Pierce and his associates. This document carries the signatures and seals of the Duke of Lennox, the Marquis of Hamilton, the Earl of Warwick, and Sir Ferdinando Gorges. It bears the date June 1, 1621, and is still preserved in the Pilgrim Hall at Plymouth. Under certain conditions it granted to Pierce and each of his associates a hundred acres of land. It remained in force for a year only, and was then superseded by another.

When the *Fortune* returned to the mother country she took back a cargo of the value of about £500, consisting largely of beaver fur and prepared timber. Unfortunately, it never reached its destination, for it was seized by the French. The cargo was retained, though the ship's company were released. Robert Cushman, who was on board, managed to secure all the papers, which included the journals of Bradford and Winslow.

It was scarcely to be expected that relations with the Indians would remain peaceful under all circumstances. Much alarm was caused by the receipt of a warlike challenge from the Narragansett Indians, consisting of a sheaf of arrows tied round with a rattlesnake skin. At the same time tragic news reached them from the neighbouring colony of Virginia, where the Indians had massacred three hundred and forty-seven men, women and children. This led the Pilgrims to fortify their settlement by means of palisades and bastions. The gates were guarded by sentinels and kept locked at night.

It came to the knowledge of the Pilgrims that the Indians were preparing to make an attack upon a new colony which had been established at Wessagusset, since known as Weymouth, by Thomas Weston, who has been referred to above as helping the Pilgrims at the beginning of their enterprise. These new settlers appear to have had little sense of discipline, and to have provoked the Indians by robbing them, and in other ways. In consequence, the Indians were plotting a general massacre of the Wessagusset settlers, and also of the whole Plymouth colony; the latter were to be included in the massacre because the Indians naturally supposed that they would otherwise take vengeance on them for such an act against fellow-settlers.

The situation was seriously discussed in an assembly of the whole people. On the one hand, the Pilgrims were unwilling to shed blood if it could be avoided. They had sought in many ways to establish peaceable relations with the Indians. On the other hand, they could not allow their fellow-countrymen at Wessagusset to be massacred if it could be prevented. They decided therefore to strike first. Miles Standish was sent, as if on a trading expedition, to warn the colony at Wessagusset of their danger, and then to strike at those who had plotted the massacre. There was a brief but fierce encounter, and the Indians were put to flight. The Wessagusset settlers had not the stamina of the Pilgrims, and in view of the hardships and dangers which threatened them they abandoned the country.

We must note here an important change that was now introduced into the life of the colony. Since their arrival, life had been on a communistic basis. All had shared alike in the proceeds of the total effort of the community. It was soon seen, however, that such a system involved much unfairness. It was not reasonable that the hard-working and thrifty should fare in all ways like the idle and the spendthrift. It was therefore decided to allot to each family for one year a piece of land in the proportion of one acre to each person; the division to be made by lot. The results were soon visible in the much greater amount of corn sown than under the old system.

The times were hard, and it was necessary that each should do his utmost to increase production, and to conserve the stocks. But when they had done all they could in these respects, by the time they had finished the sowing in the spring of 1623, the stores of food were spent, and they knew not how they would live until the next harvest was ready. Things were made more difficult by a severe drought which lasted for seven weeks from the early days of June. Winslow reports that before harvest-time came he saw men staggering for want of food. We read of William Brewster sitting down to a table with nothing but a platter of boiled clams and a pot of water before him. Nevertheless, for this meagre diet he gave thanks to God.

To add to their disappointment they heard of a supply ship that had been sent to them many months previously but which had not arrived. Signs of a wreck were seen on the coast, and they could only conclude that the vessel had perished.

Now indeed their faith was tried to the utmost. Even the most courageous felt some discouragement. Winslow says it seemed as if God, who had so many times intervened to help them, had now turned against them. Every good man was therefore moved privately to examine his condition between God and his conscience. The public authorities also appointed a day to be set apart from all other employments that all might humble themselves before God, and beseech Him of His mercy to grant them deliverance. Soon their prayer was answered. In the morning when they assembled the heavens were clear, and it looked as if the drought was as likely as ever to continue. But after their public service of intercession had lasted some eight or nine hours, before their departure, the weather was overcast, and the clouds were gathering on all sides. And the next morning the clouds distilled such soft, sweet and moderate showers of rain, which continued some fourteen days, that it was hard to say whether the withered corn or their own drooping affections were more quickened and revived.

Having received such manifest tokens of God's favour the Pilgrims thought it would be base ingratitude if they should fail to make public acknowledgment of their indebtedness and gratitude to God. They therefore appointed another Solemn Day for this purpose, and on it they returned glory, honour and praise to the good God who had dealt so graciously with them.

Before long other events occurred to cheer them. In July (1623) two more ships came, bringing reinforcements. These two ships, the *Anne* and the *Little James*, between them brought about one hundred new emigrants to the colony.

Governor Winslow concludes his narrative of these events with the remark that if ever any people in these later ages were upheld by the providence of God in a special manner these emigrants were. Oftentimes in the morning, in addition to other labours, they had their food to seek for the day. At noon he had frequently seen men stagger by reason of faintness for want of food. But ere the night came they had enjoyed such plenty that it seemed as if the windows of heaven had been opened. Often they had been at the very brim of the pit, and in danger of being swallowed up, without even knowing of their peril. But God preserved them. Wherefore he could not but conclude that God had a purpose to give that land as an inheritance to our nation.

The total number of the emigrants was now two hundred and thirty-three, and these comprise the company known in America as the Pilgrims or the Forefathers.

Chapter Eight

THE EARLY CIVIL AND RELIGIOUS ADMINISTRATION OF THE COLONY

DURING these early years the government of the colony was of a very simple and elementary character. The town meeting was the main source of authority. This laid down the rules and regulations which were held to be desirable for the well-being of the community. Fresh laws were added as they were needed, the statute-book being the Governor's notebook. By the time at which we have now arrived, however, that is, towards the end of 1623, things had begun to take a more permanent shape. The colony Record-book was started, and in it were entered the various acts and decisions of the authorities of the colony. In the case of the trial of any member of the community the whole number of the townsmen were assembled as a court; and the Governor presided and carried out the sentence. This method was now superseded by a trial by jury, as in the old country.

Another change was made in the government of the colony. This year William Bradford was a third time elected Governor; in spite of his protests that another should have the honour. In yielding to the pressure of the colonists, he urged that the Governor ought to have the assistance of a Council. The colonists acted on his suggestion, and a Council of five was created.

Up to this time the religious situation had also been one of simplicity and harmony. Elder Brewster had been their pastor and preacher, and right well had he acquitted himself of his task. In a letter that now arrived from their old friend and pastor, John Robinson, there was a hint of coming change. Some of the Merchant Adventurers, who had financed the enterprise, were inclined towards sending over an episcopalian clergyman to control the religious life of the colony. For this reason, Robinson thinks, they had put obstacles in the way of his coming over with more of the Pilgrims. It was soon manifest that Robinson's fear was not without foundation. For in this same year Robert Gorges was commissioned by the Council of New England as Governor-General of the whole country. When he left to take up his office he took with him another company of settlers to the village of Weymouth, formerly known as Wessagusset, which has been referred to above as having been deserted by the first settlers. With him travelled also an episcopalian clergyman named William Morrell. To him the Council had given general powers to regulate and control the religious affairs of the country. Morrell, however, proved to be a man of commonsense and tolerant temper, and though he spent a year at Plymouth he made no attempt to interfere with the religious life of the colony, and said nothing on the matter until he was on the point of leaving. Only after he had left them was it fully realized that all the time he had been with them he was authorized to compel them to conform to the rites and ceremonies of the Church of England.

A group of the emigrants, who had come over in the *Anne*, and who insisted on keeping themselves as "particulars"—as a colony within the colony—began now to introduce an element of contrariness into the communal life. They sent complaints to London to the effect that the ordinances of religion were being neglected in the colony, with the result that in 1624, when the ship *Charity* arrived from England bringing supplies, she brought inquiries on certain points mentioned by the complainants, and also another episcopalian clergyman named John Lyford. He had been chosen by the Adventurers who were opposed to Free Church principles to set matters right. Edward Winslow and Robert Cushman were present at the meeting of the Adventurers when the matter was under discussion and objected to his being sent out. Their objection was overruled, but they managed to secure an agreement that he should have no official position in the colony until the Church at Plymouth should voluntarily choose him as their pastor.

John Lyford was respectfully received, and he on his part professed great friendliness towards the Pilgrims, and after a time sought Church membership with them. Indeed, his fulsome effusiveness induced suspicion that he was not quite what he appeared to be. It was soon discovered that he was in the habit of writing letters home of the most mischievous character. Before despatching them he showed them to his friends among the "Particulars", who were seen to laugh and to chuckle over them. The Governor realized that letters of such a character might cause serious trouble among those who supported, and in a measure controlled, the colony at home. The letters were therefore intercepted. They were found to contain many slanders and false accusations against the Pilgrims. In one of the letters Lyford asserted that he, and another man named Oldham, intended very shortly to set up worship on the episcopal model.

Without knowing that their mischievous plotting had been discovered, these men sought occasions of quarrel with the leaders of the colony. Brewster now thought it was time to confront them with the evidence he had collected. For this purpose he summoned a court of the townsmen, and in the presence of all he charged Lyford and Oldham with secretly plotting to destroy the harmony and government of the colony. They denied the charge until the intercepted letters were produced, and some of them read. These letters showed that not only had Lyford complained of mismanagement in the colony, but he had also urged that John Robinson and the rest of the Church at Leyden should not be allowed to join the colony. He likewise suggested that another kind of colonists should be sent over, and in sufficient numbers to outnumber the original settlers. He further advised that the new-comers, known as "Particulars", though of their own free choice separating themselves from the rest, should nevertheless have an equal voice in all the courts and elections of the colony. He concluded his letter by urging that his own part in these matters should be kept secret.

The townsmen reminded him that when he sought admission to the Church of the colony he declared that he no longer regarded himself as a minister, despite the fact that he had been episcopally ordained, until he received a call by them. Yet now he had been discovered separating certain persons in the colony from the rest and setting himself against the authorities.

When he realized that his villainy had been discovered, he confessed his sins, called himself a reprobate, and said that he doubted whether God would ever pardon such iniquities.

The decision of the court was that Oldham must go home at once, leaving his family until he could make arrangements for them. They proposed to give Lyford another chance. He would be allowed to remain six months longer. He confessed with tears that he was leniently dealt with. Very soon, however, it appeared that his duplicity was incurable. He was discovered again writing secretly letters of complaint that there was no ordained ministry in the colony, Elder Brewster being still their preacher.

The townsmen continued to exercise great patience with

this importer of mischief. The letter just referred to was written in August, 1624. Lyford was allowed to remain at Plymouth throughout the following winter, drawing his food from the public stores. The townsmen, however, thought it fitting to reply to the charges made against them on the ground of faulty religious oversight, and as to their having no ordained minister.

"We answer", they wrote, "the more is our wrong, that our pastor is kept from us by these men's means, and then they reproach us for it when they have done. Yet have we not been wholly destitute of the means of salvation, as this man would make the world believe: for our reverend elder hath laboured diligently in dispensing the word of God unto us, before he came, and since hath taken equal pains with himself in preaching the same. And be it spoken without ostentation, he is not inferior to Mr. Lyford (and some of his betters) either in gifts or learning, though he would never be persuaded to take higher office upon him."

Oldham later returned to Plymouth Harbour, but only to vilify the colonists. So outrageous was his behaviour, among other things calling the colonists rebels and traitors, that the only thing to do was to put him under lock and key until he grew more reasonable. Then he was led out between two lines of musketeers and ignominiously expelled the colony. Ultimately Lyford joined him at Nantasket.

It has been objected to these proceedings of the colonists that they were high-handed and intolerant, and an infringement of the principle of freedom of religious worship. A reasonable view of the facts does not bear out the accusation. We have shown above that the leading principle of the Episcopalians at the time was uniformity. Once let this principle become established in the colony, and be sustained by the religious and civil authorities of the homeland, then all hope of freedom of religious worship in New England would be at an end.

It is one thing for an established government to be willing to concede freedom of worship to a small minority in a civilized community; it is another thing for a small community, with but a provisional form of government, to be asked to allow a form of religious administration and worship to establish itself in their midst, when that form of Church government has been for centuries notorious for its exclusive claims, and shamefully cruel in its endeavours to establish a rigid system of uniformity, and to this end has persecuted and done to death the noblest and the best. In judging the action of the Pilgrims all the facts must be taken into consideration; and, when this is done, they will be seen to have exercised only the most elementary right of self-preservation. If the episcopal system, backed by Royal power, were once established among them, there was no probability that the Pilgrims would be able to retain the freedom for which they had sacrificed so much.

The trouble with Lyford brought in its train trouble with the Merchant Adventurers in England. When Edward Winslow returned from a visit to England in 1625, he brought from them a warning to the effect that they would only consent to continue their connection with the plantation upon certain conditions. They insisted that they should not only be partners in trade but also in the government of the colony. They likewise demanded that the Presbyterian system of Church government should be adopted, and that Brownism or Congregationalism should be abolished. Another condition was that John Robinson, and the remaining portion of the Church at Leyden, should not be allowed to come over and join the colony, unless they recanted their errors and became reconciled to the Church of England.

These demands were very stern, and altogether unreasonable in view of the past history of the Pilgrim Fathers. It could not be expected that these should assist in establishing in New England any form of Church government which demanded rigid uniformity, a demand which had been the source of so many woes in Old England, and to escape from which they had fled, first to Holland, and then across the Atlantic to their new home.

To these unreasonable demands the colonists made a reasonable reply. Throughout all these contentions it is remarkable how ready these Puritans were "to give a reason for the faith" that was in them, without acrimony, despite great provocation. They urged that in substance they did hold and practise the discipline of the French and other Reformed Churches: but to bind themselves to carry out every detail of the system would involve the surrender of the liberty which was theirs in Christ Jesus. Even the Reformed Churches differed in details among themselves. Paul did not claim that any man should follow him save as he followed Christ. Bradford, however, in relating these matters, fails to state what reply they made to the suggestion that John Robinson should sign a recantation.

One section of the Adventurers still remained favourable to the Pilgrims. From these Winslow brought a reply which stated that the joint account had been closed, and that £1,400 remained due from the colonists. Goods sufficient to meet this debt were to be shipped home as means became available. Words of encouragement were added, urging them to carry on with the work of colonization, acting in accordance with the directions of conscience.

Finding that the relations with the Merchant Adventurers hindered them in developing their colonial enterprises, the authorities of the colony resolved to place their enterprise upon a new footing. They conceived the idea of hiring the trade of the company for a certain number of years, and during that time of paying off the sum of £1,800 that was now due to the Merchant Adventurers, as well as some trading debts which amounted to about £600. To carry out these designs, Isaac Allerton was sent over to England in 1626 and returned the following year. He had managed to raise a loan of £200 for the colony at the rate of thirty per cent interest. By the arrangement made with the company in London, for the sum of £1,800 the Merchant Adventurers were to surrender all claim upon the shares, land, and merchandise of the colony. The sum of £200 was to be paid each year beginning with the year 1628. The agreement was favourably received by the colonists and confirmed by them, the responsibility being borne by Bradford, Brewster, Standish, and five other leaders. A deed was duly drawn up, signed and sealed, and sent to England.

Another important arrangement was made among the colonists themselves. These men who made themselves responsible for paying off the debt to the Adventurers also came to an agreement with their brethren to pay off the debt in six years, and at the same time undertook to import every year £50 worth of hose and shoes. These were to be sold to the colonists in exchange for corn at the rate of six shillings the bushel. Certain conditions were laid down, the chief being that all the trade of the colony with the outside world should be carried on by themselves alone. After the passing of the six years the whole of the trade was to return to the use of the colony as before. The arrangement was therefore a temporary trading agreement, and not a means employed by the authorities for enriching themselves at the expense of the rest of the community. The men who undertook these responsibilities were later known as "Undertakers". There was, however, a proviso that if the trading profits were not sufficient to meet the yearly payments to the Company in London, the deficiency should be equally made up by all the colonists.

A further change made at this time was that the land was divided into shares of twenty acres, and each settler or purchaser was to have one share in addition to the land he already possessed; the heads of the households were to have as many shares as they had persons in the families. The more recent comers to the colony were to share on the same basis as the rest. The meadow-land was to be regarded as a common possession. An agreement was also made as to the possession of the few cattle.

I shall only briefly refer to the fact that in 1623 a Dutch colony was established at Manhattan, the modern New York. For several years there was no intercourse between the Dutch and the English settlers. But in March, 1627, Bradford, as Governor of the English colony, received a friendly letter from Isaac de Rassières, the Secretary of the Dutch colony. The Dutchman congratulated the English on the success of their undertaking, and expressed the wish that trade relations between the two colonies might soon be established. An equally friendly letter was returned by the English, who expressed their readiness to trade with them as opportunity offered. In the autumn of the same year the Dutch Secretary paid a visit to Plymouth, and remained there for several days. The wished-for trade relations were established.

Chapter Nine

LATER PURITAN ARRIVALS AND DEVELOPMENTS

AS our subject is the Pilgrim Fathers, their sufferings and sacrifices in the winning of religious freedom, their flight from England, and settlement in Holland and America, and the legacy of courage and devotion to a high religious ideal which they have left to the world, I shall deal only very briefly with the further developments which took place in the New World as successive groups of colonists found their way from the Old World to the New.

During the twelve years lying between 1628 and 1640 a number of groups of colonists followed the Pilgrim pioneers. These founded settlements round Massachusetts Bay and along the Connecticut River. Like the Pilgrims, many of these also came from Lincolnshire, which county therefore has the honour of providing the first and like-wise the main elements which have made the great continent of North America predominantly English in language and sentiment. These later elements were generally of a different type from the pioneers, who, as we have seen, were chiefly drawn from the humbler walks of life. Those who followed where they led the way were frequently drawn from better-class homes. About ninety of them had passed through the University, the greater part through Cambridge. The great majority of the later emigrants were drawn from the eastern counties of England. It was appropriate therefore that the chief city of New England should receive the name of Boston. The earliest counties of Massachusetts were called by the names of Norfolk, Suffolk and Essex.

The chief centre of this later puritan movement was Lincolnshire. It owed much to the influence of Theophilus Clinton, the fourth Earl of Lincoln. Two of the family seats of the Earl—Tattershall Castle and Sempringham—became centres where the puritan-minded often met for conference. Two of the earl's sisters actually went over to New England. Many of the clergy in this area were of the puritan persuasion, and suffered for their Nonconformity under the grievous rule of Laud. From the address to the King presented by the new Parliament, we gather that these later emigrants, though puritan in sympathy, were not Separatists as the Pilgrim Fathers were. They were loyally attached to the Church of England, and wished this fact to be clearly understood. The general attitude was expressed by Francis Higginson who, as the ship in which he sailed was off Land's End, called his family and others round him to take a farewell look of their beloved land, and said: "We will not say, as the Separatists were wont to say, at their leaving England, 'Farewell Babylon, farewell Rome'; but we will say, 'Farewell dear England, farewell the Church of God in England, and all the Christian friends there! We do not go to New England as Separatists from the Church of England, though we cannot but separate from the corruptions of it; but we go to practise the positive part of Church reformation, and to propagate the Gospel in America.'"

Another centre of this later puritan movement was Dorchester. In this, John White, the puritan Rector of Dorchester, was one of the leading spirits. Funds were offered by friends both in London and the west if a suitable party could be secured. John Endicott, of Dorchester, a man of strong puritan convictions, emerged as leader, and a patent was obtained from the Council of New England, in March, 1628, by which the Council sold to some knights and certain other gentlemen about

Dorchester the part of New England which lay between the Merrimac River and the Charles River on Massachusetts Bay. Endicott and his party sailed from Weymouth in the *Abigail* and arrived at Naumkeag (later called Salem) on September 6 following.

Much sickness was caused on board ship by the fact that impure salt had been used in the provisions. On arrival Endicott appealed to Bradford, Governor of the Plymouth Colony, for the services of a physician. Dr. Fuller was sent, and thus was established a lasting friendship between the colonies of Plymouth and Naumkeag. This friendship had a direct bearing on the ecclesiastical establishment of the Naumkeag colony. Endicott's objections to the Separatists' views were softened or removed by his conversations with Fuller. He wrote upon the subject to Governor Bradford, declaring that he had been satisfied by Fuller touching the Pilgrim's judgments as to the outward form of God's worship. "It is," he said, "as far as I can gather, no other than is warranted by the evidence of truth, and the same which I have professed and maintained ever since the Lord in mercy revealed Himself to me; being far from the common report that hath been spread of you touching that particular."

Endicott also expressed the wish that the two colonies should be bound together in a loving fellowship. For all God's people, he says, "are marked with one and the same mark, and sealed with one and the same seal, and have for the main one and the same heart, guided by one and the same Spirit of truth, and where this is there can be no discord, nay, here must needs be sweet harmony."

Largely through the favourable report of the new colony which was sent back by Endicott, a considerable number of influential people became interested in it and joined the enterprise, and in March, 1629, a royal charter was obtained which constituted the Company a legal corporation with the title of the "Governor and Company of the Massachusetts Bay in New England". The members of the corporation thus formed were to elect annually a governor, deputy-governor, and eighteen assistants. They were to hold monthly meetings and four general meetings during the year. Matthew Craddock was elected as Governor. Very soon a second government was elected which was to be resident in the colony. This consisted of a governor, deputy-governor, and twelve councillors. This second government was to be free from control on the part of the Company at home, both as to legislation and in the appointment of officers. For every £50 invested each shareholder was to be allotted a plot of land of two hundred acres, and fifty acres more for himself and each member of his family if he settled in the colony in addition to investing his money. Emigrants who were not shareholders were also assigned plots of land.

Three ministers were sent out to minister to the spiritual needs of the community—namely, Samuel Skelton, Francis Higginson, and Francis Bright. Higginson was the son of the Vicar of Claybrook, in Leicestershire, and a graduate of Cambridge University. He was a man of puritan convictions, and had been removed from a living in Leicester for not conforming to ecclesiastical requirements. He had many followers and was greatly beloved.

Five vessels were chartered to take the company out, including the famous *Mayflower*. These emigrants were well equipped with large supplies of provisions, and such things as would assist in the establishment of a strong colony. The puritan tone of the colony may be judged from the fact that it was laid down that labour should cease every Saturday at 3 p.m., and that the rest of the day should be spent in catechism, and in preparations for the Sabbath as the minister should direct. The Company also charged the settlers to take special care that family prayer should be observed morning and evening, and that a watchful eye should be kept over each family that disorders might be prevented. The vessels sailed at various dates in the spring of 1629.

On their arrival at Naumkeag (or Salem), the three ministers discussed with Endicott and those with him the further ecclesiastical constitution of the colony. Two of them agreed with the procedure which had been adopted after consultations with the Pilgrims at Plymouth. The other (Francis Bright) dissented and removed to Charlestown. Three weeks after they had landed, a Solemn Assembly was held to make choice of a pastor and teacher. Voting was by ballot; Skelton was chosen as pastor, and Higginson as teacher. When the two ministers had signified their acceptance of the offices they were commended to God in prayer. Mr. Higginson and three or four of the gravest members of the Church prayed and laid their hands on Mr. Skelton. Following this there was an imposition of hands on Mr. Higginson. It would be a mistake, however, to see in such a solemn service a reordination in the usual sense of the word, of men already ordained. We conclude this from the fact that, concerning a similar service and ceremony held during the following year, Winthrop says: "We used imposition of hands, but with this protestation by all, that it was only as a sign of election and confirmation; not of any intent that Mr. Wilson should renounce his ministry he received in England."

August 6 of this year (1629) was observed as a day of fasting and prayer. Elders and deacons were ordained, and the two ministers gave their assent publicly to a Confession and Covenant which they had drawn up beforehand. Towards the end of the day likewise the Confession and Covenant were solemnly read and assented to by the people generally. The use of a Confession and Covenant as a basis for a Church constitution was evidently borrowed from Presbyterianism, in which it played a prominent part, as we shall see when we come to deal with the affairs of the Scottish Reformation.[1] It was clearly stated. however, that the assent given was not to the details or form of words but only to the substance of the declarations. For instance, according to Mather, they covenanted with the Lord and with one another to walk together in all His ways, so far as He reveals Himself to them in His Word. They avouched the Lord to be their God, and themselves to be His people in the truth and simplicity of their spirits.

In the following years the Covenant was renewed from time to time on special occasions. It became the basis of Church fellowship, members being admitted to the Church by expressed assent thereto. This procedure, however, was not carried through with full agreement. Some complained that the Book of Common Prayer was not used, and that the ordinances of Baptism and the Lord's Supper were not administered according to the ceremonies that were observed in England. These dissentients, who were led by two members of the Council, John and Samuel Browne, carried their protests so far as to separate themselves from the assembly of the other colonists, and conducted a service agreeable to the Prayer Book. Governor Endicott called the two brothers before him and listened to their complaints. They charged Skelton and Higginson with being Separatists, and said that they would soon become Anabaptists. The two ministers denied the charge. They affirmed that they were not separating from the Church of England, but only from its corruptions; that, after suffering much for their convictions, they had left their native land that they might get away from the Prayer Book and

[1] See pp. 172ff., 184f.

the ceremonies, and now being in a place where liberty could be enjoyed, they should exercise their liberty, holding that the imposition of these things was a sinful corruption of the worship of God.

The answer of the two ministers was well approved of by the Governor and the Council, and finding that the brothers, John and Samuel Browne, were determined to follow a course that would lead to faction, they told them that New England was no place for them, and shipped them back to England the same year. This procedure has frequently been condemned as intolerant and inconsistent with their profession of religious freedom. But Professor Gardiner has rightly pointed out that the action of the Governor and Council should be viewed rather as one of self-preservation. At that time it must have seemed to the colonists that the question to be settled was not whether they were to tolerate others, but whether they were to give others the chance of being intolerant to themselves. Their own religious liberty would certainly have been in danger if they had allowed a population to grow up round them ready to be the instruments of oppression in the hands of the government at home.

It seems clear that in making these changes these Salem colonists did not suppose that they were ceasing to be members of the Church of England. In explaining the situation to their friends they admitted that on a number of points they had changed their views since leaving England. Certain things which they had regarded as matters of indifference, and to be at least tolerated, they had come to see were not warranted by the Word of God.

It should also be remembered that the conception of episcopal government was not then what it became later. Opinion as to the nature and necessity of episcopacy was fluid. Many of the prominent episcopalians were in relations of intimacy and friendliness with the presbyterian reformers on the Continent. Under the influence of Cartwright, large numbers of the clergy favoured a presbyterian form of Church government, and actually established that system in some of the English parishes. Yet they claimed to belong to the National Church.

Again, until the time of Laud the doctrine of the divine right of episcopacy was a comparative novelty. It was subscribed to by only a minority of the clergy. The first modern expression of it is found in a sermon preached by Bancroft at St. Paul's Cross, in 1588, and even then it was put forward rather as a counter-claim to the claim of the Presbyterians, who were claiming divine right for their system of Church government. We shall understand better the nature of that claim when we come to consider the progress of the Reformation in Scotland. When the question was referred by Lord Burleigh to Dr. Hammond, then chancellor of the diocese of London, the latter replied that the authority of the bishops was derived solely from the statute passed in the twenty-fifth year of Henry VIII, and that it was unreasonable for the bishops to make any other claim. He said also that "if it had pleased Her Majesty with the wisdom of the realm to have used no bishops at all, we could not have complained justly of any defect in our Church." When, several years later, Laud asserted that there could be no true Church without diocesan bishops, Dr. Holland, the Regius Professor of Divinity, remonstrated with him for having cast a bone of contention between the Church of England and the Reformed Churches. The position Laud took up was denounced as "a novel Popish position". One modern authority admits that "there was not one leading divine from Hooper to Hooker who ever claimed more than historic and primitive usage as the ground of episcopal authority, or pretended that it was of the essence of a Church."

There was ground therefore for the contention of the Pilgrims and their successors that such things as episcopacy, the use of the Prayer Book, the use of vestments, and the practice of ceremonies were still open questions, and that their own views were more in accord with the principles of the Reformation than were those of their opponents.

It was acknowledged, however, that these early episcopal puritans had come to accept certain principles which distinctly looked in the direction of Separatism. First, they insisted that to be true members of the Christian Church men must be Christians; not a very novel idea, one would think. Secondly, they held that a company of Christian people, that is, Christian in character as well as in name, are capable of exercising discipline among themselves in accordance with the teaching of the New Testament, without having to call in the help of the secular or civil power. There is certainly very much in the New Testament to support this position.

Chapter Ten

THE BUILDING UP OF A FREE CHURCH IN A FREE STATE

BY the year 1630 three large bands of emigrants had settled in Massachusetts. A development now took place which was of great moment for the future of the colony. The controllers of the Massachusetts Bay Company, realizing that the work of the colony might at any time be interfered with and gravely injured by the Crown, conceived the idea of a Free State beyond the sea, and invested with the power of self-government, instead of being controlled as now by a Company with headquarters in London. They realized, however, that great caution would have to be exercised if they were to achieve their ideal. Laud and the other ecclesiastical authorities were not at all likely to favour such a break away from civil and ecclesiastical control.

At a general meeting of the Company, held in 1629, the apparently innocent proposal was made that in order to induce a better type of emigrant to share in the colonial enterprise, as well as for certain other unspecified reasons, it was expedient to transfer the government of the plantation to those who should actually go to live in the colony, and that the colony should not continue in the same subordination to the Company as was then the case. After some discussion it was agreed to leave over a final decision till the next meeting. In the meantime the matter was to remain one of secrecy.

Before the next meeting took place, twelve of the governors held a private meeting at Cambridge, and bound themselves by a written agreement to be ready by March 1 to embark themselves and their families for the colony, if by the end of September the whole government of the plantation should have been legally transferred to those who should inhabit the colony. At the formal meeting of the governors three days later a general consent was given to the proposal, and the order was accordingly drawn up. In effect this placed the entire control of affairs in the colony in the hands of the ten members of the Company who were themselves going to the colony. As Matthew Craddock, the Governor at that time, was not going out, John Winthrop was elected as Governor for the following year. He lived to become one of the most outstanding men in early American history. He was a man of sterling character and of deep religious devotion.

Winthrop and his associates sailed from Southampton in four vessels on March 23, 1630, and reached their destination on June 12. On landing at Salem, Winthrop immediately assumed office as Governor of the colony. His responsibility was very considerable, for within a short time of his landing the number of emigrants had risen to about three thousand. He found much sickness in the colony, and a great scarcity of provisions, so that he had to feed the settlers out of the stocks they had brought with them. The new arrivals were not too well pleased with Salem as the site of a colony, and consequently they dispersed themselves in a number of localities, some going to Charlestown, others to Boston, and yet others to other places. Winthrop settled first at Charlestown, but later he moved to Boston, which came to be regarded as the centre and capital.

As the colony grew, it was found necessary to make other changes in the government. In October 1630 the legislative rights were transferred from the court of the freemen to the Governor, deputy-governor and assistants. The election of the Governor was handed over from the freemen to the assistants. This oligarchical form of government was not likely to be satisfactory for long; and very soon further changes had to be introduced in order to obtain money for the defence of the colony. The freemen of Watertown objected to a necessary levy being made unless the power to make laws was properly vested in the whole body of freemen.

At the general court it was enacted that during the following year the whole body of freemen should elect the Governor, deputy-governor and assistants. It was also decreed that each town should send two representatives to advise the Governor and his assistants on the question of taxation. Further, in 1634 the freemen in each town elected three representatives, twenty-four in all, who interviewed the general court, and claimed that according to the patent the making of laws was vested in the whole body of the freemen. After some discussion, the representatives of the freemen obtained full power of election and legislation. The decision was also made that there should be four courts a year, and that at one of these the whole body of freemen were to elect the officers of the colony. At the other courts the other necessary business, such as legislation, and the granting of land should be transacted. Shortly afterwards it became necessary to define more clearly the relations between the Governor and his assistants, on the one hand, and of the representatives, on the other.

It was natural that in drawing up the constitution of the new colony some mistakes should be made; and a serious blunder was made when it was decided that no man should be a freeman of the colony unless he were also a member of a church. Church membership was thus made a necessary qualification for voting at town meetings.

Then it was enacted that the towns should have the right of dividing their lands, of electing constables and surveyors, and of enforcing their orders by a fine of twenty shillings. The result of this procedure was that non-church members were practically disfranchised; and the control of their secular interests was given to men whose one qualification might be that they happened to be Church members. This was to offer unworthy inducements to church membership, and the arrangement was bound to result in friction between the two classes of emigrants. It was an unfortunate relic of the relations between Church and State in the old country.

By 1634 the Massachusetts colony consisted of about four thousand Englishmen, grouped in some twenty villages or towns on or near the shore of the Bay. The religious life of the colony was guided by some twenty ministers, most of them graduates of a university, Cambridge or Oxford, and many of them had held livings in the Church of England. Some of them were men of strong character, who had suffered for their puritan convictions before leaving the old country. Among these was John Cotton, who for twenty years had been the Vicar of St. Botolph's, the Parish Church of Boston, in Lincolnshire. He had openly taught that, according to the Scripture, bishops were appointed to rule no larger a diocese than a particular congregation—an indisputable fact, but the assertion of which at that time could not but land the preacher in a sea of trouble. Another obnoxious element in his teaching was that the keys of ecclesiastical government are given by the Lord to each separate Church. Moreover, not content with such assertions of Scriptural truth, he acted on his conviction, and set up a "gathered Church" within the bounds of his parish. We have seen that Bernard of Worksop had done a similar thing many years before. On July 8, 1633, Cotton placed his resignation in the hands of the bishop. In due course he arrived in New England, and was solemnly set apart to be the colleague of John Wilson, the pastor of the new Boston which had been established in the colony.

This John Wilson, with whom Cotton was thus associated, was also a man of note and of steadfast puritan conviction. He was a son of a prebendary of St. Paul's, grand-nephew of Archbishop Grindal, and a graduate of Emmanuel College, Cambridge.

Other men who made their mark upon the colony in these early days were Zachary Symmes, who ministered at Charlestown; Peter Bulkely, the founder of Concord, and an ancestor of Emerson; Richard Mather, father of Increase Mather, one of the Presidents of Harvard College, and grandfather of Cotton Mather who, in his *Magnalia Christi Americana*, has bequeathed to us important records of the colony during the first eighty years of its history.

Special mention should be made of Thomas Shepard, and of his collision with Laud, when he was Bishop of London. Hearing of the puritanic utterances of Shepard, when he was lecturer at Earl's Colne, in Essex, Laud summoned him into his presence and rated him savagely for his misdemeanours. "He looked as though blood would have gushed out of his face", said Shepard in recording the interview. When Shepard sought to soothe the narrow-minded ecclesiastical tyrant, the bishop called him "a prating coxcomb", and asked him if he thought all learning was in his brain. He ended by forbidding him to exercise any ministerial function within his diocese. After much persecution and many hardships, Shepard made his way over to New England, and became the pastor of a church at Newtown, which was later known as Cambridge. Cotton Mather reports that one reason for establishing

Harvard College at Cambridge was that students might be able to draw inspiration for a future ministry from Thomas Shepard's teaching.

We have seen that many of the colonists were well-educated men. A considerable portion of them had had the advantage of a university education. With such men to guide and inspire, it was natural that zeal for education should be one of the marks of the colony in these early days. A permanent memorial of this ever-enduring interest was left by John Harvard, who bequeathed his library and half his estate to endow the famous college which is known the world over. It was founded in 1636.

In the same year a large body of the colonists, under the leading of Thomas Hooker, travelled westwards a hundred miles and established a settlement in the Connecticut River valley. Here such progress was made that in a couple of years the towns of Windsor, Hartford, and Wethersfield declared themselves to be a commonwealth. They appointed a Governor, six assistants and deputies. The Governor and his assistants were to be elected annually by the whole body of freemen met for that purpose. The mistake made at Massachusetts was here avoided. Church membership was not insisted upon as a warrant for the exercise of civil rights. It was only stipulated that the Governor should be a member of the Church. All freemen who had taken the oath of fidelity to the commonwealth had the right to vote for the election of deputies. The constitution of Connecticut has been said to be the first written constitution known to history that created a government. American democracy looks back to it as its source. Thomas Hooker, who played a dominant part in the proceedings, may be regarded as the father of the American democratic constitution.

In the meantime, great events were taking place in the homeland. The Long Parliament began its epoch-making career in 1640. The tyrannous reign of Laud came to an end with his imprisonment in 1641; in 1645 he was executed. The Courts of Star Chamber and High Commission were abolished. Civil war began in 1642. These stirring events, and many others, brought much relief to the puritans, though the era of complete religious toleration was not yet. But so far as our subject is concerned, the changes meant that the immediate causes of exodus to the New World ceased to operate. Since the arrival of the *Mayflower* in 1620 the population had increased to twenty-six thousand persons. After 1640, emigration to this part of North America was inconsiderable.

While the events above described were taking place in the Massachusetts Bay and Connecticut Valley colonies, much progress was being made in and around the Plymouth Plantation. The original settlement expanded in various directions as need arose for fresh pasturage for the increasing stock. The first chief offshoot was Duxbury, so called after the ancestral seat of Miles Standish in Lancashire. Several of the original leaders went to live in this new home some five miles to the north. Of those who signed the compact on board the *Mayflower*, William Brewster, Miles Standish, John Alden, and various others, left Plymouth for Duxbury, which was incorporated as a town. Other towns arose, such as Barnstaple, Taunton and Yarmouth. When the time came for the Plymouth colony to enter into the New England confederacy there were eight such towns.

The relations between these various English colonies were of a very friendly character. Visits were paid, and advice given and received. Governor Bradford rejoiced at the progress of the Massachusetts Bay colony under its

Governor, John Winthrop, and pointed out "how of small beginnings great things have been produced by His hand that made all things of nothings, and gives all things that are; and as one small candle may light a thousand, so the light here kindled hath shone to many, yea, in some sort to our whole nation. Let the glorious name of Jehovah have all the praise."

In course of time it was felt that these New England colonies should be joined together for a common support against their enemies whether native or emigrants from other European countries. They had much in common to form a basis of union. They had similar reasons for leaving the homeland to find a new dwelling beyond the sea. Their religious convictions were very much alike. Under the shaping influence of a common environment in the New World they had developed a form of church life which had many common features.

A scheme of union was proposed by Massachusetts in 1638, but failed to mature. The project was revived in 1642, and eventually, in 1643, Commissioners from New Plymouth, Connecticut and New Haven met at Boston; and, after a series of conferences, Articles of Confederation were agreed upon and signed by all the Commissioners except those from Plymouth, who were under an obligation to refer the matter back to the court of the colony for ratification. The confederacy was to be called the *United Colonies of New England*. Each colony was to preserve its own jurisdiction. The affairs of the confederation were to be managed by Commissioners, of which there were to be two from each colony. It was to be a league of friendship and of mutual assistance. The Board of Commissioners had but little executive power; it was of the nature of a consultative body. It was, however, important as the first American experiment in the direction of a Federal Government.

This confederation of the youthful colonies was both sensible and justifiable. And no doubt the authorities of the colonies acted wisely in not seeking permission from the authorities at home for their action; for it was exceedingly unlikely that the King and his government would have sanctioned a step which tended in the direction of independence. When at last the action was questioned, Edward Winslow made reply: "If we in America should forbear to unite for offence and defence against a common enemy till we have leave from England, our throats might all be cut before the messenger would be half seas through." Fortunately, the situation in the homeland made it difficult for the Government to do more than remonstrate: for in 1643 Laud was in the Tower and Charles was involved in quarrels with his Parliament.

Effective interference was postponed for another twenty-one years. After the Restoration, in 1664, a Commission was sent out to inspect and to administer. Not much was done at this time to limit the freedom of the colonists; but they were left wondering how long it would be before more radical action would be taken. This happened in 1684, when a decree in Chancery annulled the charter of Massachusetts. This meant that all rights and immunities based upon it were swept away, and the titles to private property were rendered invalid. All the land was claimed for the King. The Governor appointed, Sir Edmund Andros, proved to be tyrannical. In 1692 Governor Phipps was appointed and brought with him a charter which united into one royal province of Massachusetts the colonies of Massachusetts Bay, Plymouth, the Vineyard Archipelago, Maine and Acadia. Thus began a new period in American history; a Crown Colony was established under an English Governor, and this system lasted until the Declaration of Independence in 1776.

We have now briefly outlined the series of events which led to the founding of the puritan party in England, and to the sailing of a part of them, first to Holland, and then across the Atlantic Ocean to found a new settlement in America. The profound significance of these events has been increasingly realized with the passing of time; and, particularly, in relation to the struggles of the past thirty years, during which that part of America which was first colonized by the Pilgrim Fathers and their successors has twice used her mighty power to assist in the rescue of Europe from a fearful tyranny, and is now helping to repair the damage done, and to supply the needs of impoverished peoples on an unexampled scale. The tracing of the story of these later events we shall leave to other pens than ours.

We also leave untold the story of the events in England which followed upon the puritan migration. It must suffice to say that the struggle for civil and religious liberty was still continued during the Commonwealth, and throughout the period of reaction which followed upon the Restoration in 1660. During the reigns of Charles II and James II the puritans maintained their protest, and under the later names of Dissenters and Nonconformists they endured much for conscience' sake, and to establish a purer form of religious life.

We wish rather to follow the story of another series of events which, from pre-Reformation days until the time of William and Mary, took place in the sister kingdom of Scotland. This also is a story of protest against corruption, of resistance to tyranny, and of a struggle to establish civil freedom and a worthier type of Church life on the New Testament model. There are many points of connection between the parallel series of events. A few of these have already been noticed. In England the protagonists have been the Puritans and Pilgrims; in Scotland, for the most part, the story relates to the Covenanters, their struggles, their sufferings, and their great achievements.

Part Two

THE CONTROVERSY IN SCOTLAND

Chapter Eleven

MATTERS FOR DEBATE

THE fact that the best things in life are the fruit of prolonged and oft-times bitter controversies is nowhere more graphically and powerfully illustrated than in the history of the Scottish people. Here the battle for freedom from a royal absolutism and a tyrannical and despotic Church was indeed "with tumult and much shouting", and with "garments rolled in blood". The years between the dawn of the Reformation and the firm establishment of Presbyterianism in 1688 were filled with fierce controversy and much strife and bloodshed. Was it worth while? What student of history, who is also a lover of freedom, can doubt the answer that should be given? Unfortunately, there are many who pick the fruit from the tree of life without ever thinking of the blood which nourished the soil in which it has grown through the centuries.

Let us consider the main features of the situation which gave rise to controversy in the sixteenth and seventeenth centuries.

Long before the outburst of new life which we call the Reformation, there had been in Scotland many expressions of dissatisfaction with the condition of things. Bonds about a living organism grow continually tighter until they break, or the organism perishes. The hungry soul of man cries out for appropriate nourishment and turns away from the things which fail to satisfy. Spontaneous revolt takes place under the historical conditions which develop. This happened in Scotland, as elsewhere.

As this account is to be a very brief one I shall not dwell

here upon the early mutterings of discontent which become audible to the students of early medieval history. Early in the twelfth century we can find traces of ideas and protests which we may regard as the beginning of the controversy with which we are now concerned. Even so early as this period no country in Europe was a self-contained unit. Ideas and beliefs travelled from land to land by means which are not now always discernible. It is known, however, that before the end of the fourteenth century the influence of Wycliffe had begun to make itself felt beyond the Border. In 1382 Richard II forbade the chancellor and proctors of Oxford University to molest the Scottish students; and these, on returning to their own country, were doubtless one main source of the Lollardism which soon made its appearance in Scotland.

A lollard, who was tried in 1407, is said to have preached the Gospel in the north of England for twenty years, and it is natural to suppose that his teaching would soon cross the Border. Andrew of Wyntown, who began his Chronicle about this time, uses the word "lollardy" as equivalent to heresy.

The account given of the trial and burning of James Resby at Perth in 1407 makes it clear that his offence was the propagation of lollard doctrine. The first of a list of forty heresies with which he was charged was his assertion that the pope is not the vicar of Christ. The second was that no pope is the vicar of Christ unless he is holy. These errors, and many others, are said to have been drawn from the heresies of John Wycliffe. John Bower, the chronicler, gives us an interesting glimpse of the arguments which were used by the inquisitor to convict Resby of his errors. It is clear to every one, the inquisitor asserts, that some one is in fact Christ's vicar; otherwise the Church would have no head for administrative purposes. The pope is such a vicar of Christ. Further, the pope is in fact the vicar of

Peter, and to be the vicar of Peter is to have power to bind and loose in heaven and on earth. This can be proved by the saying of doctors approved by the Church. If it be objected that the present pope does not resemble Peter in life and morals, the objection is not valid, because it rests upon the false idea that Peter's vicar must be holy like Peter, and implies that only a saint can be chosen pope, or can bind or loose in Peter's stead. If holiness were required it would be impossible to elect a pope, seeing that according to Scripture we cannot be sure that any man is free from mortal sin.

These specious but inconclusive arguments were completed by the burning of both Resby and his writings.

One main item in the indictment of the Papacy was the evil character of many of the popes. In England, Germany and Bohemia, it had been asserted that both priests and popes were disqualified to discharge their sacred functions by their cruelties and immoralities. The claim of church officials to exercise authority was held to depend upon their personal worth. According to the chronicler whose words we have already quoted, the pope is never so evil that he loses the power to bind and loose the souls of men. Those who have taken the papal side in the controversy under consideration have frequently admitted that no defence could be offered of the grave faults and crimes of the popes. Their view has been that the pope is a necessary part of the ecclesiastical machinery which Christ established whereby to secure the salvation of the world. Though one part be faulty, it must still be held that the machinery operates to convey to men the divine grace whereby alone they can be saved. The supreme heresy is to dispute the efficacy of the machinery. Spiritual faults are of little moment, moral crimes are of small account, as compared with a state of mind which disputes, or even doubts, the claims or the power of the pope, or of those who receive authority from him. The one thing to be preserved at all costs is the unity of the Church; and this unity is conceived of, not as a spiritual thing depending on spiritual qualities which are created by the spirit of Jesus in the lives of men, but rather as an external and mechanical thing which depends on whether a person recognizes and submits himself to the authority of the pope.

Unfortunately, those who rebelled on account of the claims of immoral popes did not yet perceive the nature of the true answer to the questioning of those times. They did not realize that a sacrament may convey the blessing of salvation without this being in any degree dependent upon the authority of the man who administers it; that it is faith and willingness to receive Christ's gift which saves, and that this grace can be received apart altogether from the machinery of the papal Church.

After the burning of Resby, the graduates of St. Andrews were forced to take a pledge to oppose heresy; and Laurence of Lindores was appointed inquisitor. In 1425 an injunction of parliament directed the bishops to seek out heretics and lollards and to punish them according to the law of the Church and with the support of the secular power. Laurence gave himself to his mission with great zeal.

About 1427 the pope called upon England to help to suppress the Bohemian heresy, which had begun to spread in Scotland, and several people were put on trial, the charge being usually that they had asserted it to be wrong to kill lollards or Bohemians. Cardinal Beaufort was sent to Scotland to obtain the co-operation of James I in the maintenance of orthodoxy. The doctrines of Wycliffe which had found most favour in central Europe had been shaped into four propositions known as the Articles of Prague. These Articles summed up the convictions of those who were opposed to the Papacy in Bohemia. This anti-papal movement led to the calling of the Council of Basel (1431–49). Before the Council opened, the Bohemians sent deputies to all European countries to show that their doctrines rested exclusively upon the Scriptures. When the Council met, the Hussite tenets were discussed. Though James I sent delegates to the Council, which challenged the authority of the pope, he had no intention of tolerating heretics in his realm. It was at this time that a notable martyr was burnt at St. Andrews, thus connecting Scotland's fight for freedom with the similar movement in Bohemia.

Paul Craw or Crawar was a Bohemian doctor of medicine who had been sent by the heretics of Prague to introduce their teachings into Scotland. He was an enthusiastic Wycliffite, and upheld the Articles of Prague. He was confuted by Laurence of Lindores, and the argument was concluded by the burning of the Bohemian heretic at St. Andrews. It is evident that the ecclesiastical authorities were now greatly alarmed at the spread of lollardy in Scotland.

Lollardy was at this time largely a lay movement. For instance, four of the famous "Lollards of Kyle" were landed proprietors. Two others were ladies who were probably related to them. Thirty-four charges brought against them are reproduced in Knox's *History*. They included the following: (1) Repudiation of the claims of the pope to be the divinely-appointed successor of St. Peter, to forgive sins, and to grant indulgences. Both he and his ministers are asserted to be robbers and murderers. (2) Rejection of the Church's ordinances and usages. The assertion that Christ did not ordain priests to consecrate; and bread still remains bread after consecration. Images and relics of saints should not be worshipped. Every faithful man and woman is a priest. (3) Disregard of civil authorities. Christ has taken away the power to judge. Oaths are never lawful.

Such, in brief outline, were the charges brought against the Scottish heretics at this time. They were accused of having completely broken away from the Church. It is interesting to observe that when they were impeached before James IV and his Council in 1494, by Blackadder, Archbishop of Glasgow, they were not condemned, although they refused to recant, but were allowed to return to Kyle and Cunningham. There is evidence that Ayrshire and district remained a centre of freedom of thought and anti-papal influence until the later days of the Covenanters.

This lollard movement in Scotland may be regarded as the first attempt to break openly with the Roman Church. It insisted upon the right of every Christian to read the Bible for himself, and maintained that every faithful Christian man and woman is a priest. These leading principles were destined to bear fruit in later days. They challenged the religion of ceremonialism which then, and much later, allowed a man to believe that he might revel in immorality and at the same time remain a pious member of "Holy Church", and be assured of salvation without turning his back upon evil life.

The evil lives of the clergy of all ranks were at this time, and for many years to come, an open scandal hardly to be conceived of in these days. When David Betoun was raised to the cardinalate in 1538, his kinsman, Archibald Hay, sent him a congratulatory panegyric which faithfully reflects the grave corruption which was spread throughout the Church. It contains many urgent injunctions to virtuous living which, if they had been effective, might have changed the course of Scottish history. In this address the ignorance, corruption and rapacity of the clergy are sternly denounced, and the urgent need for improvement is set forth. The cardinal is enjoined to set about this noble work of reform and to check ecclesiastical abuses. "I often wonder", the writer says, "what the bishops were thinking about when they admitted such men to the handling of the Lord's holy body, when they hardly know the order of the alphabet. Priests come to that heavenly table who have not slept off yesterday's debauch." Again, he says: "I judge it to be intolerable that an entrance to the Church lies open to all without selection, and that some of the entrants bring with them utter ignorance, others a false pretence of knowledge, some a mind corrupted by the greatest sins and trained to commit all the most scandalous excesses, certain of them a studied intention to do harm, so that there is no greater danger to be feared from the most noxious animals than from this offscouring of most abandoned men."[1]

But how could a man of this character be expected to initiate such a programme of reform? Though a celibate priest he had numerous children, which were described as "bastards" in the letters of legitimation. Not without good reason did Knox refer to him as "the cardinal's graceless grace" and as "the carnal cardinal". Yet this man became shortly afterwards the Archbishop of St. Andrews, the head of the Scottish Church.

In 1549 a provincial Council of clergy was summoned to meet in Edinburgh, the avowed object of which was to extirpate the many heresies which attacked the Lord's flock. It was resolved to follow the example of the prudent physician and first of all seek by careful study to discover the causes and occasions of the sore maladies which for so long a time had corrupted the morals of churchmen. "Two causes and roots of evils" were plainly indicated, namely, "the corruption of morals, and profane lewdness

---

[1] For a longer account cf. D. Hay Fleming, *The Reformation in Scotland*, 1910, pp. 41ff.

of life in churchmen of almost all ranks, together with the crass ignorance of literature and of all the liberal arts." From these two sources, it was said, sprang the many abuses which they were concerned to remedy. Many similar frank confessions of the evils which prevailed in the pre-Reformation Church could be cited.

One of the statutes of this council provides for the punishment of any cleric, even if he be of episcopal rank, who was "notoriously the keeper of a concubine". Another forbids prelates or subordinate clergy to keep their offspring, born of concubinage, in their company, or to allow them to be promoted in their churches. Mention is made of deans who received bribes from concubine-keeping and adulterous persons. Diocesan bishops are exhorted to reform their own life and morals so that occasions of heresy in the realm may be obviated, and they may be the better fitted to take measures to repress like evils in others. The largest proportion of heresy is declared to be traceable to clerical disorder and depravity.[1]

From head to foot the Scottish Church was at this time corrupt. Archbishop Hamilton, who presided over the council in 1549, has been described by a sober historian as "a dissolute scoundrel". Himself a bastard, he had a number of children by the dishonoured wife of his kinsman, and she was not the only victim of his lust.

Nine years later Bishop Gordon of Aberdeen was sternly criticized in writing by the dean and chapter of his See on account of his scandalous life. He had numerous children by various women. Patrick Hepburn, Bishop of Moray, had many children by different mothers. Another bishop was described by Archbishop Spottiswood as a "wicked and vicious man". This by no means exhausts the lists of

[1] For much other evidence see D. Hay Fleming, *The Reformation in Scotland*, 1910, pp. 49ff.; cf. A. R. Macewen, *A History of the Church in Scotland*, vol. I, 1913, pp. 247ff.

highly-placed clerical offenders against the laws of morality which were recognized at that time.

Very shortly afterwards—in March 1559—another provincial council was called in Edinburgh, and was presided over by Archbishop Hamilton. To this council the Queen-Regent, Mary of Guise, sent certain Articles which had been proposed by temporal lords and barons who wished to see the reform, though not the overthrow, of the Church. In these Articles it was pointed out that James V, in his Acts of Parliament, had thought it necessary to make public exhortation to the prelatic lords and the rest of the Spiritual Estate for the reforming of their lives and for the avoidance of open scandal given to the whole of the Estates through the ungodly and dissolute lives of the clergy. Little or no fruit had, however, followed from these attempts at reformation. This council of 1558–59 therefore adhered to the statutes of 1549 and ratified the decree of the Council of Basel again clerical concubinage. That decree was to be enforced upon all sections of the Spiritual Estate—the prelates as well as the lower clergy.

Another statute of the same council forbade "any of the prelates or lower clergy to bring up or keep in their household or society their offspring born of concubinage, so that they should stay in their household for more than four days in every three months—and even then they must not do so openly." For a first offence an archbishop must pay a fine of £200; a bishop or other prelate £100. The lower clergy must pay a discretionary fine. For a third offence the penalties were to be quadrupled (cf. Fleming, *The Reformation in Scotland*, p. 61).

Archbishops and bishops were also prohibited from collating their offspring to any kind of ecclesiastical benefice in their churches, and the Queen was implored to write to the pope and beseech him never to grant any dispensations from this statute. Again, if prelates or other clergy marry their daughters to barons they are prohibited from giving them a dowry out of the patrimony of Christ, that is, out of ecclesiastical property.

Other statutes of a similar character were passed, all pointing to terrible abuses which cried aloud for reformation. The legislation, however, remained ineffective. Princely dowries continued to be provided for the daughters of even the poorest bishops. The lives of the clergy still remained openly scandalous until a much later date, as we shall see.

Another matter touched upon in these statutes was the immorality that was practised in the nunneries. Indisputable evidence of the evil situation which prevailed at that time is provided by a letter addressed by Cardinal Sermoneta to pope Paul IV in 1556 on behalf of Mary Queen of Scots. Here it is declared that the nunneries of every kind of religious women had come to such a pass of boldness that they utterly contemned the safeguards of chastity: "(For) not only do they wander outside the monastic enclosures in shameless fashion, through the houses of seculars, but they even admit all sorts of worthless and wicked men within their convents and hold with them inchaste intercourse. (Thus) they defile the sacred precincts with the birth of children, and bring up their progeny about them, go forth abroad surrounded by their numerous sons, and give their daughters in marriage, dowered with the ample revenues of the Church."[1]

The evils of which loyal churchmen were thus driven to complain were of long standing. The evidence comes from many sources and is indisputable. Thus in a letter of James I of Scotland, written in March, 1424–25, to the abbots and priors of the Benedictine and Augustinian

[1] *Papal Negociations with Mary Queen of Scots during her reign in Scotland*; cited from D. Hay Fleming, *The Reformation in Scotland*, 1910, p. 65.

Orders, the King reminds them that the religion in the monasteries is everywhere being defamed and brought into disgrace.

Again, in a foundation charter of a chaplainry in the parish church of St. Andrews it is stipulated that "If it happen, which God forbid, that the said chaplain shall keep any concubine or common wench, or adhere to such publicly, and shall not effectively put the same away, after being thrice warned by the lord bishop or his ministers, then let the said chaplainry thereby and thenceforward, without further process, be reckoned vacant."[1] The founder of the chaplainry was the same inquisitor of heretical pravity in Scotland who was the prosecutor in the cases mentioned above when James Resby and Paul Craw were burned to death for their religious convictions. One of the most notorious facts throughout these centuries was that the ecclesiastical leaders were far more tolerant in cases of gross immorality than in cases of even slight deviations from the dogmas and usages of the Church. Overwhelming evidence of this is found throughout the history of the Inquisition wherever its operations have been recorded.

Dr. Joseph Robertson, in his preface to the *Statuta Ecclesiæ Scoticanæ*, says: "One great evil, it will be seen, the incontinence of the priesthood, stands confessed deplored, condemned through all the three centuries of Scottish ecclesiastical legislation. Here, as elsewhere throughout Western Christendom, every code of Provincial, every code of Synodal canons, calls, but calls in vain, upon the clergy to separate themselves from their 'concubines', as they are styled—their 'wives' rather as we may charitably hope that in most cases they would have been regarded, but

---

[1] *Papal Negociations with Mary Queen of Scots during her reign in Scotland*; cited from D. Hay Fleming, *The Reformation in Scotland*, 1910, pp. 69f.

for the law which forbade the churchmen to marry"
(i. 1866, p. ccv).

In Scotland, as elsewhere throughout the Middle Ages,
the dire effects of the unnatural law which forbade the
marriage of the clergy force themselves upon the student of
history.

Here then was a great matter for controversy. Should
this law of celibacy, the occasion of so much immorality,
and of the defaming of the Church, be allowed to continue?
Were not any alleged advantages far outweighed by its
evil effects? What scriptural foundation was there for this
unnatural separation of the clergy from the innocent joys
of family life, and from its lessons of mutual help, and
from the opportunity of learning how to live together?
Great claims were made by the heads of the Roman Church
as to the special divine authority which had been trans-
mitted through Peter "prince of the apostles" to his
successors. But was not Peter a married man, and do we
not read of "Simon's wife's mother" who lay sick of a
fever (Luke 4: 38)?

Debate on this subject was inevitable as soon as the
eyes of men were opened and they were able to read the
primitive records of the life of Jesus and of the foundation
of His Church for themselves. This, no doubt, was one
reason why it was held to be dangerous for the people to
read the Scriptures in their own language. Ruthless
attempts to prevent men from reading the Scriptures led
to some of the saddest scenes in the history of mankind.

One of the first results of the Lutheran reform movement in Germany was the abandonment of this man-made
rule of priestly celibacy. In his work on "Monastic Vows"
Luther sought to show that the obligations which had been
blindly incurred by young monks and nuns could be, with
a good conscience, laid aside. Luther assisted in the release
of some nuns from a captivity which had become irksome.

Many other nuns followed their example, and made their escape. A great outcry from the papists followed, and Luther wrote at length defending his action and the action of the nuns. Not long after (in 1525) the reformer married Catharine von Bora, one of the escaped nuns. The marriage proved to be one of great happiness.

The example of Luther was followed by many other reformers both at that time and later, in Scotland as elsewhere. None of the Reformed Churches to-day enforces the law of celibacy. Even the Anglican Church, which has retained so many elements of the teaching and discipline of the Roman Church, does not enforce this rule. The majority of the highest dignitaries have taken upon themselves the obligations of matrimony. Who can doubt that generally speaking the results have been salutary?

Surely we are warranted in saying that this controversy arose naturally out of the situation which was created by the intellectual shortcomings and gross moral failures of those who had, in various ways, gained control of the papal Church. The revolt was not at first primarily an intellectual one led by men who delighted to challenge authority, and to tear to pieces the fabric of scriptural and traditional teaching which had been so ingeniously woven together through the centuries. In the first instance it was a moral and spiritual revolt against evils which cried aloud for a radical remedy. Internal reforms proved to be impossible owing to the general set-up of the Medieval Church. More drastic reforms, involving the break-up of Christian social life as it existed at that time, were therefore initiated; and it is impossible to see how the precious fruits which resulted from the reform movement could have been gained in any other way.

Chapter Twelve

ROMANISTS AND REFORMERS (I)

HAVING viewed the general situation in the Scottish Church which gave rise to controversy, we shall now consider how the movement for reform gained in momentum, and take note of its main principles as they were set forth by some of its great leaders.

The first herald of the Reformation in Scotland is said to have been a Frenchman named Monsieur de la Tour, belonging to the staff of the duke of Albany, a devoted champion of Rome. On his return to France, after a visit to England, between 1524 and 1527, he was executed for having sought to spread Lutheran errors while in Scotland. He was burnt in the pork-market near Paris. A few months later a more notable martyrdom took place which greatly impressed the mind of the Scottish people and accentuated the pace of the struggle with Rome.

Patrick Hamilton was born in the year 1503 or 1504 at Stonehouse in Lanarkshire or at Kincavel near Linlithgow. He was the son of Sir Patrick Hamilton. His mother was a granddaughter of James II. He was thus closely linked with nobility and royalty. He was carefully educated, and in his fourteenth year he was appointed lay-abbot of Ferne in Ross-shire. The rents of the abbacy served to maintain him during his years of study abroad. He was a born student, and appears to have made good use of his time. In 1520 he took the degree of M.A. at the University of Paris. Thence he travelled to Louvain, perhaps to enjoy intercourse with Erasmus. The time was one of great intellectual ferment. Dynamic ideas of reform were in the air. In 1517 Luther had issued his ninety-five theses, and in 1520 he had burned the papal bull of excommunication. The students of Paris and Louvain would doubtless soon learn of these bold actions of the German monk. In 1522 or 1523 Hamilton returned to Scotland to study at St. Andrews.

Already Scotland had caught the contagion of the new ideas of religion. In July 1525 parliament passed an Act against the new opinions. It laments the fact that the "damnable opinions of heresy are spread in divers countries by the heretic Luther and his disciples" and enacts that "no manner of strangers who happen to arrive with their ships within any part of this realm (shall) bring with them any books or works of the said Luther, his disciples or servants, dispute or rehearse his heresies or opinions unless it be to the confusion thereof."

Evidently Aberdeen had become infected by the new teachings, for the King wrote to the sheriff intimating that the bishop had complained to him that there were certain men within the diocese who had in their possession books by the heretic Luther, and who favoured his false opinions. The sheriff was enjoined to publish the above-named Act, to search for the offenders and to confiscate their goods. A Dominican monk now arrived, who had been sent by the pope, Clement VII, to confirm the kingdom in its loyalty to Rome. Early in 1526 James replied, declaring that he was firmly opposed to that "accursed Lutherism" and assuring the pope that his realm was still unstained by the pollution of heresy.

This very year, however, another source of infection appeared. Copies of Tyndale's translation of the New Testament into English were brought over from the Low Countries by Scottish traders. In the absence of the archbishop, James Betoun, many of these were circulated in St. Andrews, and at the same time Patrick Hamilton came forth as a preacher of evangelical truth. On his return, the archbishop was soon made aware of Hamilton's activities. Although he knew the danger of giving offence to the powerful friends of the heretic, early in 1527 he resolved to call him to account. Probably, however, he was more concerned that the heretic should take himself off rather than that he should suffer extremer penalties. Yielding to the advice of his friends, as well as to the suggestions of some of his opponents, Hamilton made his way to the continent. While at Marburg University, in the summer of the same year, he issued a series of theses in Latin. They are believed to have been the original form of a little treatise afterwards well known as *Patrick's Places*. It is of much interest as being the earliest doctrinal treatise of the Scottish Reformation.[1] Its emphasis upon faith as the means of salvation is to-day shared by all the Evangelical Churches.

In the autumn of 1527 Hamilton returned to Scotland, knowing well the dangers which awaited him. His heart was in Scotland and he felt called to be a witness there to evangelical truth. His preaching made many converts. He was a young man of blameless life and of an attractive personality. Though he received warnings of the dangers which threatened him, and there is evidence which suggests that the archbishop would have been pleased if the accused had saved himself by flight, Hamilton this time stood his ground. He declared that he had come to St. Andrews to establish the pious in true doctrine, and if he turned his back he would cause them to stumble. He continued to bear a faithful witness until he was summoned to appear before the council of the archbishop.

On his examination he frankly admitted his belief in the greater part of the following articles, and allowed that

[1] A good account of this work is given by Knox in his *History*, Vol. i (Laing's ed. 1846), pp. 19ff.

others were disputable points: (1) that a man is justified not by works but by faith alone; (2) that good works make not a good man but that a good man doeth good works; (3) that every true Christian may know himself to be in a state of grace; (4) that the corruption of sin remains in infants after their baptism; (5) that it is reasonable that all men should read and understand the Word of God, especially the New Testament; (6) that the Confessional is not necessary to salvation; (7) that there is no purgatory; (8) that the pope is antichrist; (9) it is devilish to teach that remission of sin is purchased by penance.[1] It will be allowed that these are mere commonplaces of Protestant theology, although the truths enshrined might perhaps to-day be expressed in a different form.

When the news arrived at St. Andrews that Hamilton's brother and a friend of the family were approaching with some armed forces the proceedings were hastened. The reformer was arrested, and next day led to the cathedral church, where he was forced to listen again to the accusations made against him. He was condemned for maintaining Lutheran heresies. On the same day (February 29, 1528), having been deprived of his church office he was delivered over to the secular power for punishment. According to his friend Alesius, who was a sorrowful witness of the event, through the blundering of his executioner he was roasted rather than burned alive. His torment lasted for six hours, during which time he was taunted by the monks.

The cruel death of this brave martyr bore lasting fruit. Hamilton was not an original thinker. He had simply given expression to the teaching of Martin Luther. But he was a young man of noble birth, of blameless character, and a Scot; whereas Craw was a foreigner from Bohemia,

[1] For further charges see Macewen, *A History of the Church in Scotland*, 1913, Vol. i, pp. 420f.

and Resby an English lollard. Hamilton thus belonged to a different category. Nothing was known against him save that he had given expression to opinions which did not harmonize with the tenets of the Roman Church. His fellow-countrymen could not but reflect upon the contrast —on the one side, the corrupt and abandoned lives of a large part of the clergy, who were tolerated by the Roman authorities; and, on the other, the blameless young man cruelly done to death because of his religious opinions. The death of the martyr was a powerful element in the controversy which after many years was to produce so much precious fruit. Throughout the whole realm, it is said, the question was discussed: Wherefore was Master Patrick Hamilton burned? Then followed further questionings as to whether the articles or dogmas, for the denial of which the martyr had suffered, were necessary to be believed for salvation. Knox relates that a certain gentleman cautioned the archbishop in these words: "My lord, . . . if ye will burn them, let them be burned in deep cellars, for the reek of Master Patrick Hamilton has infected as many as it blew upon" (*History*, Laing's ed., i, 42). Foxe affirms that the testimony of his blood left the truth of God so firmly fixed in the hearts of many that it could not afterwards be plucked away.

One of the first persons to be influenced by the martyrdom of Patrick Hamilton was Alexander Alane, a canon of the Augustinian priory of St. Andrews. He is better known by the name Alesius (the fugitive or wanderer) which was given him by Melanchthon. Discussions with Hamilton helped to open his eyes to the weak points in the orthodox creed; and the trial and cruel death which followed completed his separation from the Church. For his criticism of the dissolute lives of the clergy he was arrested and condemned; but he escaped and made his way to the continent. After much wandering and many strange

experiences, he at last found himself at Wittenberg about
the year 1531. While there he rendered great service to the
Reformers by his bold defence of the use of the New
Testament in the vernacular, which he heard had been
prohibited by the Scottish bishops. He was greatly
admired by Melanchthon, who sent him with letters to
Henry VIII. He took a prominent part in the controversies which then raged in England. On returning to
Germany he became Rector of the University of Leipzig.
As a supporter of Melanchthon he played a noteworthy
part in the Lutheran controversy.

In the meantime the struggle between orthodoxy and
heresy in Scotland grew more intense. Many persons were
arrested and punished for being in possession of heretical
works, including the vernacular New Testament, or for
showing any degree of sympathy with reforming views.
In 1532 and again in 1534 there was much persecution,
the King taking a prominent part in the proceedings.
Many were convicted and their goods were forfeited.
Some were burned to death, and others fled to distant
lands. In the neighbourhood of St. Andrews seventy
Lutherans are said to have been apprehended. Numerous
fugitives found their way to England where they awaited
the coming of better days.

We must pass over many who suffered in those days,
whether by imprisonment, confiscation, or death, and
consider only a few outstanding events which clearly
advanced the cause of the Reformation a stage further.
How great was the need for enlightenment and reformation
may be illustrated by an incident which took place about
this time. Thomes Forret, a canon of Inchcolm, had been
convicted through a study of the writings of St. Augustine,
and was made Vicar of Dollar. In the persecutions of
1533 he had been censured by his bishop for preaching
every Sunday. He was told to be satisfied with "any good

epistle or any good gospel setting forth the liberty of Holy Church". When he informed the bishop that having read both the Old Testament and the New he found them both good, the bishop declared that he thanked God that he never knew what the Old Testament and the New Testament were. He had resolved to be guided by the breviary and pontifical. Thomas Forret wrote a little catechism which, it is said, led many to embrace the truth. When pardoners came to his parish to sell their wares, he faithfully warned the people of their deceit and imposition, pointing out to them that no pardon could come from the pope; it could only come from the blood of Christ.

In 1539 Forret was summoned before his bishop and Betoun to give an account of his teaching. When accused of having given defective teaching concerning the Lord's Supper, he replied: "I never ministered the Sacraments without saying, 'As the bread entereth your mouth, so shall Christ dwell by lively faith in your heart.'" One of his accusers discovered a New Testament in Forret's coat and exclaimed, "See the heretic! this is what makes all the trouble in Holy Kirk and among the prelates thereof." Forret was condemned to be hanged and his body burned.

We must now give some account of the life and work of a man who became one of the most famous of the Scottish controversialists and martyrs. George Wishart was born about 1512–13. He received his university training in King's College, Aberdeen. He acquired a knowledge of Greek, an unusual accomplishment at that time. He was a friend of John Erskine, laird of Dun, and for a time lived at Montrose. He was employed in reading the Greek New Testament with some of the pupils of Marsillier, a Frenchman whom Erskine had brought from France to teach languages.

Soon the suspicions of John Hepburn, Bishop of Brechin, were aroused, and Wishart was summoned to appear before him. Instead of obeying the summons Wishart sought refuge in England, as many others had done. He was excommunicated and outlawed. For a time he lived at Bristol and associated with Bishop Latimer of Worcester, whose diocese then included that city. But soon fresh troubles arose and he betook himself to the continent and made his home for a time in the cities of Zurich, Basle and Strassburg. He became familiar with the teaching of the great Reformers.

In 1543 or 1544 Wishart returned to Scotland and for some two years he zealously preached the Gospel, especially in the towns of Montrose and Dundee. The great success which attended his ministry in Dundee won for it the name of the "Scottish Geneva". In Dundee he expounded in detail St. Paul's Epistle to the Romans, whose message has so profoundly influenced the lives of so many Protestant Reformers. One of the magistrates, in the Queen's name, and at the instigation of Betoun, bade him depart from the town. After a manly protest he left Dundee, travelled west, and preached in the open air and wherever he had an opportunity. Soon, however, at the call of the citizens he returned to Dundee where a plague had broken out. Fearlessly he ministered to the stricken people and won their gratitude. But the clergy still resented his presence, and a priest attempted to assassinate him as he walked in the street. When the passers-by would have slain the would-be murderer, Wishart protected him, and said: "He has hurt me in nothing, but has let us understand what we may fear in the days to come." From that time when he went to preach a two-handed sword was always borne before him.

Wishart now began to lay a doctrinal basis for the Scottish Church that was to be. His adherents had begun to meet in separate congregations. They received the Lord's Supper from him in both kinds. Wishart translated the

Zurich Communion Service and also the First Helvetic Confession for their use. The Scottish Reformed Church was beginning to take shape.

Wishart's successor was now also being prepared to carry on the work of reform when he should join the Church triumphant. The bearer of the two-handed sword before Wishart as he proceeded to Leith, and thence into East Lothian, was a church notary, by name John Knox. Knox has left an account of a sermon preached by Wishart at Haddington just before he was captured by Bothwell, at the instance of Betoun. Knox asked to be allowed to remain with him; but Wishart replied, "Nay, return to your bairns and God bless you! One is sufficient for one sacrifice." Despite his pledge to protect him from Betoun, Bothwell handed him over to this arch-enemy, who carried him to St. Andrews, where he was placed on trial before the Church Council.

During his trial, and especially at the final scene, Wishart bore himself as nobly as Patrick Hamilton had done. On the first day of March 1546 he won the martyr's crown. Betoun, it is said, watched the martyrdom from his window, and apparently had no presentiment that his own doom was sealed, and his own tragic death would swiftly follow. Tradition states that after praying for his executioners Wishart declared that he expected to sup with his Saviour before the night was passed. Some of those who witnessed the death of one of the noblest saints vowed vengeance upon the cruel-hearted cardinal.

Stern and terrible was the judgment which soon befell the cardinal. After witnessing the death of the martyr, Betoun went to Angus for the wedding of one of his daughters. Not long before he had burnt a priest for marrying; now before all the world he acknowledged the bride as his daughter. Then, hearing that the English were preparing to make a descent upon the Scottish coast he hurried to Edinburgh, and thence to St. Andrews, to arrange for the defence of the realm. The enemies he had most to fear, however, were not aliens. The Scots by this time were roused to anger by his cruel policy. A number of determined men were resolved to exact the utmost penalty. Forcing their way into the castle of St. Andrews, they slew the cardinal after a fierce struggle, and afterwards hung his body out of the window. His corpse is said to have been left unburied for several months. This was not the work of the Reformers. Political rather than religious motives inspired the deed. Nevertheless those who favoured the reformation of the Church had good reason to rejoice that the arch-persecutor was no more. The death of the cardinal meant a great weakening of the political power of the papacy in Scotland.

The leadership of the Reform movement now passed to Wishart's sword-bearer John Knox. At this time he was probably about forty years of age. The date of his birth is uncertain. It is generally placed between the years 1505 and 1515. Until he appears as the sword-bearer of Wishart in 1545–46 we have little information concerning his life. When he appeared, however, he was a papal notary and in priest's orders, and he was evidently well acquainted with all the main elements in the political and religious situation. He was probably about thirty-two years of age and was fully qualified to become the leader on the reforming side of the controversy which was then raging.

When it became known that the conspirators who assassinated Betoun intended to hold the castle of St. Andrews they were joined by a considerable number of people who favoured the Reformation, and determined to use the tragic happenings of the day as an opportunity to further their cause. Among these, in 1547, came John Knox, to whom the castle was a haven of refuge from the machinations of his enemies. Though there were reckless adventurers within the castle, the convinced believers in the movement for reform were dominant; and for them the public worship, with daily exposition of Scripture, had been established. The leader was John Rough, a friar, who had acted as chaplain to the Regent, the earl of Arran, at a time when he favoured the Reformers. The situation in St. Andrews was now very interesting. In the city the old order of things was defended by the champions of the papal Church; in the castle the new message was being delivered which was destined to shake the ancient system to its very foundations, and eventually to destroy it. Occasionally John Rough forced his way into the parish church and proclaimed his message there.

On settling in St. Andrews Knox followed the method which he had found so successful in East Lothian. He showed great ability and persuasiveness as a teacher, with the result that there were many who thought he ought to become the colleague of John Rough. Eventually the latter, in the name of other notable people, gave him a call to the ministry. For a time Knox hesitated to assume the role of preacher; but at length he yielded, and gave all his heart and strength to the work. By his teaching, preaching and catechizing he so instilled the new doctrine into the minds of the people that it was retained through all the troublous years which followed.

The general nature of Knox's teaching at this time may be seen from the following summary which was set forth in a discussion which, in 1547, at the instigation of Hamilton, soon to be consecrated Archbishop of St. Andrews, had been arranged between Knox and Rough, on the one hand, and Vicar-General Wynram and Friar Arbuckle, on the other. The Reformers contended that: (1) No mortal man can be head of the Church. (2) The pope is an antichrist, and so is not a member of Christ's mystical body. (3) Man may neither make nor devise a religion acceptable to God, but is bound to observe and keep the religion received from God, without chopping and changing thereof. (4) The Sacraments of the New Testament ought to be administered as they were instituted by Christ and practised by His apostles; nothing ought to be added unto them: nothing ought to be diminished from them. (5) The mass is abominable idolatry, blasphemous to the death of Christ, and a profanation of the Lord's Supper. (6) There is no purgatory, in which the souls of men can either be pained or purged after this life; but heaven remains for the faithful and hell for the reprobate and unthankful. (7) Praying for the dead is vain, and praying to the dead is idolatry. (8) There are no bishops unless they preach even by themselves without any substitute. (9) The teinds by God's law do not appertain of necessity to the kirkmen.

With but slight modifications Knox continued to affirm these teachings until his death.

The day of triumph for this reformation doctrine was, however, not yet come. With French assistance the castle was captured and its occupants were treated as the worst kind of criminals. With many others Knox was carried away to France where, for nineteen months, he was compelled to work as a galley-slave. He was chained to the rowing benches by day, and compelled to sleep under them by night. Few situations could have been fuller of cruel torment. But to his terrible experiences at this time Knox made only a few references in later days.

At the end of nineteen months Knox and his friends were released on the intervention of the English government. He reached England in April, 1549. For nearly five years he remained in this country and preached reformation doctrine at Berwick, Newcastle and London. On two occasions he was offered preferment—namely, the Bishopric of Rochester and the Rectory of All Hallows, in Bread

Street, London. When he was called before the Privy Council to justify his refusal of the latter offer Knox stated that he thought he could be more useful elsewhere. He did, however, accept appointment as one of the chaplains of Edward VI, and was consulted on the preparation of the English Prayer Book.

When King Edward VI was succeeded by the bigoted Mary (in 1553), there was no place in England for such a reformer as John Knox. He therefore crossed the Channel and eventually reached Geneva. There he spent some time with Calvin. He also went to Zurich to see Bullinger. Apart from a short visit to Scotland, which lasted for some nine months in the years 1555 and 1556, the next five years (1554–58) were spent on the continent. How fruitful they were in study and preparation was manifested when at last he was called upon to assume heavy responsibility for the direction of affairs in his own country. Already when he went to Geneva he was well-established in the new doctrines; but there he saw ideas and principles of church government more fully worked out than had yet been possible in Scotland. In Geneva a form of church life was developing which eliminated sacerdotalism, and gave an opportunity to the members of the Church to play a responsible part in church life. There also the Book of Common Order was in use which was to become the directory of the new Scottish Church.

The death of Mary Tudor (1558) made it possible for the English exiles to return home. The English congregation at Geneva was dissolved. Knox also desired to visit England on his way north, and he made application to Cecil for permission. This, however, was refused, because Knox had given great offence to Queen Elizabeth by his book, *The First Blast of the Trumpet against the Monstrous Regiment of Women*. He therefore sailed directly from Dieppe to Scotland and arrived in Edinburgh on May 2, 1559. From

Edinburgh Knox proceeded to Dundee, and there his presence is said to have "put more life into his hearers than five hundred trumpets continually blustering".

When Knox returned to Scotland he found the country in the throes of the Reformation. Since 1556 the people had become increasingly hostile to the ancient Church, and had made attacks upon church furniture and decorations. An image of St. Giles had been seized while it was being carried through the city of Edinburgh according to custom; it had been thrown into the North Loch and afterwards burnt. In March and again in October, 1557, certain of the barons and gentry had written to Knox urging him to return. In December of the same year five lords signed a document, which was later known as the First Covenant, in which they pledged themselves to assist forward the reformation of religion, to establish the most blessed Word of God and His Congregation with their whole power and substance, and, if need be, with their very lives. The custom of signing a "band" for the accomplishment of a common purpose had been familiar to the Scots for many years. It was simply an adaptation of an idea found in the Old Testament where we frequently read of the Hebrew people entering into a covenant of loyalty to God.

It will be well here to notice that by the expression "the Congregation" in this document and elsewhere, is meant, not as at present a local gathering of Christian people for worship, but rather the whole of such people in each community as have separated themselves from the papal Church and made common cause on behalf of the Reformation. This is in accordance with the phraseology of the Augsburg Confession in which the Church is defined as *Congregatio Sanctorum*. As the Reformation progressed, those who, in each locality, accepted the reformed doctrine were gathered into fellowships or local branches of "the

Congregation", and elders were chosen by election to guide and oversee the Church. Eminent laymen who played a prominent part as leaders came to be known as the "Lords of the Congregation". Laymen also for the time being supplied the lack of a publicly recognized ministry. The first Reformed Church in Scotland to be organized on these lines was in Dundee, to which city Knox proceeded on his return to Scotland in May, 1559.

Earlier in that year the Queen-Regent had resolved upon a policy of stern repression towards the reforming preachers. On March 23 she published an edict throughout the country which decreed that no one should preach or administer the Sacraments without a licence from the bishops. The penalty for disobedience was to be death. So bold a front did the preachers show, however, that a summons to them was adjourned, and the preachers zealously continued their work. At last she issued a fresh summons to all the preachers to appear before her at Stirling on May 10. The Congregation prepared to answer the challenge. Realizing that they had now arrived at a critical moment in the movement of reform they decided that the preachers, when they attended the conference, should be accompanied by laymen who would act as their protectors.

Such was the situation which Knox found on his arrival. He resolved to make common cause with the preachers and their protectors, and to attend the conference. From Dundee they travelled to Perth, and thence sent Erskine of Dun on to Stirling to intimate their attitude and intentions to the Queen-Regent. It is stated that she promised Erskine to abandon the prosecution of the preachers. Nevertheless they were condemned and outlawed in their absence. A great assembly of the friends of the Reformation was held at Perth. The Lords of the Congregation were present and Knox acted as their secretary. When Erskine reported the result of his mission to the Regent to the Reformers much anger was expressed. The next day Knox preached against idolatry. When at the close of the sermon a rash priest proceeded to celebrate mass there was much disturbance, and great damage was done to the furniture of various churches by the people, the majority of whom favoured the Reformers.

When the Regent heard of these happenings she declared that she would destroy Perth and its people. On hearing that she was marching upon Perth, the Congregation fortified the city, and issued three manifestoes addressed to the Regent, the prelates and the nobility. The claims and intentions of the Reformers were set forth. They disavowed any seditious purpose, and asserted that the issue was the question of true or false religion. They claimed the liberty which Jesus had purchased by His blood, to have His Word truly preached, and the holy Sacraments rightly administered. In the defence of this liberty they were ready to take the sword against their persecutors.

Welcome reinforcements now reached the Reformers from the south-west, where the reforming spirit had continued to exist from the days of lollardy. Some two thousand five hundred Reformers, under the Earl of Glencairn, arrived. An agreement was now reached with the Regent. It was arranged that the Congregation should disperse, and the Regent be allowed to enter the city on the condition that no citizen should be punished on account of the recent outbreak, and that the reforming movement should be allowed to go forward. After a covenant of mutual assistance in case of need had been signed the Congregation dispersed. It was soon manifest that the pledges of the Regent were of little worth. Reformers were removed from their positions in the city, and mass was reinstated in the churches. When the nobles remonstrated, the Regent replied that she was not bound to keep promises made to heretics.

The work of reform went forward in many places, particularly at St. Andrews, to which place the leaders of the Congregation resorted. There Knox preached in the parish church, and thus he realized the hope which he had expressed when he was a slave in the French galleys. The main subject of his sermons was the evil of idolatry, as expressed in the mass and in the worship of images and relics, and the necessity of removing such things as conduced to false worship, such as crucifixes and images. Many of these things were gathered together and burnt on the spot where an old man, Walter Myles, had been martyred.

The Congregation moved to Perth, Stirling and Linlithgow, and then to Edinburgh, the Regent having gone to Dunbar to await reinforcements from France. At Edinburgh Knox preached in St. Giles Church, and was elected Minister of Edinburgh by the local congregation.

The "cleansing" of the churches from "the dregs of popery" was a part of the settled policy of Knox. It is not difficult to understand this aspect of the work of the Reformation when we recall the fact that the minds of all the reformers were saturated with the ideas enshrined in the literature of the Old Testament, and remember that they were fully convinced that this was verily the Word of God. The idea of development in the process of revelation had not yet been born. In the Old Testament much is said about the destruction of graven images. There are many stern denunciations of those who wished to retain these things, and customs associated with baal-worship, and merge them in the worship of Jehovah. There are many lamentations over the folly and sin of otherwise good kings who failed to root out and destroy the sacred "groves" and "high places", which had been centres of idolatrous worship. And in the New Testament also the Reformers read of Jesus driving the buyers and sellers and the money-changers from the temple, though these things had long been regarded as indispensable adjuncts of Hebrew religion. Early Christian literature likewise contains many references to the loathing aroused in Christian missionaries by idolatrous worship.

For many centuries the policy of the Roman Church had been a very different one. The ecclesiastical authorities had followed the practice of "baptizing" Jewish and pagan elements into the service of the Christian Church. Many elements had been assimilated or absorbed into their teaching, and into the practice and constitution of the Church. In view of the corruption which prevailed when the work of Reformation began it was quite natural that such elements as were not directly sanctioned by the Bible should be discarded. And Knox was profoundly convinced that it was the duty of those who accepted reformation doctrine to cleanse their churches from all those things which by their associations might be a stumbling-block to the more ignorant or weaker brethren. At the same time he was of the opinion that this should be done systematically and by those acting under authority, and not by the violent mob.

Chapter Thirteen

ROMANISTS AND REFORMERS (2)

IT is not possible in this brief narrative to follow the ebb and the flow of the reformation movement from this date to its final victory. We must be content to give a very brief outline of events. As the Roman party had the help of France it was impossible for the Reformers to make headway without assistance. They naturally looked for this from England, where the Reformation had already made so much progress. Both in England and in Scotland leading statesmen had recognized the need for an alliance between the two countries. For some time, however, Elizabeth hesitated to espouse heartily the cause of the Reformers. She was anti-papal, but also autocratic. She had small sympathy with the democratic principles which lie at the basis of Presbyterianism. Though she refused the title "Supreme Head of the Church", she claimed to be "Supreme Governor" in ecclesiastical affairs. Her policy of balance in spiritual and ecclesiastical affairs, as in political matters, made it difficult for her advisers to pledge that active assistance to the Scots which alone could enable them to withstand the might of France, Rome, and the strong papal party which existed, especially in the northern parts of Scotland. Moreover, in matters of doctrine and usage her personal taste inclined rather to a moderate Romanism. She felt none of the repugnance to the mass which found expression in all the writings and sermons of the Reformers. A strong personal dislike to Knox increased the difficulties of the situation.

Knox laboured to remove these difficulties, and to this

end he emphasized the religious aspect of the Reformation. So urgent a matter did an alliance of the two kingdoms appear to him that he wrote to Elizabeth to explain that his *First Blast of a Trumpet against the Monstrous Regiment of Women* was not intended to refer to her. He also wrote to Cecil and others declaring that if assistance from England was not forthcoming some of the Lords would abandon Scotland, and others would join the French cause.

In the meantime the doctrines of the Reformation were spreading further and further. Forceful preachers were everywhere carrying the liberating message of the Gospel. A number of powerful nobles also crossed over to the side of the Reformers, notably the Earls of Lennox and Huntly, Maitland of Lethington and the Duke of Chatelherault. At last the Lords of the Congregation marched to Edinburgh, and at a meeting held in the Tolbooth on October 21, 1559, the Regent was suspended from the regency, and the government was entrusted to a council composed of Argyle, Lord James, Glencairn, and various others. The Regent was ordered to leave Edinburgh with the French ambassador and soldiers. When she removed to Leith, it appeared as if the Reformers had triumphed.

Soon, however, the Regent rallied her forces and marched upon Edinburgh. The Lords of the Congregation fled to Linlithgow and then to Stirling. There Knox, by his fervent eloquence, roused the drooping hearts of the Congregation. A messenger was sent to England to appeal for help. Some of their forces went to Glasgow, and others to St. Andrews. In the latter place Knox was the guiding spirit and he succeeded in persuading the Congregation to die rather than to relinquish their enterprise.

English statesmen saw the serious nature of the situation and the danger to England if Scotland became subject to France. Cecil therefore wrote urging the Lords to stand fast, and promising to bear the costs of the army, and to check the French fleet. All this, however, had to be done with the greatest secrecy, as offence must not be given to France. Elizabeth, in fact, made promises both to the Regent and to her rebellious subjects. Such progress was made by the Regent at this time in ravaging the estates of the Lords that Knox described himself as in greater torment than during the months which he spent in the galleys. Yet his courage did not fail, and he urged the Lords "still to row against these contrarious blasts till that Jesus Christ should come, being assuredly persuaded that God would deliver them from the extreme trouble."

Soon the tide turned. An English fleet appeared in the channel and a force was landed. Commissioners from the Lords met the English ambassadors at Berwick to draw up an agreement between the two nations. Though the action was informal, it was a matter of the utmost importance, since England now recognized that the Protestant Reformers, not the Regent, represented the country. The agreement at Berwick soon became a treaty, and according to its terms the English undertook to defend Scotland against France, the Scots giving a similar undertaking to assist England.

Fighting still continued around Leith. In the meantime a hundred and fifty of the Reformers signed a fresh Covenant in which they bound themselves to continue the work of the Reformation according to God's Word, and to assist the English army to expel the Frenchmen. They also instructed certain of their number to set forth in a book their judgments on the subject of a reformation of religion in the realm.

The French now recognized that their cause was lost, and Francis and Mary appointed commissioners to make a treaty of peace. At this juncture the Queen-Regent died after summoning the Lords of the Congregation to her bedside and bidding them a friendly farewell (June 11, 1560).

On her death the Lords presented to the ambassadors a document entitled a "Declaration of Requests", setting forth the terms which they held to be essential for a peaceable settlement. These included the expulsion of French troops, the demolition of fortresses, the exclusion of foreigners from public office and an Act of Oblivion. They also requested royal sanction for the meeting of parliament on July 10, and that it should be authorized to establish such laws and ordinances as should be necessary for the quietness of the realm, both with reference to civil policy and religion. Most of the demands of the Lords were granted and embodied in the Treaty of Edinburgh on July 6.

The French troops began to embark and on July 19 Knox conducted a thanksgiving service in St. Giles' Cathedral. The Estates had already met on July 10, but had adjourned their proceedings till August 1. In the meantime matters concerning the religious situation were considered. Preachers were planted in the great cities. A supplication was drafted and presented to parliament by the barons, burgesses and others. This demanded: (1) that the doctrinal errors of the Roman Church, such as transubstantiation, indulgences, purgatory, pilgrimages, and justification by works should be abolished by Act of Parliament; (2) that the discipline of the ancient Church should be revived; (3) that a remedy should be found for the situation which had resulted from the claims of the pope to be vicar of Christ and head of the Church, and from his possession of the whole patrimony of the Church; (4) that the clergy should be examined, and those found to be unworthy should be expelled.

When the Estates met they confirmed the Edinburgh agreement and appointed a committee, known as the

Lords of the Articles, who considered the supplication of the reforming barons and others. The latter were summoned, together with the ministers, and ordered to draw up a summary of the doctrine which they desired the parliament to establish as wholesome and necessary to be believed. Six ministers, including Knox, were entrusted with this important task, and within four days they submitted a summary of the Protestant faith. This document became known as the First Scottish Confession. It included, in addition to a summary of evangelical doctrine, a definite repudiation of the leading dogmas of the Roman Church. The Lords of the Articles gave their approval, after which it was presented to the Estates. No definite objections were raised.

On August 24 parliament completed the revolution by passing three enactments. The first abolished the authority and jurisdiction of the pope within the realm of Scotland, and the bishops were forbidden to do anything in his name. The second nullified all Acts of Parliament contrary to God's Word; and the third decreed that no one should henceforth administer the Sacraments except those who should be duly authorized. Severe penalties were provided for those who transgressed these laws, including death for a third offence.

It is a matter for amazement that so profound a change in the religious life of a nation should have been achieved with so little bloodshed, and with so much speed. There was little opposition to the doctrinal settlement, even on the part of the ecclesiastical authorities. This is largely to be accounted for by the fact that, whilst a strong papal and French faction still remained in the north, Protestant ideas had become firmly rooted in the southern and eastern parts of the country. A spirit of sturdy independence had grown up. Patriotic motives mingled with religious ideas, and nearly everywhere there was a readiness to throw off the ecclesiastical yoke, and to fashion anew the life of the Church more in accordance with New Testament principles.

Now that the papal control of the Scottish Church had been destroyed, there still remained the great task of ordering the life of the Church upon its new basis, and of so shaping its constitution that it should be a more efficient instrument for the establishment of Christ's kingdom in the life of the people. Many years were to pass, and much blood was to be shed, before the aims of the Reformers could be realized, and the precious fruit of the Reformation could be enjoyed in peace and quietness. Aided by the wiles of a Roman Catholic Queen, and by powerful forces operating from England, the forces of reaction fought hard, and at times it seemed as if they must prevail.

The first General or National Assembly of the Church met in Edinburgh in December, 1560. It comprised six ministers and thirty-six lay commissioners. The second meeting was held in June, 1562, and was attended by sixteen ministers and an equal number of lay commissioners, besides five superintendents. These figures indicate the very important part that the laity were to play in the life of the reconstituted Church. It was to be a democratic Church, rooted in the affections and confidence of the people.

The Confession of Faith and Doctrine which was now drawn up is a clear statement of evangelical doctrines which were held by the Reformed Churches abroad. It emphasizes the authority of the Scriptures contained in the Old and New Testaments. Justification is said to be by faith, and sanctification by the influence of God's Holy Spirit. The *First Book of Discipline*, prepared about the same time, and revised in 1564, was a manual of Church policy for clergy and laity. Unfortunately it was not passed into law. It sets forth a scheme for the complete government of the Church. Congregations were to elect their own office-bearers; that is, elders and deacons, annually. Ten superintendents were to be appointed in the place of the bishops. Though bishops are not condemned outright, they are given no place in the new constitution. Each preacher must confess to have received an inward call of the Holy Spirit and ask for trial as a minister. The Church was to judge of his qualifications. The offices of elders and deacons were held to be permanent and of scriptural authority.

In view of the scarcity of ministers, two other offices were created and held to be expedient under the conditions then existing, those of superintendents and readers. The readers might also become exhorters, and when their qualifications justified, they might become ministers. The ministers were supported, and the church fabrics were maintained, partly out of the ancient patrimony of the Church, and partly by voluntary contributions.

A directory of public worship and of religious rites was also prepared. This was variously called *The Book of Common Order*, or *The Order of Geneva*, or, in its later form, *Knox's Liturgy*. It was in use as a guide to worship until 1645.

We have seen that the Queen-Regent died in June 1560. In the months following her death parliament had passed important measures to establish the Reformation. On August 19, 1561, Mary Stuart, the widowed Queen of France, a girl of eighteen years, returned to her native land to assume the sovereignty. The Scottish people had good reason to expect that the coming of the Queen would greatly intensify the struggle between the forces of progress and reaction. Communication between Scotland and France was very close. The Reformers knew the temper of the Queen; the Queen was well acquainted with the dour determination of Knox and his associates.

Behind the Queen stood the papal Church, ever watchful to seize an opportunity of regaining its supremacy, and the power of France was available to enable it to achieve its designs.

The contrasting elements of the situation which existed at this time have often been powerfully portrayed. On the one hand, there was the beauty, pathos and fascination of the young bereaved Queen, endowed with great capacities, and filled with a resolute determination to re-establish the papal Church, if need be, by the help of the arms of France. On the other hand, there stood the Reformers, inspired by an overpowering conviction of the righteousness of their cause, and fully persuaded that the papal Church was a tyrannical Church which had usurped an authority that was without scriptural warrant, and that this must be ended in order that Christ's true Church might carry out its redemptive mission among the Scottish people.

The details of the struggle which now began cannot be recorded here. The forebodings of Knox and his friends were soon justified. Papal modes of worship were speedily re-established at Holyrood Palace. Papal agents and Roman Catholic priests gathered round the young Queen. The members of the Privy Council were induced to enact an Edict of Toleration which forbade any inter-ference with the worship of the Court under pain of death, and announced that parliament and the Queen were to consider the state of religion. It soon appeared that no real toleration was intended. The measure adopted was but a subtle ruse, inspired by the Jesuits, to re-establish papal authority. A loving letter was brought to the Queen from the pope, urging her to purge her realm of heresy. The policy of the Queen was to feign tolerance until her party was strong enough to gain the desired end.

Many and long were the discussions which now took place between the adherents of the ancient and the reformed religion. Perceiving the drift of things, the leaders of the Reformed Church thought it was time to remind the government to carry out the terms of the royal proclamation which had been made to the effect that there should be no interference with the state of religion existing on the arrival of the Queen; and forty-eight Roman Catholics who had transgressed the law were prosecuted. Thus the reactionary movement was for a moment checked.

On July 29, 1565, Mary married her cousin, Lord Darnley, an incapable youth who had not yet attained his majority. The marriage was sanctioned by the pope on the condition that the Queen and her consort should defend the Roman Catholic religion. Realizing that the Protestant cause was now directly menaced, the Lords of the Congregation protested against the marriage, and consequently were chased into England and branded as outlaws.

Mary made it clear that she had no intention of ratifying the Act by which the Protestant Church was to be established. The phrase "the maintenance of the state of religion found on her arrival" was to be interpreted very differently by the opposed parties. By Mary it was used as a convenient phrase which would enable her to maintain the authority of the ancient religion.

A new party now emerged whose object was to free the Queen from the influence of her favourite secretary, the Italian, David Rizzio. He was murdered in the Queen's presence in March 1566. Darnley was involved in this incident, and in order to achieve his object he had made overtures to the exiled Lords of the Congregation. The safety of the Protestant faith was one of the articles included in the bonds that were exchanged. Events, however, soon favoured the Queen, and the new Protestant party collapsed. Knox was compelled to retire afresh from the capital. Mary's estrangement from her husband was foredoomed to end in tragedy. Darnley was murdered in February 1567, and within three months Mary married Bothwell, who was alleged to be responsible for Darnley's death. These tragic events still further alienated her Protestant subjects. Members of the nobility banded themselves together to avenge the death of Darnley. Mary, having assembled some thousands of sympathizers, marched to Carberry Hill, near Musselburgh. There she was confronted by a host of enraged subjects to whom she surrendered, whilst Bothwell fled.

Mary was carried off to Edinburgh, and then imprisoned in Lochleven Castle where, on July 24, 1567, she abdicated in favour of her infant son Prince James.

Murray was appointed Regent, and the Covenanting Lords, rejoicing much at their great deliverance, proceeded to have their Church established by law. In a few months time, however, Mary made another bid for freedom; but the battle of Langside (May 13, 1568) went against her and she sought refuge in England, where she became the prisoner of Queen Elizabeth for eighteen years, and at last met her death at Fotheringay Castle on February 8, 1587.

Chapter Fourteen

PRELATISTS AND COVENANTERS

AT the coronation of the infant King, at Stirling, on July 29, 1567, the Earl of Morton, acting as sponsor, took an oath to the effect that the King would serve God and "maintain the true religion of Jesus Christ, the preaching of the Holy Word, and the due and right ministration of His Sacraments now received and practised in this realm, and shall abolish and gainstand all false religion contrary to the same. . . ." Murray, who was appointed Regent, took an oath to maintain the Reformed Church. The General Assembly met and appointed George Buchanan, the Principal of St. Leonard's College, St. Andrews, to be the Moderator. Thus the stage seemed to be set for the firm and speedy establishment of a self-governing Church. Articles of Establishment were submitted to the Privy Council for approval. A Covenant was signed by a number of lords who bound themselves to take measures to secure support for the Reformed ministers from the patrimony of the Church, and also the abolition of the mass and idolatry. They likewise undertook to march over the land and to obliterate every trace of popery.

The first Parliament of Murray, which met in December, 1567, ratified the previous abolition of papal jurisdiction (1560), and passed a series of eleven Acts, all tending in the direction of a radical reformation of the Church. The Reformed Churches of the realm were declared to be "the only true and holy Church of Jesus Christ within this realm", and they were recognized as such by the public officials. The Church was to be autonomous and be able to act independently within its own sphere.

Soon, however, the forces of reaction set to work to hinder the consummation of this programme of reform. The murder of the Regent Murray in 1570 deprived the Reformers of the guidance of a strong and wise man when strength and prudence were most needed.

Much intrigue now began for the maintenance or restoration of the power of the prelates, and this was supported by the policy of Morton, who was soon to be appointed Regent. It then became manifest that there was a considerable party who favoured a compromise between Presbytery and Episcopacy, and the Leith Concordat was the result. We here see the beginnings of the conflict which was to be waged for more than a century between those who stood for the spiritual independence of the Church, governed in scriptural fashion by a group of elders, and those who wished the papal rule to be superseded by kingly rule operating through the bench of bishops.

By the Leith Concordat of 1572 a joint-committee had agreed that archbishops and bishops should exercise the functions of superintendents and have charge of the former dioceses. They were to be subject to the Assembly in spiritual matters, and to the King in temporal concerns. An Assembly, convened at Perth, accepted the Concordats as a temporary measure; and Knox himself acquiesced in view of the fact that the bishops were to be of the primitive Pauline type, and the office was to be derivative from the Church, like that of the superintendents who had been appointed. Unfortunately, at this difficult stage in the position of affairs Knox died (November 24, 1572).

The Regent Morton now secured the passing of a statute which decreed uniformity of worship under the direction of the bishops, archbishops and superintendents (1573). The Confession of Faith was transformed into a test.

Many unsuitable men, both ignorant and immoral, were appointed to the vacant Sees, though they were unordained and exercised no authority. An arrangement was made whereby the lords obtained most of the profits of the benefices, the bishops receiving only a small share. Hence the bishops were called "tulchan bishops", a "tulchan" being a calf's skin stuffed with straw, which was set up beside a cow to induce her to give her milk more freely. The attempt to change these nominal bishops into real bishops was a fruitful source of conflict in the years which followed. The Assembly repeatedly asserted its right to test such persons as were presented by the Regent to bishoprics, and affirmed that, according to Scripture, the bishop is only the pastor of one flock. On the other hand, the Regent was a thorough Erastian and sought to assert his absolute will and control over the Church, even challenging the right of the Church to hold its Assemblies.

At this juncture of affairs Andrew Melville came upon the scene, and soon proved himself to be a worthy successor of John Knox. After studying at St. Mary's College, St. Andrews, and at various other colleges on the continent, from 1569 till 1574, he had been a professor of Humanity in the Academy of Geneva. He was a man of amazing capacity and of strong moral character. He arrived in Scotland in 1574, and was appointed Principal of the College of Glasgow, at that time in a very poor condition. Such was the energy and the fame of the new Principal that the University became crowded with students. As Principal of the University he had a place in the Assembly and soon attained to a position of great influence.

On his arrival Melville found in the Scottish Church a strangely complicated condition of affairs. At the basis there was a presbyterate on the Pauline model. Then there were also superintendents who had oversight over large areas where there were few ministers. It was their duty to see that services were conducted by readers or exhorters. But thirteen bishops had also been re-established under the Leith and Perth Concordats. Melville quickly perceived that there could be no real harmony or progress in the Church while such conflicting elements were so strangely intermingled. The presbyterate was thoroughly democratic. On the other hand, the bishops were appointed by the crown. The bishop was the King's man. On his appointment the bishop was required to say: "I confess to have and to hold the said bishopric and possessions of the same, under God, only of your Majesty and Crown Royal. . . ." Such antagonistic elements could only produce discord and confusion. In the final result, under such conditions, the will of the people must yield to the will of the King working through his creatures the bishops.

Melville was a great scholar, and during his years of study abroad he had made some important discoveries. He had discovered, for example, that in the Greek New Testament the term "bishop" is synonymous with "presbyter" and "pastor". Thus in the New Testament period the name "bishop" belonged to every pastor of a flock. Melville held as tenaciously as did Wycliffe that the only sure foundation in Church life is the Word of God. According to this, he affirmed, the people are the source of governmental power. A hierarchy is both unwarranted by Scripture and dangerous to the rights of the people.

A debate upon Episcopacy took place in the Assembly held in August 1575. That Scripture was opposed to Episcopacy was urged by Melville and others. As a result of the debate a clerical committee was appointed to examine the situation, and it was agreed that a primitive bishop was the pastor of one flock only. He might, however, be appointed to act as overseer in a special sense and have certain duties entrusted to him by his fellow presbyters. The next Assembly ordered each of the bishops to enter on a pastorate. To this none of the six bishops present dissented. But the King and Morton still remained of the contrary opinion. The main points for which the Covenanters contended were eventually embodied in the *Second Book of Discipline* which obtained the force of statute law.

In 1578 the Regent Morton was compelled to resign and the King reigned with the help of a Council of twelve. From this time onward strenuous efforts were made by the pope to undo the work of reformation and to regain control in England and Scotland. In 1587 Queen Mary was executed at Fotheringay Castle. The Armada sailed in 1588 and was destroyed. In the meantime the Reformed Church of Scotland was busily occupied in combating the reactionary elements which hankered after the old order of things. Previous to 1580 the Assemblies had reduced bishops to the level of pastors of congregations, yet they refused to resign their episcopal dignity or their place in parliament or their estates, which they claimed to hold direct from the Crown. In October, 1579, King James had ratified the Act which declared that there was no other kirk in Scotland than the Reformed Kirk; yet the bishops still clung to their positions. The Assembly of 1580 therefore passed an Act which declared that the office of bishop had neither warrant nor hint in Holy Scripture, and demanding that the bishops should forthwith relinquish their functions and seek re-admission as simple pastors under pain of excommunication. Nevertheless the bishops still clung to their posts with the approval of the King.

Much perturbation was caused by the news which spread everywhere of the arrival from the continent of papal emissaries which came with gold to purchase the support of the nobles. The King's counsellors were suspect. News also came of a plot to depose the King and to restore

Catholicism. The King himself appears to have become alarmed with the trend of things. He appointed John Craig, one of the most outspoken of the Reformers, as Court Chaplain, and authorized him to draft a Confession of Faith which could be used as a test of loyalty to the Crown and Church. In January 1581 the King and his household subscribed the Confession, which was afterwards known as "The King's Confession", and, in later days, when some additions had been made, as "The National Covenant". It repudiates popish doctrine, law and ceremonies, whilst diocesan Episcopacy is simply ignored, but not abjured. It marks a distinct stage in the history of the Scottish Church. Though many bonds and covenants had preceded it, it was the first covenant which could be called national. The King commanded that it should be signed by all ministers and their parishioners, and that those who refused should be punished. It was generally signed with enthusiasm.

In 1584 Melville, for criticizing the doings of the King too severely, was sentenced to be imprisoned in Blackness Castle, but made a successful flight to England. Arran now became the King's confidant and tool for the reduction of the Church to submission to the royal will. The King prevailed upon the Assembly to appoint fourteen ministers to act as commissioners for the Church. The parliament gave the commissioners the dignity of bishops, with votes in parliament. The way was thus prepared for parliament to obtain effective control over the Church. In 1584 a series of Acts, known later as "The Black Acts", were passed. By these Acts the bishops were restored and it was declared to be treason to impugn their dignity or to lessen their authority as one of the three Estates of the realm. One Act made unlawful any meetings not convened with royal licence, and any jurisdictions not approved by parliament. Another Act made it possible for any minister, for any kind of offence, to be removed by a bishop or royal commissioner, who were no longer subject to the Assembly. Thus was the autonomy of the Church destroyed. It had become but a department of the State. The King had now become the virtual head or pope of the Scottish Church. The bishops could only administer the affairs of the Church in accordance with the King's will.

The next step towards the absolute subjection of the Church was to pass an Act of Uniformity, which decreed that pastors, readers and teachers should subscribe these Black Acts of 1584, and take an oath of obedience to the bishops and King's commissioner. The penalty for infraction of these laws was loss of function and benefice. Magistrates were given the power to imprison any minister who criticized the Acts in question. As the result of this repressive policy many ministers and teachers fled to England and Ireland. Others felt that the best thing to do under the circumstances was to submit; and yet others began to meet in secret conventicles.

During the years which followed, the Church petitioned in vain for the repeal of the Black Acts. The petitioners were simply accused of the crime of non-allegiance, just as the papists were, whereas one of the most outstanding characteristics of the Covenanters was the tenacity with which they clung to the Stuart dynasty, even when it had been repudiated in the southern kingdom. In 1585 the King issued an Irenicon, and made various shifts to establish a working relationship with the Church. For a time persecution was relaxed. An attempt was made to persuade the Assembly to accept Episcopacy under a mask of popular Presbytery.

At times it seemed as if the Reformed Church was to enjoy the King's favour. Thus, on his marriage, in 1589, to Anne, Princess of Denmark and a Lutheran, James thanked God for his birth in Scotland, and for the

Presbyterian Church, which he described as "such a Kirk, the sincerest Kirk in the world". In 1592 parliament passed an Act which restored a large measure of freedom to the Church. It re-established the Protestant, Presbyterian, and parochial system of religion in Scotland. But it was soon discovered that the King was favouring the Catholics at the very time they were being repressed by the Covenanters in accordance with the law.

The King's real attitude to the Covenanters, and his secret intentions, were clearly manifested in one of his books entitled, *Basilikon Doron*, or *Royal Gift*, which contained his instructions to his son, prince Henry. It was to be privately printed in seven copies, but became known to some of the leading Covenanters. Classing the Covenanters with the puritans, he described them as "brainsick and headie preachers like Anabaptists in contempt of the civil magistrate." He advised his son to beware of and to hate them. While pretending to be favourable to the establishment of Presbytery he advised the prince to restore Episcopacy. Such teaching doubtless profoundly influenced the mind of his other son, prince Charles, who was born in 1600. By this time Queen Anne had become a professed Roman Catholic.

Throughout the remainder of his reign the King lorded it over the Church. Ecclesiastical commissioners were appointed, some of whom afterwards became bishops; and were afforded special privileges of approach to the King. Visitors were appointed over districts, which were practically dioceses, and these had power to examine pastors and other people. Obnoxious ministers were imprisoned or they fled. In this way the Church was subjected to the King's absolute will.

On the death of Queen Elizabeth in 1603 James VI of Scotland became James I of England. It was hardly to be expected that the change would be productive of any good to the Scottish Church. The King was now freed from the robust check of the democratic Presbyterians of the north who had been for ever curbing his despotic temper. The attitude of passive obedience of the English hierarchy was much more to his mind. James was soon tasting to the full the sweets of episcopal adulation. On his accession, about a thousand puritan preachers presented what was known as the Millenarian Petition, in which they begged for some reforms in the ceremonies of the episcopal Church. The Hampton Court Conference was called in 1604 to deal with the matter. The archbishop is reported to have blessed God, on bended knee, for setting over his country a King "so wise, learned and judicious" who spoke "by the special assistance of God's spirit". According to the Bishop of London they now had "such a King, as since Christ's time, the like, he thought, had not been seen." A passing reference to presbyters by one of the puritans present called forth the angry remark of the King that "a Scottish Presbytery agreeth as well with a monarchy as God and the devil."

Very soon the decree went forth that all persons must conform to the official religion, namely, Episcopacy. There was to be "one doctrine, one discipline, one religion, in substance and ceremony." The favourite maxim of the King now was: "No Bishop, no King." At a convocation convened in Canterbury he was declared to be supreme in both jurisdictions, spiritual and civil.

With the troubles between the King and his puritan subjects in England we are not here immediately concerned, although they have a bearing upon our story. In Scotland the King's policy resulted in the complete restoration of the hierarchy. The bishops became the ready tools of the King, little more than civil servants. At first appointed to be Constant Moderators of synods, Archbishop Spottiswood confessed that they were creatures of the King. Such ministers as rebelled against the King's interference in ecclesiastical matters, for example, in the actions of the Assemblies, were persecuted and imprisoned. In 1606 eight ministers, who were invited to London for consultation, were imprisoned, and compelled to hear Anglican sermons on the virtues of Episcopacy. One of these, Andrew Melville, was committed to the Tower for sneering at the "Romish rags" of Bishop Bancroft, and there he remained for four years. He ended his days in France in 1622. James Melville, his nephew, was ordered to reside in Newcastle-on-Tyne; and others were confined to certain parishes in Scotland.

Before the death of James VI in 1625 Scotland could rejoice in having what the prelatists conceived to be a valid hierarchy. But the King had earned the hearty contempt of his people. In the words of Bishop Burnet: "It is certain no king could die less lamented or less esteemed than he was" (*History of His own Times*, Everyman ed., p. 5).

From his training, and the atmosphere which he had breathed from his earliest days, it was hardly to be expected that the accession of Charles I would bring any improvement in the bitter controversy over ecclesiastical affairs which had for so long raged in Scotland. In outward appearance, and in many other ways, he was very different from his father. But in his passion for absolutism, his capacity for double-dealing, and his obstinate refusal to learn from experience he was his father's true successor. Cost what it would—and in the end it cost him dearly—Charles was resolved to destroy Puritanism in England, and Presbyterianism in Scotland, and to establish uniformity of worship throughout his kingdoms. To assist him in carrying out his programme he had the expert assistance of the evil genius William Laud. With all his great capacity and considerable education this rigid ecclesiastic appears to have been almost constitutionally incapable of knowing the meaning of spiritual religion. For him, religion was primarily a matter of form and ritual, and of passive obedience to the King and to the ecclesiastical authorities. Dissent of any degree he counted a horrible crime. Machine-made men, without any capacity for freedom of thought would alone be fit subjects of a kingdom ruled over by Charles I and William Laud.

In 1633 Charles went to Scotland to be crowned, and also to attend to other matters. He was accompanied, among many others, by Laud, and James, Marquis of Hamilton; men whose influence was to count for much in the history of the Scottish Church. Laud was Master of the Ceremonies, and so was able to arrange for the coronation to be after the episcopal fashion, with the full splendour of ceremonial, and regardless of Scottish ideas concerning vestments and the "smell of popery". On the Sunday following the coronation the English Liturgy was read in St. Giles'.

This same year Laud was raised to the Primacy, and discerning men were soon able to see the shape of things to come. The preparation of a Scottish Liturgy had for some years been under consideration. Laud now conceived the idea of binding the English and Scottish Churches together by the use of a common Liturgy. A Book of Canons for the government of the Church of Scotland was also drawn up and sanctioned in 1635. It set forth the absolute authority of the King as head of the Church. Those who denied his supremacy, or who asserted that there were errors in the Liturgy, were to be excommunicated. There were many innovations in the canons, and names of institutions which had been hallowed by long usage were suppressed: for example, "presbytery", "eldership", "ministry" and "kirk-session".

One of the first men to suffer under these new rules was

Samuel Rutherford, the saintly minister of Anwoth, whom Sydserf, Bishop of Galloway, caused to be summoned before the Commission in Edinburgh for ignoring the regulations. He was sentenced to be banished from the parish and transported to Aberdeen, a place which at that time was well known to favour Episcopacy.

At last the Service Book, or Book of Common Prayer, was published at Edinburgh in 1637. It largely followed the English Prayer Book of Edward VI, though there were some changes. From the first the book was suspect. It was not that the Scots objected to the use of a Service Book or of forms of prayer. John Knox himself had prepared a book of prayers which had been based on the Genevan Service Book, and these had been in use for more than seventy years. The main objections were: (1) that it had its origin in England; for though Laud had obtained the assistance of certain Scottish bishops, these were an English creation; (2) that it contained many Romish features; (3) that it was imposed upon a people who did not want it, and without the assent of either pastors or people.

It was decided to make use of the new Service Book for the first time in St. Giles' Church, Edinburgh, on July 23, 1637. The service was to be a model which was to be followed by churches throughout the country. The church was crowded with an excited people, many of whom were seated upon their own three-legged stools, after the fashion of those days; for at that time churches were not furnished with seats. No sooner did Dean Hannay appear at the desk carrying the Service Book than the pent-up indignation of the people broke out into tumult. Some shouted, others wept. Jenney Geddes is traditionally reported to have been the first to throw her stool at the dean and the bishop (Lindsay), who had gone to his assistance; though there is some doubt whether she is entitled to this distinction. Many followed the example set.

Eventually the rioters were expelled, and the service was completed by the dean and bishop. Similar tumults took place in other city churches, and many petitions were signed calling for the suppression of the obnoxious book. The first blow had now been struck in the great national struggle for freedom of conscience which, after a conflict which lasted for fifty years, resulted in the establishment of civil and religious liberty.

So great was the tumult caused by this attempt to foist the new Service Book upon the Scottish people that the Privy Council and the bishops agreed to suspend the use of both the old and the new Service Books until the King had been consulted. The new Liturgy, however, continued to be used in some places. Whiteford, Bishop of Brechin, for example, is reported to have entered the pulpit with a pistol in one hand and a Prayer Book in the other, supported by an armed body-guard. But the angry temper of his flock was so manifested that he never durst repeat the unchristian performance.

The King was greatly enraged by what he called "the barbarous tumult", and he sent commands for the punishment of the rioters. He also gave orders that the Liturgy should continue to be used. The authorities, however, were paralysed by the popular feeling, and durst not attempt to enforce the King's commands. It was one thing for the King and Laud to bluster and threaten when so far out of the reach of the mob as London was; it was quite another to brave its fury so near at hand. The righteous wrath of the people was now fully aroused, and they were in no mood to yield to further bludgeoning without fierce retaliation. More than one savage attack was made upon responsible ecclesiastical dignitaries, who had to be protected by the Covenanters themselves.

For some months the situation grew worse. The leaders of the Covenanters became "Supplicants" and prepared

a reasoned statement of their case. They were now
supported by a formidable number of nobles. At length
a Covenant was drafted by "The Tables", that is, the Commissioners of the Covenanters, who had been appointed
a little before this time as a permanent body sitting in
Edinburgh to deal with the situation. The name was
derived from the fact that they met in four sections and
sat at four tables. The leaders realized that only popular
support could enable them to resist the forces of England,
should they be brought against them. The Tables therefore
requested Henderson and Johnston to prepare a Covenant
for signature by the people. The Lord's Day, February 25,
1638, was set apart as a day of fasting and public humiliation.

The Covenant now drawn up consists of three principal
parts. Part I is a repetition of the King's Confession of
1580–81; for the national troubles were traced to the
breach of that Covenant. Part II specifies the Acts of
Parliament by which popery was suppressed and the
Protestant religion established. Part III is the new Covenant adapted to the situation then existing. Those chiefly
responsible for the drafting were Sir Archibald Johnston,
also known as Lord Warriston, and the Rev. Alexander
Henderson, minister of the country parish of Leuchars.

The day of the signing of the Covenant, February 28,
1638, was one of the most memorable days in Scottish
history. It belongs to the same category of events as the
day on which Magna Carta was signed. The Covenant
bound the people to abjure the papacy and to defend the
Reformed religion, while at the same time defending the
King and their co-subscribers, if need be with their lives.
The Covenant was signed in Greyfriars Church and churchyard, where a vast congregation had assembled.

The National Covenant, as this enlarged edition of the
King's Confession came to be called, was read by Johnston

and the Earl of Loudoun exhorted the people to be loyal to the bond. The congregation, with uplifted hands, swore allegiance to the Covenant. Then the signatures were appended, those of the nobles and barons coming first. The signing in the church went on into the night. The parchment was then carried into the churchyard and laid upon a flat table-stone, and was there signed by the eager multitudes of people. Some, it is said, signed in their own blood. Copies of the Covenant were afterwards made and sent throughout the kingdom and were signed everywhere with enthusiasm. Within a few weeks the greater part of the kingdom had subscribed the momentous document.

When the Primate Spottiswood saw the turn which events had taken he gave up all for lost. Seeking safety across the Border, he exclaimed: "All which we have been attempting to build up during the last thirty years is now at once thrown down." When the news reached London the King was both angry and alarmed, but he was not so apt to read the writing on the wall. Some of his short-sighted advisers, lay and clerical, tried to persuade him to believe that the use of a little force would soon reduce the Scottish rebels to submission. He was quick enough to see that he could not now draw back without much loss of prestige—a matter of great moment to a King who claimed to rule by divine right, and who had been so often assured by his flatterers that he possessed divine wisdom. After consideration the King temporized and resolved to send the Marquis of Hamilton to compose the quarrel with his subjects. Private instructions given to the commissioner, however, did not agree with those made public. Hamilton was instructed to maintain an appearance of friendship until the English fleet had sailed, and sufficient power was at hand to coerce the rebels.

Still further to dupe the people a Royal Proclamation was put forward to encourage no popery. The Privy

Council also passed an Act abolishing the Liturgy, the Canons and the Court of High Commission. But a London spy informed the commissioners that these things were being done merely to keep the people quiet until the King should be able to answer "from the mouth of the cannon". Various schemes were also brought forward to divide the Covenanters. The Privy Council even went so far as to subscribe the King's Confession of 1581. The Covenanters, however, issued a Protestation which explained why they could not accept the King's explanations or intentions, or be satisfied with the King's Confession, since it did not abjure Episcopacy. Nothing now would satisfy them but the calling of a Free Assembly. The Assembly had not met for twenty years and was practically defunct.

The Assembly was regularly summoned and met in Glasgow Cathedral towards the end of 1638—the first really free Assembly in forty years. Soon disagreements arose as to the powers of the Assembly, and Hamilton, the King's Commissioner, ordered the Assembly to dissolve. As he attempted to withdraw, the Rev. Alexander Henderson, of Leuchars, protested, and the members formally declared: "In the name of the Lord Jesus Christ, the only Head and Monarch of this Church, we cannot dissolve this Assembly." The Proclamation issued the next day dissolving the Assembly was ignored. The Assembly continued its sitting until it had swept away Service Book, bishops, papal rites and ceremonies, and had restored the Presbyterian system. In his report to the King, Hamilton, while advising the use of force to suppress these rebels, yet acknowledged that the situation had been brought about by the folly, pride, illegalities and unworthy living of the bishops.

Detailed charges were preferred against the bishops, including various forms of dereliction of duty, and numerous vices and acts of oppression. Some of the accused were excommunicated; others were both deposed and excommunicated.

It is a most remarkable fact that this thorough revolution in ecclesiastical life was carried through with a total absence of bloodshed, and with an amazing rapidity. It serves to show that the decisions of the Covenanters were in harmony with the will of the mass of the people. It is largely to be accounted for by the fact that Episcopacy had been thrust upon the people against their will, and that first the Reformers, and then the Covenanters, made use of the recognized legal procedure to undo the evil which had been done. To a remarkable degree the Covenant represented the will of the people.

The first reaction of the King, and of his evil genius Laud, was to propose to send an army into Scotland to overcome the rebels, as they were called. The Committee of the Estates, which had been appointed and given legislative and executive functions, accordingly prepared for war. A military organization was speedily built up, and Field-Marshal Alexander Leslie was given the command. When the King's army prepared to invade Scotland, however, the King realized that the opposing forces were so strong that, after a skirmish, in which his forces were worsted, peace was arranged, and the Pacification of Berwick was signed on June 18, 1639. By this treaty the Scots gained nearly all they asked for. The Acts of the Assembly were confirmed.

The affairs of Scotland became now even more closely linked with momentous events in England. Charles had no thought of giving up the struggle, and regarded the Treaty of Berwick merely as affording a breathing-space. The Scots observed closely the troubles which had arisen between the King and his subjects in England, and which found expression in the Short Parliament of 1640. The English recognized that the Scots were fighting for English as well as Scottish liberty. As Charles prepared for war, so did the Scots. The Scottish army entered England and took possession of Newcastle in 1640. Eventually the Treaty of Ripon was arranged, and Charles summoned the Long Parliament, which met on November 3 of that year.

Civil War broke out in August, 1642, when Charles unfurled the national standard at Nottingham. Commissioners of the Long Parliament soon appeared in Scotland to seek the help of the Convention of the Estates, which had taken the place of parliament and the General Assembly. They proposed the formation of a solemn bond of union between the three kingdoms as the best means for securing the safety of the cause of the Reformation. On August 2, 1643, the General Assembly met in St. Giles' Church, Edinburgh, with Henderson in the Moderator's chair. The English commissioners gave an account of the progress of the Reformation in England, and presented a request for assistance. Henderson produced the draft of the famous document which came to be known as "The Solemn League and Covenant", which was welcomed by the Assembly. The English had favoured a civil league only, but they yielded to the Scots insistence that this should be accompanied by a religious Covenant. It was soon approved by the Convention, and, at a later date, by the Westminster Assembly, and by both Houses of the English Parliament.

The Solemn League and Covenant of 1643 differed considerably from the National Covenant signed in Greyfriars Church in 1638. Both were anti-papal; but the Solemn League and Covenant was more anti-prelatic, and was intended to make Presbyterianism supreme in Scotland. It also aimed at achieving a definite uniformity of religious belief and Church constitution in all the three kingdoms, despite the wish of the English to secure toleration for Independency. In this attempt on the part of the Presbyterians to secure uniformity lay the seeds of much future trouble. It was a fateful inheritance from the false conceptions of the Church which had prevailed since she became wedded to the Roman Empire. To the enlightened mind of Cromwell we owe the first effective attempt to withstand the intolerance of Presbyterianism, as of Episcopacy, and to establish the principle of toleration in religious beliefs.

Into the details of the Great Civil War we shall not here enter. On the execution of Charles I in 1649, his son was proclaimed in Scotland King of Great Britain, France and Ireland. At first Charles II was unwilling to accept the conditions with regard to the establishment of Presbyterianism laid down by the Scots. After the defeat and execution of Montrose in May, 1650, however, he saw that there was no other way of attaining the crown, and therefore signed both the *National Covenant* and the *Solemn League and Covenant* on June 23, 1650. These he subscribed again when he was crowned at Scone on January 1, 1651. In a few months, however, the King was a fugitive. After being defeated at the Battle of Worcester, on September 3, 1651, he sought refuge in France.

In the meantime an unfortunate split took place in the ranks of the Covenanters between the Resolutioners and the Remonstrants or Protesters. The Resolutioners were willing to accept the service of certain persons—called "Malignants"—who did not agree with the dominant party in politics and church affairs. The Remonstrants or Protesters opposed this policy, and held that only unbending Covenanters should be allowed to engage in this warfare. A wrangle took place in the Assembly when the Remonstrants voiced their protest. The leading Protesters were deposed. Thus began a bitter quarrel which was a source of great weakness in later years.

Scotland was subjugated by 1652, and from this date

until the eve of the Restoration the country was annexed and treated as if it were a conquered province. The will of Cromwell and of the English parliament was supreme. The Edinburgh Assembly was dissolved in 1653 by Colonel Cottrel, and the ministers were expelled from the town under threat of imprisonment. A meeting of the Protesters was also dissolved, but before the dissolution they drew up a protestation against the unlawful suppression of the Assembly. The Covenant ceased to be enforced, and the people were allowed to worship God as they pleased, so long as they did not interfere with affairs of State. Cromwell made certain attempts to settle the religious troubles of Scotland, but without success.

The presbyterian system of religion proved to be unpopular in England. It was established there in June, 1646, and elderships, presbyteries and provincial and national assemblies were constituted. But the English people did not take kindly to the oversight of presbyters; and the principle of toleration, favoured by Cromwell, rendered the system unworkable. In Scotland the feuds between the various parties continued. Both Resolutioners and Protesters appealed to Cromwell who, after listening to their representations, bade them return home and live in peace.

Cromwell died on his "lucky day", September 3, 1658. His most valuable contribution to the religious controversy which we are considering was his firm enunciation of the principle of toleration. To the Irish he had said: "As for the people, what thoughts on religion they have in their own breasts, I cannot reach, but shall think it my duty if they walk honestly and peacefully, not to cause them in the least to suffer for the same." It was a long time, however, before this became an accepted principle of English or Scottish religious and political life.

Cromwell's son Richard was appointed to succeed him,

but he proved to be utterly incapable of carrying out the duties of his high position and was forced to resign.

General Monk, the friend of Cromwell, declared himself in favour of a civil rather than of a military régime. Taking advantage of the religious divisions of Scotland, and of the slight hold which the presbyterian system had upon the affections of the English people, Monk was able to secure the support of the Scottish Resolutioners and of the English Presybterians for the Royalist design to restore Charles II to the throne of his fathers.

Chapter Fifteen

CHURCHES AND CONVENTICLES

CHARLES II landed at Dover on May 25, 1660. It was not unnatural that his return should have inaugurated a period of reaction. The people were tired and exhausted by the long period of struggle and war. Military rule had proved to be irksome to a liberty-loving people. Even the stern unbending Covenanters were monarchists, and had proclaimed Charles as King immediately on the death of his father. They had never heartily accepted the rule of Cromwell. They had some ground for hope that the King would have learned some wisdom during the years of exile from home. Charles, however, was not of the type that learns lessons even from adversity. Vain, foolish and lustful, he was the last man in the world to lead his people to gather the fruits of the controversy which had raged throughout his kingdom for so many years.

In Scotland the people were generally still firmly attached to their Protestant and Presbyterian faith. But James Sharp, the representative of the Resolutioners in London, deceived them and soon attained to a dominating position in ecclesiastical affairs. Shortly after his return to Scotland he was appointed Archbishop of St. Andrews, and speedily led the way to the undoing of the work of the Covenanters.

The government of Scotland was reconstituted, with the Earl of Middleton as commissioner. He had been a Covenanter, but had been won over by Charles. The first Restoration parliament met on January 1, 1661, one of the blackest days in Scottish history. Middleton had received instructions to assert the ancient royal prerogative; the right of the King to call parliaments, and to annul the Covenanting legislation of 1643–49. He was also to secure the passing of an Act of Oblivion, and to annul confiscations. The question of Episcopacy was also to be considered. The Oath of Allegiance taken acknowledged Charles II to be supreme in all causes and over all people. It was required of all public officials and burgh magistrates. Sympathizers with the Covenanting Cause in vain demanded the insertion of the word "civil" before "supreme authority". The Act was passed and the King became practically pope of Scotland.

Nearly four hundred enactments were speedily passed, including one which repudiated the League and Covenant, and forbade any renewal of it without royal warrant. The series was consummated by an Act—called "the Act Rescissory"—which rescinded all the legislation of the period 1640–48. The very foundations of the Reformed Church were thus destroyed. The Commissioner also considered whether to proceed immediately to re-establish Prelacy, but was dissuaded by the more cautious Clerk Register, whose advice was: "Bring the bishops in; let it be done surely, but let it likewise be done slowly." As Bishop Burnet says, this legislation was "only fit to be concluded after a drunken bout". The same authority describes the period as "a mad roaring time, full of extravagance; and no wonder it was so when the men of affairs were perpetually drunk". This parliament is fitly known to history as Middleton's "Drunken Parliament".

The government next proceeded to punish those who had given offence to the King by seeking to establish the reign of law in place of the absolute will of the King, and also to displace Prelacy by Presbytery. The first selected victim was Samuel Rutherford, formerly Professor, and now Principal of New College in St. Andrews, who had given mortal offence by the publication of his book *Lex Rex*, in which he had argued that law is the true king by which the country should be governed. It was decreed that all copies of this famous book should be burned. It was intended that its author should also share the same fate. But a more kindly death intervened. To those who brought him the summons of the Privy Council to appear and answer to the charge of treason, he replied: "Tell them that I have a summons already from a superior Judge and judicatory, and I behove to answer my first summons; and ere your day arrives I shall be where few kings and great folks come."

The Marquis of Argyle was the next prey to be marked down. He was accused of nearly all the offences in the statute book—treason, arson, rebellion, murder, and accession to the murder of the King. Yet it was he who had set the crown upon the King's head, after vehemently opposing the execution of his father. Perhaps the greatest count in the indictment was his compulsory submission to Cromwell's government. The trial was but a farce, and in the end he was condemned to die on the scaffold.

Only a week later James Guthrie also received the martyr's crown. He had been one of the most zealous adherents of the Covenant. Even Cromwell admired his courage, and referred to him as "the short man who could not bow". He was accused of many offences, and particularly of writing a pamphlet entitled *The Causes of the Lord's Wrath against Scotland*, which was alleged to amount to treason. Though the fact was not mentioned in the indictment, he had committed the unforgivable offence of excommunicating Middleton in 1650. He was a man of simple piety and transparent sincerity. His loyalty was manifest, and he had opposed Cromwell as a usurper. His virtues, however, availed nothing. He was condemned to be hanged and his head fixed on the Nether Bow. He met his death with the utmost composure and gave his testimony, according to Bishop Burnet, who saw him suffer, "with the composedness of a man that was delivering a sermon". His final words, "The Covenants, the Covenants shall yet be Scotland's reviving", were long a rallying cry for the Covenanters.

Another notable victim of the reactionary enthusiasm now prevailing was Archibald Johnston, Lord Warriston. We have already noticed the prominent part he played in the signing of the Covenant in Greyfriars Church in 1638. The Glasgow Assembly which followed appointed him to be the Clerk of the Assembly. Later he was made Lord Clerk Register of Scotland. He also served as one of the eight Commissioners from Scotland to the Westminster Assembly. Although he tried to save the life of Charles I, he refused to sanction the calling of Charles II to the throne. He was elected a member of Cromwell's House of Peers, and under him continued to act as Lord Clerk Register. These facts were sufficient to seal his doom at the Restoration. A warrant was issued against him, but for a time he saved his life by flight.

Whilst at Hamburg he fell ill and was treated by a doctor who was said to be in league with his enemies. He never recovered from this sickness, and remained but a shadow of his former self. He went to Rouen to see his wife and while there he was arrested by the agents of Charles, carried to London and thrown into the Tower. Thence he was transported to Edinburgh and cast into the Tolbooth. He was sentenced to suffer the doom of traitors—to be hanged at the Mercat Cross, and to have his head affixed to the Nether Bow. As he mounted the ladder, on July 22, 1663, he spoke cheerfully to the people, saying: "The Lord hath graciously comforted me."

The Drunken Parliament had transferred all power, civil and ecclesiastical, into the hands of the King. The

King speedily announced his resolve to restore bishops to the Church. Neither the Church nor its ministers were consulted in the matter. Charles was now pope of the Church, and re-established Prelacy on his own authority alone. The clergy must obey the bishops, and the bishops must obey the King. This was the idea embodied in the Royal maxim: "No Bishop, no King." It was a return to the condition of things under King James, when the feeble Spottiswood had acknowledged Prelacy to be the creation of His Majesty.

Fourteen bishops were nominated, of whom four—Sharp, Fairfoul, Hamilton and Leighton—were summoned to London for ordination in Westminster Abbey, and thus to receive the grace of Episcopacy, which they, in turn, were to transmit to the rest of the creatures of the King. So little account was taken of the previous ministry of two of them—Sharp and Leighton—who had been set apart by presbyters only, that they had to submit to ordination as deacons and presbyters before receiving ordination as bishops.

In November, 1661, Sharp had been appointed Primate in succession to Spottiswood, the last occupant of the Metropolitan See, and in the May following parliament formally restored Episcopacy, and gave to the bishops all their former powers. The right of Scottish congregations to call their own ministers was taken away, and patronage was re-introduced. Benefice, stipend, manse or glebe were to be taken from all ministers who had been appointed since 1649, unless they received presentation from a patron and collation from a bishop. This implied a renunciation of Presbyterianism and submission to episcopal authority. An Act was passed which declared Covenanting to be treason. Rebels and their families were deprived of the very means of life, and all who supplicated mercy on their behalf rendered themselves liable to prosecution for

195

disloyalty. Fines amounting to nearly two million pounds were imposed upon a number of leading Covenanters who were excepted from an Act of Indemnity and Oblivion.

In 1662 the Privy Council decreed that the clergy should meet their bishops, and that those failing to do so would be held guilty of contempt of authority and liable to censure. The ministers showed much reluctance to obey this injunction, and many of those in the west country refused to acknowledge episcopal jurisdiction. In order to remedy matters, Middleton, accompanied by numerous members of the Council and other influential supporters of the government's policy, made what amounted almost to a royal progress through the western districts. When they arrived at Glasgow, Archbishop Fairfoul made loud complaints about the obstinacy of the ministers who had failed to take the necessary steps for remaining in their charges. Asked to suggest a remedy the archbishop advised coercion. All ministers were to be commanded immediately to submit to the bishop or leave their manses. He assured the Commissioner that no more than ten pastors would refuse to comply. An eviction order was thereupon issued and signed by all present. According to Burnet they were all so drunk that they were incapable of realizing what they were doing. The position of the ministers was aggravated by the fact that it was winter-time. Even so, few of the ministers were willing to comply.

Between three and four hundred ministers, about a third of the total number of ministers in Scotland, prepared to leave their homes. Alarmed by the situation created by their own rash action the Council agreed to a short postponement of the eviction. When it took place the ministers were deprived even of the stipend which was due at the time when they left their parishes.

Many notable ministers were driven from their charges

about this time; for example, Alexander Peden, Donald Cargill, John Welsh, and John Blackadder. Many others were summoned to appear before parliament, and commanded to sign the oath of allegiance. They expressed their willingness to do this with the proviso that the King's authority did not embrace things spiritual. Their scruples were held to be treasonable, and they were thrown into prison. Others were exiled, like John Livingstone who, when his request to be allowed to say farewell to his wife was refused, said: "Well, although it be not permitted me that I should breathe my native air, yet I trust, what part of the world so ever I go to, I shall not cease to pray for a blessing to these lands, to his Majesty, and the government, and the inferior magistrates thereof, but especially to the land of my nativity." Such men were of noble mould, and deserved something better of their fatherland than cruel exile.

The places left vacant by these deprived ministers had somehow or other to be filled. As no qualified ministers were available the bishops went to the north and offered special inducements to young men to offer themselves to fill the vacant charges. A host of highland lads responded to the appeal, most of them having no pretence to the usual qualifications; they were ignorant, worthless and contemptible, for the most part. "They were the worst preachers that ever were heard," says Bishop Burnet, "ignorant to a reproach, and many of them openly vicious —a disgrace indeed to their function, and the very dregs and refuse of the North" (*History*, Everyman ed., p. 75). So great was the exodus from the north that the farmers complained that they could not get lads to tend their cows. And of such a poor type were they that they were treated by their parishioners with contempt, and received the nickname of "The King's Curates". It was not surprising that the intrusion of these unworthy men into the places of well qualified and beloved pastors was in many cases bitterly and forcefully opposed. Some of these "curates" were stoned, others found their church doors barricaded against them.

Coercive measures were now adopted to force the parishioners to attend the churches manned by these uncouth intruders from the north. By an Act of Parliament passed in 1663 heavy penalties were imposed upon such persons as absented themselves from the kirk on the Lord's Day. The Privy Council decreed that husbands were to be responsible for seeing that their wives attended the church. These measures became known as the "Bishops' Drag Net". On August 13, 1663, the "Twenty Mile Act" was passed. This decreed that deprived ministers and their households should remove twenty miles from their churches, six miles outside a cathedral city, and three miles outside a royal burgh. The natural result was that the "outed ministers" and their sympathizers began to meet in private places and in the open air. Thus originated the "Conventicles" which became so famous in Scottish Church life. Large numbers of people who refused to hear the obnoxious curates of the King gathered in secret places to hear their beloved pastors.

At the instance of those whose ministers were thus treated with contempt further repressive measures were instituted. Those who would not meet for worship in the churches were not to be allowed to meet in private house, barn, or on the hillside. Archbishop Sharp was implacable, and complained bitterly that "the gangrene of separation from the Church" was spreading, nullifying the efforts of the prelates. Travelling to London in 1664 he secured the establishment of the Court of High Commission for executing the laws in Church affairs. Of this new instrument of tyranny Sharp was the president. It was to have cognizance of every kind of ecclesiastical offence, and to have the power to fine or imprison at will. In 1665 Conventicles were altogether forbidden.

One of the members of this court was Sir James Turner, a soldier of fortune, who had served as a mercenary in the wars on the continent. He was a drunken, brutal-minded man who, eventually, was dismissed by the Privy Council for his shameless cruelties. When it was learned that Conventicles were still being held in the south-west this man was sent, with a hundred and forty horse and foot guards, to put them down. In the most barbarous fashion these forces preyed upon the people. The most exorbitant fines were imposed. Men were beaten, and women violated. Then, that they might have no hope of redress, when the soldiers withdrew the sufferers were compelled to sign a certificate affirming that Turner had used them civilly and discreetly.

These brutal oppressions, frequently repeated, naturally produced a spirit of rebellion. Revolt broke out on the morning of November 13, 1666, when four starving Covenanters near the village of Dalry were informed that a company of soldiers had bound an old man and were brutally ill-treating him because of his refusal to pay some fines which had been imposed. The Covenanters hurried to the scene and remonstrated with the soldiers. A struggle took place in which one of the soldiers was killed. The remainder were overpowered.

Fearing reprisals, the Covenanters decided that their best plan was to capture Turner, the commander of the soldiers, before he was aware of what had happened. They hurried to Dumfries, where they found Sir James still in bed. Without much trouble he was taken captive. They then assembled at the Town Cross, and to show their loyalty, they drank the King's health, whilst reviling the bishops. Messengers were sent into Ayrshire and to Edinburgh to report these incidents and to solicit assistance.

The revolt, however, was premature, and the greatest strength of the revolters did not exceed about 1,100 horse and foot. Colonel James Wallace of Auchans was appointed commander. He had served with distinction in the civil wars, and had joined the Covenanters from a stern sense of duty. He agreed to lead the ill-armed company, though he fully realized the danger of the situation. They marched to Lanark, where they renewed the Covenant, and again asserted their loyalty to the King.

The rising gave great alarm to the Privy Council, of which Archbishop Sharp was then the acting President. Lieutenant-General Dalzell, the Commander-in-chief of the government forces, was sent west to deal with the situation. The insurgents made for Edinburgh, from which city they had hoped for sympathy and help; but they found the city closed against them. They then took up a position in the Pentland hills, above Rullion Green. Here Dalzell's forces came upon them and defeated them, killing fifty men and capturing about one hundred. The rest escaped into the darkness. Wallace made his way to Holland.

The prisoners were treated in the most barbarous fashion. Some were speedily executed. Others were crowded into a dungeon called "Haddock's Hole". Their trial soon followed; and when they pleaded that they had surrendered on the promise of quarter, the archbishop replied: "You were pardoned as soldiers; but you are not acquitted as subjects." They were hanged, and their heads were fixed to the city gates. Before they died, however, they gave striking evidence of their piety and patriotism. They rejoiced in being martyrs for the cause of Christ, and gave their farewells without bitterness. Not one was willing to purchase life by abjuring the Covenants. "If I had many worlds", said one of them, "I would lay them all down, as now I do my life for Christ and His cause."

One of the most notable martyrs at this time was Hugh Mackail, a young minister of only twenty-six years of age. Though he had joined the insurgents, he had left them before the fight took place on account of ill-health. He was captured, taken before the Council, and subjected to the torture of the "Boot". He was found guilty of treason and sentenced to death. Throughout the cruel ordeal his faith was exultant. In his final words he exclaimed: "Welcome, blessed Spirit of grace, God of all consolation! Welcome, glory! Welcome, eternal life! Welcome, death!"

As the repressive measures put in force failed to intimidate the Covenanters, Lauderdale decided to take matters into his own hand, and try what could be done by a change of policy. During a brief period, later known as "The Blink", the sufferings of the persecuted were greatly eased. In 1669 a conditional Indulgence was authorized by the Privy Council. Parish ministers were allowed to resume duty in their old charges when these were vacant, providing they received collation at the hands of the bishops and attended the ecclesiastical courts, and in other ways showed a more subservient spirit. They might even be appointed to new parishes on certain conditions. Even those who refused collation were allowed the use of manses and glebes, and might receive a grant from the government. On the other hand, an indulged minister must confine his ministrations to his own parish, and refrain from preaching against Prelacy. The great majority of the ministers refused to accept this Indulgence, as it meant the recognition of the right of the State to govern the Church. Only forty-three returned to minister under these conditions.

In 1672 a further Indulgence was offered. By this ministers were allowed to work in pairs in selected parishes. They must minister only to their own parishioners. They must not leave their parish without a licence from

the bishop. Private preaching and attendance at conventicles were declared to be criminal. Some eighty
ministers accepted these terms for the resumption of their
ministry.

The granting of these Indulgences had most unfortunate
effects within the ranks of the Covenanters. It produced an
attitude of mutual recrimination as bitter as that between
Resolutioners and Remonstrants or Protesters ten years
before. The strict Covenanters would have nothing to do
with the Indulgences, and regarded the indulged ministers
as traitors to their cause. On the other hand, some of those
who had accepted the Indulgences were men of noble
character and great gifts, who sincerely thought that
under the circumstances their acceptance of the opportunity to minister under the conditions laid down was the
best thing that could be done. Another result was that the
partial submission of many of the Covenanters encouraged
the government to pursue its policy of persecution. They
resolved to persist in their policy of repression until they
had completely stamped out the conventicles.

An attempt which had been made upon the life of the
hated Archbishop Sharp in 1668 had only served to
intensify the struggle. In 1674 the would-be assassin,
James Mitchell, was apprehended. On the promise of the
Council to spare his life he confessed that he had fired the
shot which had missed the archbishop, but had wounded
his companion. After being confined in the Bass Rock
prison for two years, he was subjected to the horrible
torture of the "Boot" to force him to incriminate his
companions. Ten years after the shot was fired, on the
insistence of the archbishop, he was condemned to death,
despite the promise of the Council to spare his life.

Still further repressive measures were devised by the
archbishop. He had persuaded the Council to give all
military officers the power to kill anyone found going

to and from a conventicle, and that without any form of trial. But before going to London upon this business he had occasion to visit St. Andrews. He set out from Edinburgh with his daughter and an escort of four soldiers. In this district twelve men were on the look out for William Carmichael, Sheriff-Depute of the country, who had been specially zealous in the persecution of the Covenanters. Angered and outraged by the series of robberies, rapes, and much other ill-treatment to which the people of the district had been subjected, the twelve men had resolved to seize Carmichael and teach him a lesson, thus forcing him to leave the district. Perhaps because he had been warned, the Sheriff-Depute was not to be seen. Whilst, however, the twelve men were holding a consultation as to what was to be done, they were informed that the archbishop's carriage was approaching. Here, they felt, was a heaven-sent opportunity to deal with the chief instigator of all the sufferings which so many innocent people had been compelled to endure. Forthwith the band of determined men, now reduced to nine, set upon the archbishop on Magus Moor, and, though he begged piteously for his life, he was murdered on the spot. It was hardly to be expected that he who had shown no mercy should receive mercy when he fell into the hands of those who had been his victims.

Chapter Sixteen

REVOLT, SUFFERING AND VICTORY

THOUGH the murder of Archbishop Sharp was condemned by the leaders of the Covenanting-party, the immediate result was a great increase in the sufferings of the Covenanters generally, and some were put to death who were in no way responsible for the deed. The former test question put to prisoners had been: "Do you hold by the Covenants?" Now this gave place to the question: "Do you hold Sharp's death to have been murder?" The King's Advocate, known as "the Bloody Mackenzie", succeeded to Sharp's place as President of the Privy Council. Ten thousand merks were offered for the apprehension of the assassins. Conventicles were declared to be seditious assemblies. Lauderdale gave orders for the assembling of a great army, largely composed of rough, cruel men from the north. Carrying shackles and instruments of torture for the prisoners, they were let loose upon whole districts. The sufferings caused, and the losses endured by spoliation, were indescribable.

The army which was raised to exterminate the Covenanters was supported by means of a cess or tax. The Covenanters naturally objected to the payment of such a tax, and some went so far as to refuse to pay it. A further division was thus introduced into the ranks of the Covenanters. The more rigid among them denied the right of the magistrates to levy the tax. They thus became rebels in a double sense. In 1679 a small company of them entered Rutherglen and put out the bonfires which were blazing in honour of Restoration Day, May 29. They also made a

Declaration at the Cross against all the proceedings of the government since 1660, and burned the Acts which had been directed against the Reformation.

Graham of Claverhouse was sent to quell the insurrection which thus found expression. This man was a worthy successor to Turner, whose doings have been indicated. He was a fanatic, thoroughly unprincipled, who rejoiced to be known as "a terror to the godly", and gloried that his mission was to exterminate the opponents of Episcopacy. About a month after Sharp's death this ruffian soldier found a company of Covenanters, including those who had taken part in the incident at Rutherglen, holding a meeting near the moorland tract of Drumclog. On warning being given of the approach of Claverhouse, the Covenanters resolved to stand and fight with such arms as they possessed. The rudely armed men fought to such effect that Claverhouse's troops were put to flight, and he himself escaped on a trooper's horse after his own had been killed. Thus ended the battle of Drumclog, the only battle won by the Covenanters.

This humiliating defeat of the government's forces was, however, speedily avenged. The Duke of Monmouth was sent from England with a considerable army to put down the insurrection. He was known to be a Protestant, and on his arrival he made known his kindly intentions to arrange a reasonable peace. He refused, however, to treat with the insurgents unless they laid down their arms within half an hour. The half hour passed in disputings between the indulged and non-indulged. A fierce fight followed near Bothwell Bridge, in which the Covenanters were heavily defeated (June 22, 1679). About four hundred Covenanters were slain and twelve hundred taken prisoners. The latter were treated with the utmost cruelty. They were confined in Greyfriars churchyard for five months without any shelter from the elements until some sheds had been erected. They stood by day and lay on the earth by night. An Act of Indemnity was proclaimed to all who would take an oath to rise no more in arms. Certain of the prisoners took the oath and were released. After a trial nine of the prisoners were hanged in chains on Magus Moor for the slaughter of the archbishop. Two hundred and fifty-seven were sentenced to be transported to Barbados to work in the plantations. The ship's holds were crammed with suffocating prisoners. The vessel, however, foundered off Orkney, and not more than fifty survived the wreckage to be transported.

On June 29, 1679, largely through the efforts of Monmouth, a Third Indulgence was proclaimed. It denounced field conventicles, and declared those who preached at them to be traitors. House conventicles, however, were to be allowed, except in Edinburgh, Glasgow, St. Andrews, and Stirling. Ministers who had taken part in the last rebellion were excluded and those who availed themselves of the Indulgence had to give a bond of good behaviour.

The Indulgence became a further occasion for division and dispute among the Covenanters. A number accepted the opportunity thus offered to exercise a limited ministry; the others refused. The latter were led by two determined men, Donald Cargill and Richard Cameron. They believed that the government, by its interference in the affairs of the Church of Christ, and by its policy of persecution, had forfeited all claim upon the allegiance of the people, and asserted that the killing of the King as a tyrant would be a justifiable act.

Richard Cameron was a remarkable man. Converted from Episcopalianism to Presbyterianism, he became an ardent enthusiast of the extreme type. Rather than avail himself of the Indulgences he went to Holland for a time, and there he was ordained. He returned to Scotland in

October, 1679, having felt the call to help his persecuted fellow-countrymen.

This bold determined man soon gathered round him a band of like-minded men who were determined to go to the limits of resistance to the cruel and oppressive government. On June 22, 1680, Cameron, at the head of twenty horsemen, with drawn swords in their hands, marched down the High Street of Sanquhar, and published and fixed to the Cross a Declaration which disowned allegiance to Charles II and declared war upon him.

The government was immediately stirred to vigorous action. A reward of five hundred merks was offered for Cameron dead or alive. Large sums of money were offered for his brother Michael, and for Donald Cargill. All the people of the surrounding districts were ordered to search for and deliver up the wanted men. On the other hand, Cameron was henceforth accompanied by a bodyguard of about sixty friends, many of them mounted, under the leadership of Hackstoun of Rathillet. Within a month, this small band of Cameronians was surprised by a military force at Ayrsmoss. The Covenanters fought with the utmost courage. Cameron and most of the mounted men were slain. Hackstoun was wounded and captured. He was taken to Lanark and thence to Edinburgh, where he was most barbarously executed. The atrocious cruelties practised on this occasion can scarcely ever have been exceeded.

Donald Cargill escaped for a time. In September, 1680, he boldly excommunicated the King and his advisers, an act which was a main count in the indictment when at last he was captured and brought to judgment. On the scaffold Cargill appeared serene and triumphant. He exclaimed: "This is the most joyful day that ever I saw in my pilgrimage on earth; my joy is now begun." Four others who suffered at the same time showed an equal contempt for death.

The arrival of James, the King's brother, in Scotland in 1679, as the royal representative, had served only to intensify the sufferings of the Covenanters. He was animated by all the Stuart passion for absolutism. As President of the Privy Council he induced parliament to pass an Act which declared that the Kings of Scotland derive their power from God alone, and succeed each other lineally without regard to any difference in religion. Another Act passed was known as the Test Act. It was intended to put an end to all forms of dissent. Each parish minister was ordered to send a list of those who withdrew from public worship to his bishop, who, in turn, was to sign it and send it to the magistrates who were to persecute. All individuals in places of office or trust, except the King's brothers and sons, were to subscribe an oath, accepting the royal supremacy and promising obedience, before January 1, 1682, or be attainted.

The Earl of Argyle refused to take the oath except with the proviso: "as far as it is consistent with itself or with the Protestant religion." He was condemned to death as a traitor. Taking advantage of the visit of his step-daughter, however, he escaped from the castle disguised as her page, and eventually passed over to Holland. A price was put upon his head and his estates were confiscated.

Many besides the extreme Covenanters found the Test too severe and refused to take the oath. Some eighty episcopal ministers resigned rather than bind themselves by its terms. In the diocese of Edinburgh alone twenty-one ministers preferred to suffer ejection rather than subscribe. Many aristocrats chose to surrender their hereditary jurisdictions and offices rather than take the new oath.

As for the common people, so many were brutally done to death, with or without trial, that the years 1684–85 came to be known as "The Killing Time". James, the Duke of York, himself set an example of callous cruelty. When some of the members of the Council, after decreeing that torture should be applied, found the sufferings of the tortured too excruciating to witness, and wished to leave the room, the Duke forced them to remain, and seemed to find pleasure in observing the agonies of his victims. With such encouragement, an orgy of almost unexampled cruelty began. Claverhouse became the subjugator of the westlands and set the pace for others. Excessive fines were imposed upon those who refused to attend the churches. Soldiers were given the authority to search, imprison and slay at will. Many men, women and children were left lying in foul dungeons for long periods without trial. The utmost cruelties were practised on young children to compel them to betray the whereabouts of parents or other adults. Women were imprisoned, tortured and executed, "not accepting deliverance; that they might obtain a better resurrection" (Hebrews 11: 35).

It is not possible to say how many were done to death during these years. The Martyrs' Monument in Greyfriars churchyard, Edinburgh, gives the number of those who were destroyed between the execution of Argyle and that of Renwick as eighteen thousand. There seems to be little reason to regard this figure as an exaggeration.

Space does not allow us to tell of all the outstanding personalities held in honour by the Scottish people for maintaining their witness, and upholding the banner of freedom in these dark times. Such men as Robert Baillie of Jerviswood, John Brown of Priesthill, and Alexander Peden, will ever be honoured as amongst the bravest of the brave. They will ever shine as bright stars in the firmament of Scottish life over against the shameless cruelties of Claverhouse and his associates.

In the thickest darkness which preceded the dawn of the "glorious revolution" of 1688 there were not lacking men of heroic resolution and strength of soul who were enabled to be true to the Covenants at all costs. Before the defeat of Ayrsmoss (1680) Cameron and Cargill had begun to gather the unbending Covenanters, who would have nothing to do with Indulgences, into societies which went by the names of Cameronians or Society People. Of these, on the death of Cameron and Cargill, James Renwick became the leader. Born in 1662, he studied at Edinburgh University. Soon he became associated with the Nonconformists, and was in the company which witnessed the death of Cargill. The scene filled him with a detestation of cruelty and led him to dedicate his life to the winning of liberty. He greatly impressed the Societies as a young man of ability and strong spiritual conviction. He was recommended to the care of the exiles in Holland as a suitable candidate for the ministry. There he was ordained, and in 1683 he returned to Scotland to lead the Covenanters in their undying struggle against their oppressors. He had great gifts of leadership. As a preacher he was cultured, evangelical and poetic; a very different type of man from what the Covenanters are usually represented to have been. He was entirely fearless of any fate that might befall him. Episcopal fanaticism could scarcely have chosen a fairer victim for its final onslaught. Under the leadership of this intrepid young man the Societies rallied and increased in number. His enthusiasm was tireless. When preaching at conventicles a swift horse was always kept in readiness on which he passed quickly from place to place.

The government was roused to put forth all its energies against him. A price was put on his head and he was proclaimed a rebel. No one was allowed to shelter or succour him, and death was the penalty for assisting him in any way. The wonder was that with a physique so frail he was able to endure so many hardships for so long a time.

On the death of Charles II, James II was proclaimed

King in February, 1685. It was not to be expected that
an avowed papist would be allowed to assume royal
power in Scotland without a vigorous protest from the
Cameronians. This protest was made when James Renwick
led a considerable company of armed men to the Burgh
Cross of Sanquhar, on May 28, 1685. The Declaration
made on this occasion denounced the doings of the government of Charles II, and rejected the Duke of York as King,
on the ground of his cruel oppressions, and because he was
a Roman Catholic, and was thus disqualified by many
Scottish Acts of Parliament from wearing the Scottish
crown. The avowed principles of the Societies were clear
and emphatic. They held that magistrates have no powers
except those assigned them by the people. Tyranny
and oppression justify revolt. Whatever is necessary
to achieve civil and religious freedom may be justly
done.

Before Renwick was captured and put to death the
Earl of Argyle made an attempt to raise the standard of
revolt in the western Highlands. On May 2, 1685, the earl
and a force of three hundred men set sail from Holland in
three ships, and in a few days reached Cantyre by way of
Orkney and the Hebrides. A proclamation made on his
arrival failed to win the support of the Cameronians. A
thousand men joined the earl from the Campbell clan, but
the Lowlands were unresponsive. The Privy Council were
speedily notified of the descent, and the earl was captured
at Ichinnan. He was treated with marked severity as he
was being taken to Glasgow and to Edinburgh. His doom
was a foregone conclusion, for he had been condemned as
a traitor four years previously for having taken the Test
oath with reservation. The King ordered his immediate
execution, and he was beheaded at the Market Cross,
uttering his dying testimony in the words: "I die, not only
a Protestant, but with a heart hatred of Popery, Prelacy,

and all superstition whatever." His final words were: "Lord Jesus, receive me into glory."

Intent upon the removal of all disabilities from the Roman Catholics, King James, early in 1687, issued a number of Acts of Indulgence, under the guise of toleration for the leading classes of Dissenters—the moderate Presbyterians, the Quakers, and the Roman Catholics. Certain of these parties accepted the benefits of this autocratic action of the King. In particular the Roman Catholics began to erect fresh places of worship. On the other hand, Renwick and his party rejected this absolutist method of giving civil and religious freedom. The limitations imposed were objectionable to such as claimed liberty of conscience as a divine right.

On the first of February, 1688, Renwick was captured in a house on Castle Hill, Edinburgh. At the trial which followed he justified his principles, denied that the King was a lawful sovereign according to the Word of God and the ancient laws of Scotland. He was condemned to be executed on February 10. Some measure of sympathy seems to have been felt by members of the Council for this young lad of twenty-six, and they were willing to provide a loophole for his escape from a cruel death. The King's Advocate urged him to sue for pardon. But when Linlithgow, the Justice-General, asked him if he wished a longer time for preparation, he replied that "It was all one to him. If it were protracted it was welcome, if it were shortened it was welcome. His Master's time was best." All attempts made to induce him to forsake his covenanting principles failed. On the day of execution he walked to the scaffold in a transport of joy, and gave his testimony amidst the rolling of drums intended to drown his voice.

The last man to suffer martyrdom in Scotland for his religious belief was worthy of the honour of opening the kingdom of liberty to those who should follow after.

The dawning of a new day was now rapidly approaching. I shall not here attempt to tell in detail how the Crown of these kingdoms was transferred from the foolish and obstinate James to the Protestants William and Mary. On his assumption of the government the Duke of York had given a solemn promise to the Council that he would uphold the established liberties of the State and people. Yet he immediately proceeded to override parliament; to levy customs and excise duties by his own authority. He gathered round him Jesuit counsellors, and was believed to have said that "he would either convert England or die a martyr". He suspended the Test Act and appointed Roman Catholics to ecclesiastical offices. He granted Indulgences and toleration without reference to parliament.

Even those who stood to gain most from a real policy of toleration perceived that the ultimate object of James was merely to re-establish the Roman Catholics; this done, the persecution would begin all over again. They realized, too, that the liberties of the English and Scottish peoples ought not to be at the mercy of any arbitrary monarch inspired by absolutist principles. The Nonconformists in England and Scotland therefore resolved to make common cause with their former episcopalian persecutors, and to have done with Stuart tyranny. The Primate of England and six bishops, who refused to circulate the royal Declaration of Indulgence, re-issued in April, 1688, played a noble part.

Leading English statesmen now decided to offer the Crown to William of Orange, a grandson of Charles I, and nephew and son-in-law of James VII (II). The invitation was accepted, and soon the Prince of Orange landed at Torbay, declaring that he came to maintain the Protestant religion and to secure a free parliament which should decide the destination of the Crown. James thereupon fled and sought refuge in France.

In contrast with the English bishops the members of the Scottish hierarchy still remained infatuated with the Stuart dynasty, and blind to the significance of events. Only two days before the arrival of the Prince of Orange at Torbay, all the Scottish bishops but two subscribed a letter to the King, whom they described as "the darling of Heaven", and assured him of their firm and unshaken loyalty. They prayed God to give him victory with "the hearts of your subjects and the necks of your enemies".

At the news of the invasion, the Scottish bishops and the King's officials were panic-stricken. In vain did the members of the Privy Council sound the alarm and order the beacons to be lit in order to assemble the King's forces. The majority of the people were only too glad to know that the hour of deliverance had come. The Chancellor, the Earl of Perth, fled; but he was captured and lay in prison for four years. Many Covenanters were released, and the martyrs' heads were removed from the market crosses and city gates.

The quick march of events in Scotland was largely due to the strong bands of Society Men or Cameronians which were spread throughout the country. They had long been firmly convinced of the righteousness of their cause. They had repeatedly affirmed the right of the people to dethrone tyrannous rulers and to appoint others in their place. They had been drilled in the use of arms, and had learned how to defend themselves against the onslaughts of their foes. When therefore the opportunity presented itself they were prepared to take the lead, and to give armed support to the forces of the Prince of Orange. They hastened to Edinburgh to defend the Convention of Estates when it met to deliberate on the transferring of the Crown to William and Mary. For their strong help in this time of need they received the thanks of parliament. In July 1689 parliament passed an Act abolishing Prelacy.

Troublous days still lay ahead. It was not to be expected that after so much party strife—even among the Covenanters themselves—the whole nation would settle down immediately to enjoy the fruits of the great controversy. Much disappointment was felt when it was found that the proposed coronation oath made no reference to the Confession of Faith, or to the necessity of destroying heresy and the establishment of the covenanting religion. It simply provided for the maintenance of the true religion as then received and preached. A persecuting clause was at first inserted, but King William would not bind himself to it in the sense intended. "I will not lay myself under any obligation to be a persecutor", he said firmly. The deputies, who had been sent to London to tender the oath to him, assured him that the formula implied no such obligation. "In that sense, then, I swear", the King said. Like Cromwell before him, this enlightened monarch perceived the falsity of the idol-worship of uniformity to which such untold multitudes of people had been sacrificed.

It took the Presbyterians a considerable time to accept this new code of freedom in religious matters. In the meantime there were many zealots who set out to cleanse their country from papal corruptions. The palace of Holyrood was stormed. Crucifixes, images and other Roman Catholic symbols were swept away and often burnt. The "King's Curates" and the "Bishop's Curates" were "rabbled" and ejected from their parishes. Yet considering the completeness of the revolution, and the enormous power which was suddenly placed in the hands of those who had been so atrociously persecuted, the wonder is that such power was employed with so much restraint and humanity. The Cameronian leaders exerted themselves to restrain the vengeance of their followers and very little blood was shed. After the old persecutor Claverhouse (now Viscount Dundee) had fallen at Killiecrankie, in July, 1689, it was not long before the whole of Scotland, Highlands and Lowlands alike, accepted the rule of William and Mary.

Many questions still remained to be settled, especially the question of patronage, involving the claim of local churches to an effective voice in the selection of their ministers, a matter which eventually caused the Disruption of 1843, and provoked many earlier secessions on a smaller scale. It soon became evident, however, that the vast majority of the Scottish people were firmly attached to protestant and presbyterian principles. Both Romanism and Episcopalianism had been outthought and outlived. If ever Romanists and Episcopalians were to regain their lost influence in the life of the Scottish people they must learn new ways. Their power to lord it over God's heritage had for ever been taken away.

In June, 1690, an Act was passed ratifying the Confession of Faith and settling the government of the Church on presbyterian principles. The surviving ministers who had been expelled from their churches were restored, to the number of about sixty. But the curates who had taken their places were not unkindly treated. Those who were willing to subscribe the Confession of Faith and to promise loyalty to the King were permitted to remain in their old parishes as far as possible. Those who refused to do this were removed. But so generously were they treated that twenty years after the Revolution there were many scores of episcopal ministers in presbyterian parishes who had never taken the oath to King William.

These counsels of moderation were largely due to the personal feelings and principles of the King, and to the wisdom of William Carstairs, his chief adviser. This presbyterian minister, who acted as chaplain to the King, and who later became the Principal of Edinburgh University, still bore in his body the marks of cruel torture. But a passion for revenge formed no part of his nature. Very wisely the General Assembly which, after an interval of thirty-seven years, met in October, 1690, agreed to follow his guidance, and to build the Church afresh upon the basis of New Testament teaching, while resisting the spirit of retaliation for past injuries. This studied moderation gave offence to the rigid Cameronians, but it undoubtedly assisted the process of resettlement, and it was favoured by the great majority of the people.

Part Three

THE FRUITS OF CONTROVERSY

Chapter Seventeen

THE INEVITABILITY OF CONTROVERSY

WE have now sketched the main elements of the controversies which raged for so long a time in English and Scottish life. So far as we can judge, the controversies which arose in the days which preceded the Reformation were inevitable so soon as men should learn to think for themselves. By the time of the Middle Ages the Christian Church had become a vast despotism. Its teaching was imposed upon the people by all manner of brutal force—by fines, imprisonments, confiscations and tortures—all these were used to compel people to think and act in accordance with the views of the ecclesiastical authorities. That the Church was terribly corrupt was admitted even by those who were firmly resolved to stand by the old order of things. The main difference between the latter and the Protestant Reformers was as to the means by which an improvement or Reformation could be brought about. Those who stayed in the Church held the view that bad as things were they should be changed only from within, and with all due respect to constituted authorities. Unfortunately for those who thus argued, it can be proved that this method was tried repeatedly, and failed each time because the Church was a despotism, and had both the will and the power to stamp out movements of reform as soon as they appeared. All those who thought or acted differently from what had been decreed by the Church, or from the traditions which had grown up during the centuries, were immediately branded as heretics, and condemned as being unfit to live, however virtuous their lives might be.

The only way in which a reformation could be achieved therefore was by those who were prepared to carry controversy to its logical conclusion; that is, to the point of refusing to obey the commands of those who had come to occupy high places in the Church, although they were frequently notoriously evil in their lives. When people began to think, to read, and to inquire, they found that those in the highest places of authority, that is, the popes, had frequently been men of the worst character, whose way of life set at naught the plainest precepts of the Gospel. The bishops, who were second in command, and who claimed to be shepherds of the flock, were only too often both ignorant and depraved, cruel and rapacious. It is no wonder that thoughtful men were led to investigate the complete system of Church doctrine, and the whole machinery of Church government.

The discoveries which the pioneers of reform made were surprising even to themselves. They had accepted the system of religious truth on the authority of the priests; but now that they were able to examine the most characteristic dogmas of the Church in the light of the primitive documents, they discovered that a large number of them had but the slightest foundation in New Testament teaching. Many of them indeed appeared to be in direct contradiction to the spirit and teaching of Jesus and His apostles. Transubstantiation, for example, the dogma which gave the priest control over the means of salvation, was based upon the most forced and unnatural interpretation of our Lord's words. Here the Church enforced a literalism which was not applied to any other words that Jesus ever spoke. The result was that every priest became a magician, or miracle worker. It mattered not how worthless in character he might be, according to the prevailing dogma he must be able to change the bread and wine at the Lord's Supper into the veritable body and blood of Jesus, or else men would remain for ever unsaved.

How intolerable was the strain which this system of belief placed upon the hearts and minds of those who were enlightened by Scriptural teaching can only be appreciated by those who have read through the literature of the earlier and later Middle Ages. Of the sincerity of those who revolted against this "shibboleth" of Romanist teaching there can be no manner of doubt. It is manifest that it became impossible for them to accept this teaching without stultifying their minds and doing violence to their consciences. Some of the rebels, such as Wycliffe, were amongst the most learned men of their day. They were capable of examining every point of the traditional doctrine in the light of the primitive documents and the findings of the most learned commentators. Every consideration of self-interest to induce them to think along the tracks laid down by the ecclesiastical authorities was present. Promotion in the Church depended upon implicit obedience. They knew that any sign of hesitation, and any manifestation of doubt, would be construed as heresy, to be corrected and stamped out by the most terrible penalties that men have ever been able to impose upon their fellow men. Men were thrust into dark, damp and unhealthy dungeons and kept there for months or years. They were tortured with the most cruel instruments of torture. They were barbarously executed, and their remains were exhibited in a public place as a warning to others of the doom which awaited them should they dare to follow in the same forbidden paths. Surely these deterrents were sufficient to cause any man to think many times before deciding to throw in his lot with the victims of persecution.

That such men did think long and seriously is evident to

every student of the Reform Movements in the Medieval Church. The Reformers thought out the contents of the Christian Gospel as few other men have ever done, and they were consequently able to obey the apostolic precept to "give answer to every man that asketh you a reason concerning the hope that is in you" (1 Pet. 3: 15). Often from the very steps of the scaffold they gave as lucid a presentation of evangelical truth as was ever given from the pulpit of a Church.

And not only were the pioneers of Protestantism led to examine and to repudiate the characteristic doctrines and usages of Roman Catholicism—transubstantiation, confession, purgatory, mariolatry, worship of images, pilgrimages, etc.; they were likewise led to investigate the very basis upon which this gigantic structure rested. The popes claimed to be vicars of Christ and heads of His Church on earth. To them, it was affirmed, Jesus had given a plenitude of power and authority over the whole of Christendom. But when the words of Jesus, upon which these exalted claims were based, were examined in the light of many other statements of Jesus and of His apostles, they were found not to support the meaning which had been forced upon them. It was not the most natural meaning, or the meaning which had been attached to them in the earliest days. Even the greatest Roman Catholic authorities had differed in their opinion as to what Jesus meant when He said: "Thou art Peter, and upon this rock I will build my Church, and the gates of Hades shall not prevail against it" (Matt. 16: 18). For a long period the bishops of Rome had not claimed to be the heirs of this promise made to Peter; and for centuries they had not asserted their supremacy over all other bishops. And when that claim was made it had been for a long time fiercely repudiated even by the most famous and honoured bishops in the Church. How the claim came to be made, and eventually acknowledged, became known to these investigators of the beginnings of Christianity. The claim of primacy on the part of the bishop of Rome was due, not primarily to any words spoken by Jesus, but to the historical situation in which the Church found herself. It was mainly due to the fact that at the downfall of Rome the bishop of Rome became heir, in a very real sense, to the imperial place and power. Rome was the most important city in the empire, the centre of government, and the place where the appeal tribunal was established.

Still more noteworthy was the fact that the very spirit of the papacy was changed through association with imperial Rome. No longer did the popes of Rome exhibit the spirit of the lowly Jesus of Nazareth, or the spirit of Peter the fisherman. Rather did they manifest the spirit of the pagan emperor who had built his empire upon force, and was determined to maintain it by the same despotic power. This spirit breathes throughout innumerable decrees which proceeded from the lips of the occupants of the papal throne. Jesus had said: "My kingdom is not of this world." He was content to be the man "who had not where to lay his head." But those who claimed to be His vicars, and to exercise His authority, and through whom alone, it was claimed, flowed the grace of salvation, lived in a palace, and laid claim to temporal power and to an earthly kingdom, just like other kingdoms of the world, but all-embracing and supreme. They were defended by armed soldiers, and claimed that every king in Christendom must at their bidding assist to maintain the papal power. Any prince who failed to do his duty in this respect was visited by the most awful vengeance by the friends of the popes of Rome. Whole towns and villages were put to the sword. Men, women, and children were butchered. Kings were driven from their kingdoms, and these were given to others who had no title to them except the will of the pope.

It is not surprising, surely, that when these facts became known to those who had been driven to criticize the papal Church, at first on moral, and then on doctrinal, grounds, they began to use what may seem to us, in these more tolerant days, harsh and even unjustifiable language. The Roman Church became "Antichrist"; "the great whore"; "the false prophet"; and "the beast". To those early pioneers, the system which centred in imperial Rome must have seemed the very antithesis of all that Jesus stood for. Jesus taught and practised kindliness and love, even to His enemies. The popes of Rome taught and practised the most atrocious cruelties which had ever been known. Jesus was pure in morals and holy in every part of His life; many of the popes were notorious for the practice of the most awful forms of vice, and, as was natural, a very large proportion of the clergy followed the evil example set them by those whom they recognized as the heads of the Church, and the fountain whence flowed all their supernatural powers and privileges.

Another discovery made by these early Reformers was that the very spirit and nature of Christianity had been changed with the passing of the centuries. It had become mechanized in the crudest fashion. Nothing is more impressive to the reader of the Gospels than the spiritual nature of the religion of Jesus. He declared that "God is a spirit; and they that worship Him must worship in spirit and truth" (John 4: 24). No one has ever taught so clearly as He did the immediacy of the soul's approach to God, without priestly mediation. He taught that believers in Him receive Him into their hearts and become branches of the True Vine. They abide in Him, and He in them, and thus they are saved and enabled to bear good fruit (John 15). This is not the teaching of the Fourth Gospel only, though here it is summarized and emphasized. It is also the teaching of Jesus as it finds expression in all the other Gospels. There is a total absence of anything which can be called sacerdotalism in His teaching. He severely criticized Jewish dependence upon rites and ceremonies as means of salvation. He called the religious leaders, because of their emphasis in this respect, "blind guides", who "made void" or "transgressed" the commandment of God by their traditions (Matt. 15: 3, 6, 14).

The same repudiation, implicit or explicit, of rites and ceremonies as a means of salvation is found throughout the remaining New Testament writings. No one is so emphatic as St. Paul, whose writings form, after the Gospels, the main element in the New Testament. Some of his most important writings were called forth by the activities of the Judaizers, who were intent upon forcing all Christians to conform to Jewish ceremonies. They desired, Paul says, to rob Christians of their liberty in Christ Jesus and bring them into bondage (Gal. 2: 4). The victims of this campaign he describes as "foolish Galatians"; people who had been "bewitched" by specious and false teaching (Gal. 3: 1). In passionate words he rebukes them for their folly in turning back again "to the weak and beggarly rudiments" wherein they desired to be in bondage over again (Gal. 4: 9). And as for Peter (Cephas), who had given a false lead in this respect, Paul "resisted him to the face, because he stood condemned" (Gal. 2: 11). In his later Epistles, too, we have the same emphasis, the same repudiation of Jewish ritual and ceremonies as being unnecessary and ineffective as a means of salvation (cf. e.g. Col. 2: 8–23).

In contrast to this plain New Testament teaching, the Reformers discovered that Medieval Christianity had become thoroughly externalized and mechanized. In its constitution the Roman Church had become an elaborate piece of machinery which, by means of a great variety of rites and ceremonies, produced a condition of "salvation" that had only too often no relation to a worthy moral and spiritual condition. The pope, the head of the Church, had become the great distributor-in-chief of divine grace. His principal agents were the bishops who, in turn, conveyed supernatural powers to the clergy. From these alone the people could receive the benefits of salvation. By the rite of baptism—according to the theory of baptismal regeneration—they transformed a child of Satan into a child of God. Then through an elaborate series of rites and ceremonies the individual was kept in the way of salvation. By confession to a priest, by the performance of penances imposed by him, by the payment of sums of money for indulgences, by the making of pilgrimages, by the worship of the virgin Mary and of saints and images, and above all by the reception of the literal body and blood of Jesus magically created by the priest—by all these things people were "saved", though after death they might still have to remain long years in purgatory, unless they were rescued by the payment of large sums of money for prayers and masses.

On discovering the contrast between the teachings of the New Testament and the teaching and practice of the Medieval Church, the Reformers were led to make a wholesale repudiation of the Roman Church itself. In the violence of their reaction some of the Reformers did less than justice to the many good people, lay and clerical, who adhered to this ancient system. They did not realize so clearly as we do now that a man may be much better than his creed, and that the most imperfect system may produce some good results if men are devoted to God, and are possessed by His spirit of love and sympathy. But the oversight of this fact may be excused in men who were fighting a fierce battle for truth and freedom, and who were undergoing the fiercest persecution that men have ever had to endure.

But when the majority of the people of England and Scotland had finally cast off the authority of the pope many matters still remained to provoke the fiercest controversy. Who, for example, was to take the place of the pope as the centre of authority? In England, the vacant throne was claimed by the Tudor kings; in Scotland, by the Stuarts. This transference of ecclesiastical power from the religious head of Christendom to secular monarchs was greatly assisted by the prevailing notion of the "divine right of kings", which was supported by the bishops and clergy, and which it took so long a time to eradicate. Moreover, throughout the Middle Ages the religious heads of Christendom—the popes of Rome— had been temporal as well as spiritual monarchs. They had laid claim to temporal power. They had ruled over an earthly kingdom. They had surrounded themselves with all the trappings of kingship. They had raised armies and made wars. But if popes could be kings, why should not kings be popes? The dual character of the papacy gave support to the idea that a monarch, whatever his character, might be the head of Christ's Church.

The Reformers, however, had arrived at quite different ideas as to the headship of the Church of Christ. In the New Testament they could discover no basis for the belief that the Church must have an earthly head who should direct and control all its life and activities. They were convinced that no human being was spiritually fit for such an exalted position; much less such men as many of the popes were known to have been. The conception of the pope as the divinely-appointed head of Christ's Church on earth was also badly shaken by the fact that there had been long periods when two or three popes at the same time had claimed this position. At such times Christendom had been divided in its allegiance. "Now", said Wycliffe, "is the

Head of Antichrist cloven in twain, and one part contendeth against the other."

When this idea of a papal head of the Church was rejected at the Reformation, there were many Reformers who felt that there were equal objections to making the ruler of each country the "pope" of the Church within his own realm. It was not only the conviction that men like Henry VIII and James VI were morally and spiritually unfit to occupy such a position which created opposition. The strongest opposition was based upon the fact that the idea had no basis in New Testament teaching. Here Jesus alone is King. He is the sole Head of His Church on earth and in heaven. The Church is a divine society which acknowledges allegiance in spiritual things only to Him who "purchased it with His own blood" (Acts 20: 28), and "from whom all the body fitly framed and knit together through that which every joint supplieth, according to the working in due measure of each several part, maketh the increase of the body unto the building up of itself in love" (Eph. 4: 16). The Reformers therefore contended that Christian people in every land who truly love and obey Jesus belong to His society. Groups of such people, which spring up inevitably from obedience to the laws of Christ, form local branches of His universal Church. Such groups of Christians, whether smaller or larger, are, or should be, self-governing communities, though they might join in voluntary association with other groups. Earthly kingship as such has no true place within this society. As the Covenanters and Puritans so often affirmed, to acknowledge any such authority is to infringe "the crown-rights of the Redeemer". "Sir," said Andrew Melville to King James, "as divers times before, so now again I must tell you that there are two kings and two kingdoms in Scotland. There is Jesus Christ the King and His Kingdom the Kirk, whose subject King James VI is, and of whose Kingdom not a king, not a lord, not a head, but a member."

In this attempt to reorganize the life of the Christian community, another question which inevitably arose was as to the nature of the offices in the Church, and the various functions of its officers or ministers. On the one hand, there were those who wished to disturb as little as possible the system of Church government which had grown up during the centuries. In the main these governmental arrangements had no basis in explicit Scriptural teaching. They had arisen in response to the practical needs of the Church, or they had followed the outlines of the civil government. The chief governmental centres of the empire, for example, had become the principal centres of Church government. Thus had arisen the great Patriarchates of the Church. Archbishoprics had been established in the principal cities. Each archbishopric was divided into smaller areas or dioceses over which a bishop ruled. Each diocese was divided into parishes, of which a clergyman—priest or parson—had charge. Obviously no trace of these arrangements and offices can be found in the New Testament; and the same can be said of other functionaries, such as canons, deans and chapters, and archdeacons.

At a time when revolutionary changes were being made it was inevitable that the question should arise whether, after the repudiation of the papacy, this hierarchical government of the Church should be preserved intact. In its favour it could be urged that it was of great age, and that with but slight variations it had prevailed throughout the empire. It had survived many changes and the downfall of kingdoms. It had held together in a sort of unity the whole of the Western Church. Such facts weighed heavily with the lovers of antiquity, for whom almost every ecclesiastical arrangement which had ever been made in the process of the years had a kind of divine sanction.

On the other side, it could be urged that the system had worked much ill in the life of the Church. Archbishops and bishops had frequently been no more than secular princes, who had lorded it over God's heritage. There was no gainsaying the fact that they had often been both degraded, criminal and bloodstained. Under this government the Church had become corrupt and tyrannical. It persecuted to the death, as fiercely as ever the old pagan government had done, Christians who wished simply to follow the injunctions of Holy Scripture. On the face of it there was little enough reason for regarding such a system as having any divine sanction. To many it seemed much more likely to have been inspired by Antichrist, whose evil doings are so often spoken of in the Book of Revelation, the Epistles of St. Paul, and elsewhere in the New Testament.

Moreover, the system failed to pass the supreme test of scriptural authority which, from the time of Wycliffe onwards, was the touchstone which the Reformers applied to all the affairs of Church life. Despite its antiquity it was not primitive. There is no trace of the diocesan bishop in the New Testament, or for a considerable time after the apostolic age. The earliest bishops were presbyters, and presbyters were bishops or pastors who fulfilled certain functions in the local churches. We have seen that these views were strongly urged by Andrew Melville, the great reforming leader of the Scottish Church in the sixteenth century. A committee which was appointed to study the matter declared that in primitive times a bishop was a pastor of one flock only, though he might be appointed an overseer, and have certain duties delegated to him by his co-presbyters. These views were also held by the continental Reformers, and by the English puritans. Here then was ground enough for controversy, especially in view of the claim which the traditionalists made as to the "divine right of bishops". This claim was emphatically rejected by both the Covenanters and the English puritans.

Controversy about the vestments which were worn by the clergy was equally inevitable. This was not at all "Much ado about nothing" as has often been represented. The clerical garb was not simply a "seemly garment" suitable for preaching, and fashioned according to the taste of ancient times. It had a deep significance, though much of its meaning might be unknown to the common people. In the first place it marked off the priest from the layman, and thus emphasized a distinction which is one of the most prominent characteristics of the Roman Catholic type of religion. Yet the apostles of Jesus were laymen. In His humanity Jesus was a layman, and when the Reformers came to study the record of His life and teaching it seemed to them impossible to think of Him priding Himself upon His dress, as the priests did. References made by Jesus to the priests, the scribes and pharisees, the religious leaders of His day, who wore a distinctive dress, were by no means complimentary (cf. Matt. 6: 2ff.; 23: 13ff.).

Whence then came the clerical use of millinery? Since it was not native to the religion of Jesus, it must have come either from Judaism or paganism, or from both sources. In either case it was anathema to those who wished above all else to re-establish the Church upon a New Testament basis.

On the one hand, they knew that the early Church had fought hard to free itself from the entail of Jewish usages. On this question a conference had been held at Jerusalem, and after discussion it had been decided that the unbearable yoke of Jewish regulations should not be placed upon Christian converts (Acts 15). And we have already seen that when Peter, fearing "those of the circumcision", acted in a way contrary to this principle, Paul "resisted him to the face because he stood condemned" (Gal. 2: 11). On the other hand, it was the contention of the Reformers that the introduction of pagan elements into the life of the Church had been one of the main sources of that corruption of Christianity which had made reform imperative. From the time of Constantine onwards, when Christianity was adopted as the religion of the State, the clergy, that is, Christian teachers and preachers, were given the status of the ancient priesthood. Pagan usages were taken over wholesale, including the use of priestly vestments.

In the eyes of the Reformers, therefore, priestly vestments stood for priestly claims which were repudiated because they were contrary to the very nature of Christianity as represented by Jesus and His apostles. It seemed to them impossible to establish primitive Christianity so long as false beliefs were visibly represented to the eyes of the people by the clergy. It was not without good reason therefore that the Covenanters and the Puritans alike objected to vestments as "dregs of popery"; that Hooper, on being appointed Bishop of Gloucester, objected to wearing "Aaronic vestments", and that many Puritan clergy suffered deprivation rather than appear to assume a character out of accord with their convictions. The controversy was inevitable, and profound issues were at stake.

Other alien elements in the great body of Medieval Christian teaching and practice were equally provocative of controversy. Mariolatry, and the worship of saints generally, the making of pilgrimages, the necessity of confession to a priest and absolution by him, beliefs and practices connected with purgatory—all these things could not but be repudiated by Reformers working under the conditions which prevailed at that time. Not only was it impossible to separate them from the gross abuses which had become attached to them in the course of the centuries; they also ran counter to a fundamental principle of the whole reform movement; namely, that only such things as are enjoined in Scripture are to be counted necessary for salvation.

Chapter Eighteen

ABIDING VALUES GAINED THROUGH CONTROVERSY

WE have seen that in both England and Scotland the reformation movement was first of all a moral and spiritual revolt against the evil lives of the clergy. Serious-minded people were scandalized by the obvious contrast which existed between the practice and the preaching of those who claimed to be their spiritual guides. Elementary as the preaching was at that time, it pointed to an ideal of purity and nobility of life which was embodied in the life of Jesus. The common people understood that to be a Christian was to be good, as Jesus and His disciples were. By the time of the early Middle Ages, however, the attempt on the part of the clergy to attain this ideal of goodness had been very largely abandoned. Doubtless there were exceptions; but voluminous evidence shows that only too often the clergy, of the highest and the lowest ranks, lived lives which were entirely unworthy of their high calling. They were rapacious, and fleeced their flocks unmercifully. They were worldly-minded and frequently openly immoral. The clergy were not chosen because they exhibited in their lives Christ-like goodness. Neither did they after election seek to attain such goodness. They were frequently men of the world pure and simple, though in the pursuit of their vocation as Christian priests they practised Christian rites and ceremonies.

How this condition of things had come about has been briefly indicated above. It was partly due to the vast absorption of paganism by Christianity which followed upon Constantine's recognition of Christianity as the State religion. As Dr. Foakes Jackson says: "It cannot be denied that the Christianity which took the place of the official cultus was not the pure faith of the Gospel; and that, if dogmatically it was the legitimate outcome of the teaching of the New Testament, it was often in practice a continuation of the ancient state of things under Christian forms" (*History of the Christian Church*, 6th ed., 1924, p. 420). The same writer points out that the poor were "weaned from their paganism by being instructed to give their hereditary customs a Christian significance. The old paganism of Italy was but thinly veiled by the policy or superstition of the Christian saint." So it was on a vast scale throughout the empire. Christianity was watered down and contaminated by pagan ideas and practices.

Another cause of the corruption which provoked the early Reformers into activity was that the very conception of goodness was changed. It became something artificial; it meant simply that a person had been set apart to minister in sacred things. No matter what the spiritual character of a person might be, he became "holy" once he had been consecrated or ordained to office with due ceremony. The character thus stamped upon him was held to be indelible. Once a priest, always a priest; once a bishop, always a bishop. In this way holiness or goodness came to mean not a moral or spiritual quality, such as was exhibited in the life of Jesus of Nazareth, but rather a quality imposed upon a person by an external agent. In those days of darkness and of gross superstition a magical efficacy was everywhere held to belong to all manner of rites and ceremonies. The words and imitative acts of the witch-doctor, magician or priest, for example, were believed to possess supernatural power. And this power of the magician or priest was believed to be passed on to whoever was properly initiated into the sacred office. It is well known that such ideas passed over into the Church in the early centuries, causing the most unworthy priest to be regarded with peculiar feelings of awe and reverence. It was generally believed that the priests were the repositories of divine power which they could use at will to bless or curse any individual.

This whole circle of ideas was challenged by those who found their way to the prime source of Christian teaching, namely, the New Testament. Although the name "puritan" came into vogue at a much later date, in the sixteenth and seventeenth centuries, the operation of ideas which led to the puritan movement can be traced at a much earlier period. Wycliffe was essentially a puritan in his teaching and mode of life. The germ of the Reformation is found in his claim that Scripture is to be regarded as the only rule of faith and life. Wycliffe asserted that the true type of Christian piety is to be found in following the example and obeying the precepts of Jesus of Nazareth. The value of all rites and ceremonies must be tested by apostolic faith and practice.

This emphasis upon real holiness, in the New Testament sense, as contrasted with the artificial holiness which came into vogue at a later date, remained an abiding element of Puritanism. In the heat of controversy it has not always been sufficiently recognized that under the Roman system lives of real piety and of wonderful beauty were often attained. We can appreciate better to-day the intense spirituality and heart devotion of some of the medieval saints. But that the system generally tended to make men satisfied to attain a much lower type of holiness is, we believe, indisputable. By rite and ceremony men were brought into the Church; by rite and ceremony they were kept in the way of salvation; and "outside the Church there was no salvation". It mattered little or nothing what the moral and spiritual character of a person might be so long as he was obedient to the precepts of Rome as uttered through the lips of a priest.

Evidence of the spiritual deadness and moral corruption which followed upon this type of teaching cannot be produced here. A few illustrations only have been given in the previous pages. It is to be found in very numerous works, dealing with the Church of the Middle Ages and the Reformation, written by Romanist and Protestant historians alike. It is to the lasting credit of the early Reformers that, whilst still accepting the main Romanist teachings, they revolted against the moral corruption which had come to prevail under that system. As has been explained above, intellectual revolt against the fundamental doctrines of the Church came only at a later date.

Here then is one of the abiding values of Puritanism. It takes us back to the fountain-head of our religion. The first responsibility of the Christian, it affirms, is to follow Christ and to keep His commandments. Forms and ceremonies enjoined by the Church may be of much value, and they should not lightly be cast aside. But even the most meticulous performance of them is no substitute for Christlike goodness. It may even conduce to self-righteousness, and prove hostile to the development of real goodness of heart and mind. The Puritans of England and the Covenanters of Scotland were alike in that they recalled Christians to attach the chief importance to the centralities of the faith. With the apostle Paul, they affirmed that the Kingdom of God is "not meat and drink, but righteousness, joy and peace in the Holy Ghost". They knew themselves to be in possession of the treasures of the Kingdom of Heaven, and in continual enjoyment of fellowship with their Lord and Saviour. They could not conceive of anything higher or better than the experiences which had come to them in Christ Jesus. Nothing that the ecclesiastical authorities could say or do was able to shake their conviction that this was the religion of Jesus as it found expression in the earliest days of Christianity, and as it is forever enshrined in the pages of the New Testament.

Every great revival of religion has been characterized by the same sense of immediacy of access into the presence of the Saviour which has made the use of forms and ceremonies seem to be of comparatively little account. Not that Puritanism is formless or lawless. Though in earlier days there were outbreaks of disorderliness, even as there were in the New Testament period, it would be entirely wrong to regard disorder as characteristic of Puritanism. The religion of the Puritans and of the Covenanters created its own forms; but they were simpler, and they did not quench the spirit of spontaneity. To-day, services for public worship in churches of the puritan tradition are as orderly and decorous as any of those conducted in a Romanist or State church.

Another element of abiding value in the churches which best preserve the puritan tradition is the opportunity given to the rank and file members to cultivate, within the fellowship of the Church, their God-given powers of mind and soul. In our account of the Covenanting struggle we have seen how valiantly Knox and Melville, and other leaders, contended for the right of the Christian people to have a voice in the selection of their own ministers. The Kirk-session, composed of a minister, elders and deacons, exercised oversight over a parochial congregation. There was a weekly Exercise, which developed later into the Presbytery, in which anyone possessing spiritual gifts was free to edify the brethren by prayer and exposition of Scripture. The audience was at liberty to criticize the views expressed. How nearly this approaches the primitive practice can be seen by reference to St. Paul's Epistles (e.g. 1 Cor. 12 and 14). The General Assembly had jurisdiction over all the congregations in the country, and was composed of all the clergy and one commissioner from every Church.

In England the puritans went even further towards democratizing the Church. They threw overboard the idea that any person within a given area, or parish, was a Christian because he or she had been baptized in infancy. In its place they adopted the principle of the "gathered Church". A person, they said, becomes a Christian through a personal faith in the Lord Jesus. By personal faith people are joined to Jesus and become regenerate and sanctified. Those who are thus brought into spiritual fellowship with Jesus are naturally and inevitably brought into fellowship with each other; they form a Christian society, and a local branch of Christ's Church. The puritans accepted the principle *ubi Christus, ibi ecclesia,* in accordance with the words of Jesus: "where two or three are gathered together in my name, there am I in the midst of them" (Matt. 18: 20). Such local fellowships claimed the power to select their own pastors, teachers and other officers, and to exercise discipline. Each member had a voice in the direction of the affairs of the Church, and each could exercise such gifts as he possessed for the edification of his fellow-members.

Such was the basis of the societies formed in London, in East Anglia, at Gainsborough and Scrooby, and later in Holland and New England. These societies recognized no hierarchical control. They were "independent"; which fact, however, did not mean that they refused to accept guidance or help from other groups of Christians. All such groups, formed on the New Testament model, they recognized as parts of the Universal Church of Christ. And from all such groups they were free to accept any help that did not conflict with their fundamental principle of autonomy.

The abiding value of this form of Puritanism is now recognized far beyond the borders of Congregationalism. Essentially the same principles are embodied in the Baptist Church. In the eighteenth century, with certain modifications, they found fruitful expression in the societies formed under the influence of the Wesleys and Whitefield. Despite the Anglicanism of Wesley, and the autocratic control he exercised over the societies formed within the Methodist movement, he owed much to the ideas and principles of the earlier puritans. He was himself essentially a puritan in his way of life, and in his appeal to the authority of the Scriptures. While he accepted Episcopacy as a scriptural form of Church government, he was by no means always amenable to the authority of bishops. Bishops had no authority over the life and activities of the Methodist Societies. Here we find a state of things very similar to that which had prevailed in other religious societies, from the sixteenth century onwards. Members met together for mutual edification under the leadership of laymen, subject only to the supervision and control of Wesley, which in the nature of the case could usually only be occasional. These classes were the most characteristic feature of Methodism. And the employment of laymen, whether as class-leaders or as lay preachers has remained a permanent feature of Methodist Church life.

It has long been recognized that the Methodist Movement has reacted powerfully upon the Anglican Church. According to J. R. Green, "The Methodists themselves were the least result of the Methodist revival. Its action upon the Church broke the lethargy of the clergy" (*Short History*, Everyman ed., p. 696). Mr. W. E. H. Lecky also bore a similar testimony, and affirmed that the movement exercised a powerful and lasting influence upon the spirit of the Established Church.

Anglican leaders have many times expressed appreciation for certain puritan elements in the life of Methodism, and especially for the use it makes of the ministries of laymen. In 1895 Bishop Ryle, at a Diocesan Conference, said: "As for a Church in which the clergy acted alone, settled everything, decided everything, judged everything, and managed everything, and the laity had no voice at all, I cannot find the shadow of such a thing in the Acts or Epistles of the New Testament." He went on to criticize the failure of the Church of England to give a worthy place to laymen in its activities: "From one cause or another they are left out in the cold, passive recipients, and not active members in a huge ecclesiastical corporation; sleeping partners, and not working agents, in an unwieldy and ill-managed concern. In short, in the normal action of the Church of England, lay churchmen have been left on a siding, like soldiers not wanted. They have fallen out of the ranks, retired to the rear, and sunk out of sight" (cited from a contribution by John Telford to *Our Churches and Why we Belong to Them*, 1898, p. 136).

Considerable changes have been introduced into the working of the Anglican Church since that time, particularly as the result of the passing of the Enabling Act in 1919. In parochial and other councils the laity can now make their voice heard in the direction of affairs. But this branch of the Church of Jesus is still far behind the Free Churches in the use it makes of the ministries of the laity, as leading Anglicans themselves confess. In recent discussions on the means of promoting a revival of religion in our country one of the most interesting suggestions made is that in every parish groups of people should be encouraged to meet together to form "cells", in order to promote mutual edification. Such groups or cells, it is suggested, should not be controlled or even led by the clergyman, but by such laymen as have the capacity for leadership. How closely this form of meeting approximates to the Methodist "classes" will be recognized by all students of Church life. The Methodist class-meetings, in turn, were in the direct line of succession from the puritan gatherings for religious fellowship which took place at Scrooby, Gainsborough, and elsewhere.

There were many such religious societies in existence long before the evangelical revival of the eighteenth century. A good account of these is given by Dr. John S. Simon in his *John Wesley and the Religious Societies* (1921). Wesley was converted at a meeting of such a society which had been founded under Moravian influence. But there were many similar societies within the Church of England at that time. Their members met together for mutual edification, and to encourage one another in works of charity. That they were thoroughly puritanic is seen in the fact that they set themselves to check the prevalence of vice, and were responsible for the foundation of the "Society for the Reformation of Manners".

Religious societies can, however, be traced back to a much earlier date, as Dr. T. M. Lindsay has shown in his *History of the Reformation*, Vol. I. This writer has given an interesting account of what he calls "non-ecclesiastical religion". He relates that many charitable bequests and foundations were transferred from clerical to lay management about the close of the fifteenth century. Still more important is the fact that many associations were formed, some of them definitely religious, and all of them with a religious aspect. They were not at first anti-clerical, though they were distinctively lay associations, and cultivated the religious life in their own way. Notable among these confraternities were the *Kalands* or *Kalandsgilden* in North Germany, and the *Zechen* in

Austria. They were formed mainly for the practice of religious exercises, although they also served as insurance societies and burial clubs. In these societies men and women met together at stated times for religious services. The point of special interest for the moment is that the conduct of the religious services was in the hands of the members of the brotherhood. Martin Luther refers to these brotherhoods and gives the marks of the true brotherhoods as distinct from the false.

Other groups or societies of Christian people called themselves *Brethren*, though the ecclesiastical authorities gave them such names as Waldenses, Wycliffites and Hussites. They refused to recognize ecclesiastical authority, and managed their own affairs. Even their persecutors testified to the beauty of their lives. That they were thoroughly puritanic in their mode of life is manifest from the description given of them by early writers. "The heretics", it is said, "were known by their walk and conversation: they live quietly and modestly; they have no pride in dress; their learned men are tailors and weavers; they do not heap up riches, but are content with what is necessary; they live chastely; they are temperate in eating and drinking; they never go to taverns, nor to public dances, nor to any such vanities; they refrain from foul language, from back-biting, from thoughtless speech, from lying and swearing" (cited by Lindsay, *History of the Reformation*, I., p. 152, from *Magna Bibliotheca Patrum*, 1618). With scarcely any modification the description would apply to the puritan societies at Scrooby and Gainsborough, and to the vast majority of the societies formed by John Wesley.

One marked feature of all these societies was the use they made of the Scriptures. It was for their use, very largely, that translations of parts of the Scriptures into the vernacular were made from the fourteenth century onwards. The ecclesiastical authorities frowned upon such translations, and regarded their use as a sign of heresy. But they were demanded by the members of these associations outside the hierarchical system, who invited their neighbours into their own houses, or into some room where the Scriptures were read and expounded by some of their number. These associations established schools which spread throughout Germany before the close of the fifteenth century. Thus they helped to keep alive personal religion, and their influence counted for much in the swift progress of the Reformation when it came at last.

Another element of abiding value in Puritanism was its insistence upon the exercise of civil and religious liberty. The most impartial authorities have recognized our indebtedness to the puritans in this respect. According to Lord Acton, the Roman Catholic, liberty is the golden thread of history; it is the first essential of progress. The historian Hume was no lover of puritan modes of thought, yet his knowledge of the facts of history compelled him to pay this tribute to the puritans: "So absolute indeed was the authority of the Crown that the precious spark of liberty was kindled and preserved by the puritans alone; and it is to them that the English owe the whole freedom of their constitution" (*History of England*, 1875, p. 324).

Many similar tributes have been paid since this was written. In the previous pages we have seen English Puritans and Scottish Covenanters fighting to preserve alive the soul of true religion, and to assert the "Freedom of the Christian Man". At the same time they were laying the foundation of modern democracy. Within the gathered Churches Christian people found an opportunity for the exercise of democratic rights. They prized above all things their freedom of access into the fellowship of God through Christ without priestly mediation. They valued intensely their freedom of assembly for worship, and to hear God's

Word read and expounded. They appreciated also their freedom to exercise their God-given powers of mind and heart in the affairs of Christ's Church.

As they strove for these things, so did they strive for civil freedom; that is, for the right to participate in the shaping of the laws of the country in which they lived, and in the moulding of the conditions of their daily lives. This democratic right is now usually taken for granted, and it is difficult for many people to realize that there was ever a time when it was disallowed. It is a fact, however, that this right was painfully won. Much hardship had to be endured, and many battles fought, before the common people were able to share in the privileges and responsibilities of government. In this long and costly struggle the puritans were the pioneers. They were inspired thereunto by their religious experience. Their guiding principles came from their own personal knowledge of the teaching of the New Testament. The experience they gained in the management of their religious societies was of immense value to them when they turned to deal with more general civil and political affairs.

We have seen the working out of democratic principles in the Pilgrim settlements of New England. The same struggle for liberty was carried on in England both before and after the departure of the Pilgrim Fathers. Pym, Hampden, and Milton, are names famous in the annals of human liberty. In the years that followed the Revolution of 1688, Nonconformist congregations, the direct heirs of Puritanism, sought everywhere to increase the gains so dearly won, and to extend yet further the bounds of freedom.

There are those who identify Puritanism with some transitory fashion of thought or dress, or who take a very limited view of the principles involved therein, and who consequently feel that they can rejoice at the passing of

Puritanism. But if we take the larger view, and consider fundamental principles, we see that Puritanism belongs to the very essence of Christianity. It can never pass away so long as the religion of Jesus remains an inspiring and redeeming force in the lives of men.

Chapter Nineteen

THE WARRANT OF CONTROVERSY

THERE are many people to-day who seem to regard controversy on religious matters as being an essentially evil thing. Controversy on other matters they accept as natural and inevitable. They admit that it is not to be expected that all the people of any country should agree as to the best form of government, or about the most effective means of promoting the well-being of the community. Free discussion in local meetings, in Parliament and Press, has long been regarded as among the most valued features of our social and national life. It is generally recognized also that members of opposing parties, whether Conservative, Liberal or Labour, to name only the larger parties familiar to us in the political life of our time, may hold, in all sincerity, the most diverse views. In these days no party is thought to possess a monopoly of truth, wisdom, or patriotism. An official "Opposition" is one of the most notable features of our parliamentary life; and, under the normal conditions of peace, it is generally held to discharge a useful function. By the clash of opposing views truth is discovered and established, and progress is made towards a better condition of things. Outside politics also, for example, in science, art, economics, the method of discussion and controversy is accepted as a matter of course.

In religious matters, however, this method of controversy is now at a discount. It seems to be assumed that worshippers of the one God, at least those who worship God as revealed in Jesus, ought to think very much alike.

They ought everywhere to have the same forms of prayer and worship; the same rites and ceremonies, and, especially, they ought to have the same form of Church government. That Christians should have differed profoundly in their views of such matters is thought by many to be a rather disagreeable, not to say disgraceful, fact. Religious differences are supposed to be due not so much to the many-sidedness of truth, nor to differences in the constitution of the minds of men, which naturally lead them to apprehend truth differently, but rather to the corruption of human nature through the fall of man. Moral depravity is thus held to attach to all the operations of the minds of men in relation to religious matters.

It is now suggested by some that this method of disputation and controversy ought to be abandoned, as a discredited and unworthy means of upholding and promoting the Kingdom of righteousness and truth. Enlightened Christian people ought to come together in a kind of round-table conference, or in a series of conferences; compose their differences, and agree to compromise on all those matters which have caused so much heart-burning through all the ages. Thus it will be possible to present to the world a semblance of unity which will prove to be attractive to those who have been scandalized by the diversity which has so long prevailed among Christian people and the Christian Churches.

No one who is even moderately acquainted with the chief events which have taken place in the long history of the Christian Church will be disposed to minimize the evils which have often been associated with the controversies which have arisen. "Off with his head" has only too often been the final argument used against those who have dared to think and speak differently from those who have claimed to possess the keys of the kingdom of truth. Death in its most horrible forms, indescribable torment,

long periods of imprisonment, confiscations of property—
all these have frequently been the lot of those who have
ventured to hold opinions which have deviated from those
laid down by ecclesiastical authorities.

It may be maintained, however, that the evils mentioned were not due to controversy itself, but to wrong
methods of controversy, or rather to the attempts made by
authority to prevent controversy; that is, to prevent the
expression of views differing in any degree from those
held by the dominant authorities in the Church. Such an
attitude could only be justified if Jesus, the Founder and
Head of the Church, had laid down in brief and easily
understandable form the truths and ideas which He
required His followers to accept without reasoning or
discussion. We know that this was very far indeed from
being the case. Our knowledge of the life of Jesus is
mainly derived from four fragmentary accounts which
differ from each other in important respects. In addition,
we have a number of other writings, particularly the
Epistles of St. Paul, which enable us to see the different
impression which Jesus made upon various types of mind,
and how they related His teaching to other teachings with
which they were familiar, and to the general situation in
which people lived at that time. Many different ideas find
expression in the New Testament writings. There are
profound differences, for example, between the first three
Gospels and the Fourth; between St. Paul's Epistles, the
Epistle to the Hebrews, and the Epistle of St. James. The
Acts of the Apostles and the Book of Revelation belong to
quite different categories of literature.

It was in the very nature of things that this large body of
writings should provoke discussion. The minds of men
differ in a thousand ways. They differ in their approach to
truth, and in their power to apprehend it. The mind of the
poet differs from that of the mathematician; the mind of

the historian differs from that of the philosopher or the artist, and so on. It is not suggested that these categories are clean-cut, or that they do not sometimes overlap. For our purpose it is sufficient to recognize that the minds of men do differ greatly and inevitably, and that these differences lead to a varied apprehension and statement of truth.

Racial differences must also be taken into account. The student of Church history is familiar with the profound differences which existed in the early centuries between the mentalities of the peoples of the east and west. The Greek tended to find salvation in knowledge; the Roman placed the emphasis on the observance of law and order. Clement of Alexandria and Origen viewed Christian truth in one way; Tertullian and Cyprian in another. It was quite inevitable that minds so differently constituted should expound and formulate Christian truth in a variety of ways.

The method of controversy finds a firm basis in the New Testament itself. The writer of the Fourth Gospel presents Jesus as a great controversialist. He puts into His lips many long addresses in which Jesus confutes the Jews on various points of doctrine. Even if we adopt the view, which is commonly accepted to-day, that these addresses contain summaries of the words of Jesus, spoken on different occasions, we are still confronted with the fact that the Synoptic Gospels also represent Jesus as entering into controversy with the Jews, although His addresses are not given at such length. Jesus did not hesitate to speak stern words of those who sought to frustrate His mission. He reasoned with them, and denounced them as the "offspring of vipers" (Matt. 12: 34); as "blind guides" (Matt. 15: 14); and as "hypocrites" (Matt. 22: 18). It was thus that He described the Scribes and the Pharisees, the duly constituted authorities of the Jewish Church. He reprimanded them for rejecting the commandment of God and substituting in its place the traditions of men (Mark 7: 8). He described them as a "faithless and perverse generation" (Luke 9: 41), and declared that the inward parts of the Pharisees were "full of extortion and wickedness" (Luke 11: 39). Such are but a few of many illustrations which might be cited on this subject.

The greatest of all early Christian controversialists was St. Paul, to whom we owe it that Christianity was carefully distinguished from Judaism. It is not surprising that the relation between these two expressions of religion should have been provocative of much debate. Jesus was a Jew, and most of the early Christians were Jews. It was natural therefore that the teaching of Jesus should have been regarded simply as a development of Judaism. Some of the words of Jesus seemed to look in this direction: as, for example, when He said: "Think not that I came to destroy the law and the prophets: I came not to destroy, but to fulfil. For verily I say unto you, Till heaven and earth pass away, one jot or one tittle shall in no wise pass away from the law, till all things be accomplished" (Matt 5: 17ff.).

On the other hand, much of Christ's teaching seems to imply a totally different conception of the nature of religion; that is of man's relation to God and of God's attitude to man. As exhibited both by the example and precept of Jesus, religion seems to be a much simpler thing; more homely and spiritual than that which found expression in contemporary Judaism. It is far less dependent upon rites and ceremonies, and consists essentially in spiritual communion between God and the individual soul. Christ's view of Sabbath observance, for example, was very different from that which prevailed among His fellow countrymen; and we are told how it brought Him into serious conflict with the Jewish religious authorities (see e.g. Matt. 12: 1ff.). "The Sabbath", he declared, "was made for man, and not man for the Sabbath" (Mark 2: 27).

What then should be the attitude of the followers of Jesus towards the Jewish law? Since Jesus was a Jew, must those who become Christians also become Jews? This question was bound to arise and be answered in different ways. There were those who took the Jewish view and emphatically affirmed that all Christians must take upon themselves the obligations of the Jewish law, and practise Jewish rites and ceremonies. These "Judaizers", as they are called, followed in the wake of Paul in his evangelistic work and caused much trouble among his converts. How serious Paul conceived the situation to be we see from his Epistle to the Galatians, one of the most passionate writings of the New Testament. We here see the apostle putting forth all his powers of reasoning and persuasion to undo the mischief which the Judaizers had wrought among the flock: "I marvel that ye are so quickly removing from him that called you in the grace of Christ unto a different Gospel; which is not another Gospel; only there are some that trouble you, and would pervert the Gospel of Christ" (Gal. 1: 6f.). These false brethren, he says, "came in privily to spy out our liberty which we have in Christ Jesus, that they might bring us into bondage" (2: 4f.). Even Peter (Cephas) was carried away by these Judaizers, who wished to make Christianity but another brand of Judaism. "I resisted him to his face," says Paul, "because he stood condemned" (2: 11). He proceeds to show how different was the Gospel of Jesus from the teaching of the Judaizers, which, indeed, was no Gospel at all, since it required such an obedience to the works of the law that could never be attained. He expostulates with them for their folly: "O foolish Galatians, who did bewitch you, before whose eyes Jesus Christ was openly set forth crucified?" (3: 1).

In all ages, lovers of true Christianity, who believe that it is essential to the salvation of the world, have been immeasurably indebted to Paul who risked everything to keep the society founded by Jesus from coming under the bondage of the Jewish law, and turning back "to the weak and beggarly rudiments" (4: 9), which would have frustrated the purpose of Christ (cf. Romans 1–8).

But the reduction of Christianity to a form of Judaism was not the only danger which threatened its life in the early centuries. Christians were compelled to live in a world in which many other teachings concerning God and man had already become deeply-rooted. The mind of man is never a *tabula rasa*, a clean slate, upon which a teacher or preacher can begin to write new truths without relation to the ideas and beliefs which have already found a place there. On the contrary, new ideas and beliefs must be related to the old ideas and beliefs, either in the way of comparison or contrast, or a mixture of the two.

One important result of this interaction of the minds of men, more or less Christian, is known at Gnosticism (from the Greek word *gnostos*, known). It was a system of religious philosophy which combined ideas from Greek and oriental sources with Christianity, which it professed to expound as a mystical philosophy or *gnosis*. We find an early reference to this attempt to mix Christian truth with Greek and other beliefs in Paul's Epistle to the Colossians. "Take heed," he says to them, "lest there be any one that maketh spoil of you through his philosophy and vain deceit, after the tradition of men, after the rudiments of the world, and not after Christ" (2: 8). And again, "Let no man judge you in meat, or in drink, or in respect of a feast-day or a new moon or a sabbath-day: which are a shadow of things to come" (2: 16; cf. 2: 20; I Tim. 6: 20). The reference is to a very rudimentary form of Gnosticism, containing both Jewish and pagan elements. Soon, however, gnostic ideas increased, and threatened to swamp Christianity. Very many traces of them are to be found in the literature of the second and succeeding centuries. It is impossible to give here any adequate account of the various gnostic systems which were developed. They are associated with such famous names as Simon Magus, Valentinus, and Marcion; and numerous references to gnostic philosophy are found in Christian writings of the second and third centuries, for example, in those of Ignatius, Irenæus, and Hippolytus.

Three main types of speculative thought found expression in gnostic philosophy, namely, the Judaistic, the Oriental, and the Greek. In each case an attempt was made to blend Rabbinic traditions, Zoroastrian conceptions, and Greek and Roman mythology and philosophy with the truths of Christianity. The result was a strange hotchpotch of ideas which is still very confusing to less speculative minds. The mixture includes such conceptions as the Infinite and the self-existent Being; the Demiurge, and a series of emanations called Æons. These conceptions were strangely elaborated. One of the Æons was said to have come into the world to be the Saviour of men. He united himself with the earthly body of the man Jesus, and thus Jesus became the Christ at the time of His baptism by John. Some of the Gnostics taught that the body of Jesus was not real, but only a phantom; and thus we have Docetism. Salvation was said to be attainable by knowledge, contemplation and mortification.

It is not difficult for any student of Christian truth to see how detrimental the acceptance of such a series of beliefs would have been to the simplicity and the saving-power of the Gospel. It was necessary that Gnostic ideas should be rejected, and this involved much argument and controversy.

It was under such historical conditions that the great

Christian creeds were formulated. The earliest of these, the so-called Apostles' Creed, is now believed to have originated somewhere between the years A.D. 100–150, though in its present form it dates back only to the early part of the fifth century. It is a convenient summary of the truths which, it was held, the apostles had taught— the basic truths of Christianity. It emphasizes the humanity of Jesus by enumerating the main points of His life—His birth, death, burial and resurrection—as a defence against the prevailing Docetism, to which reference has been made above. It also affirms His divinity as the only-begotten Son of God; and then recites a number of other Christian beliefs—in the Holy Spirit, the Church, the forgiveness of sins, the resurrection, and the life everlasting. It is easy to see how natural, and indeed inevitable, it was that such a summary of Christian beliefs should be drawn up. It provided a simple and convenient answer to the question, which candidates for admission to the Christian Church were always asking: What do Christians believe?

The Nicene Creed, formulated by the Christian bishops who met at the first Council of Nicæa in A.D. 325, is to be explained as a defence against sub-Christian beliefs which were being propagated by Arius, a presbyter of Alexandria. I shall not attempt to give here even a summary of the teaching of Arius. A good account can be found in Mackintosh's *The Doctrine of the Person of Christ*, pp. 175ff., and in many other works easily available. It contradicted the Church's belief in the full deity of Jesus Christ. It included such points as the assertion that God was not the Father eternally, and that there was a time when God was alone. Thus the Son came into being at a later time. Although pre-existent, He did not exist eternally. There is no identity of essence between Father and Son. At times Arius used language which seemed to imply his acceptance of the Christian belief, which had already been formulated. At other times this was as clearly denied. In the teaching of Arius we have a more definite formulation of ideas which had previously been put forward by Lucian of Antioch and Paul of Samosata. Similar ideas have found expression at various times during the long history of the Church, and in our own country they became prominent in the eighteenth and nineteenth centuries.

To deal with this controversy, which was disturbing the unity of the Empire, the Emperor Constantine, in A.D. 325 summoned all Christian bishops to assemble at Nicæa in Bithynia for the first Œcumenical Council. An account of the proceedings of this famous Council cannot be given here. Various attempts were made by the representatives of the different parties to draw up a satisfactory statement of Christian beliefs which would exclude the errors that had so much troubled the minds of Christian people. Eventually a form of words, known as the Nicene Creed, was accepted by the great majority of the members of the Council. Its terminology can, of course, only be fully appreciated by those who acquaint themselves with the heterodox ideas which Arius and his friends had sought to introduce into the beliefs of the Church. The crucial fact is that Jesus is said to be "begotten not made", and "of one substance with the Father (*homoousion*)". The Arians and Semi-Arians had been willing to acknowledge that Jesus was "of like substance (*homoiousion*) with the Father". But this, it was felt, did not sufficiently safeguard the real nature of Jesus Christ.

It is easy for the uninitiated to make sport about the Christians of those days "contending for a diphthong". But the question in dispute was one of the utmost importance for the future of the Church. Is Jesus God or man? If Jesus is God, as the *Homoousians* affirmed, we can believe that He is able to save the world. If He is merely man, a creature, as the *Homoiousians* contended, then we cannot conceive how He can be the Saviour of the world, even though He is believed to be specially endued with divine grace.

The leading opponent of the Arian views at the Council of Nicæa was Athanasius who, in the early stages of the conflict, was secretary to Alexander, Bishop of Alexandria, and also a deacon of the Church. In A.D. 326 he succeeded Alexander as bishop. Although at the time of the Council he was not yet a bishop, and therefore not eligible to be present, he is believed to have taken a leading part in the debates. He was a man of great ability and clearness of thought and speech. From the beginning of the conflict he realized that vital issues were at stake. His fundamental ideas found expression in his tract, *On the Incarnation of the Word of God*. He pointed out that Arius was teaching pure polytheism. If the Son is not identical in nature and essence with the Father it is impossible to speak of the divine unity, and it is wrong to pray to Him and to worship Him. If the Father is not Father everlastingly, but in time a Son emerges, and afterwards a Spirit lower still, who can say when this will end? Thus the Christian conception of God as a Trinity in Unity disappears.

It should be noticed that the so-called "Athanasian Creed", which is also known, from its first word, as the *"Hymn Quicunque"*, was not the work of Athanasius. It belongs to a much later date, and has reference to later controversies, e.g., to those associated with Apollinarianism, Nestorianism, and Eutychianism. Its author is unknown. Various dates have been suggested, from the fifth to the eighth century. It was at first used as a hymn or canticle, rather than as a creed. It was known as *Fides Catholica*, and afterwards as *Fides S. Athanasii*, probably simply to intimate that this was the faith which Athanasius held, and for which he contended so long. As a natural result of the title, it was later ascribed to Athanasius as the author.

Over a long period strong objection has been taken to its minatory clauses: "This is the Catholic Faith: which except a man believe faithfully, he cannot be saved." According to the modern mind it lays far too much emphasis upon correct belief as a means to salvation, and is too dogmatic as to what happens to those who have no opportunity of learning the truths laid down. Many of the statements made about the relation of the three persons in the Trinity to each other are beyond the understanding of the average person. They can only be understood by trained theologians who are well acquainted with the erroneous views of Christ's person which the creed was intended to deny. It is, in fact, a specialist's creed, and is unsuited for use in public worship.

The main point to be observed is that this, like the other creeds mentioned, was primarily intended to safeguard the central truth of Christianity: that in Christ Jesus, God Himself entered into human life to be the Saviour of the world.

Chapter Twenty

THE preceding chapters have shown how natural it was that controversy should arise within the Christian Church. In the earliest days differences of opinion and of conviction existed among the apostles as to the nature of the Gospel that was to be preached. If the Judaizers had been allowed to have their way there would, as Paul affirmed, have been no Gospel to preach. For Judaism is not a Gospel. It has none of the universal appeal that belongs to the Gospel. It is not "the power of God unto salvation to every one that believeth." Fortunately Paul opposed the misguided efforts of those who misunderstood the nature of Christianity. Controversy ensued; and this was no doubt a cause of scandal to many; but, on the long view, who can doubt that the controversy was abundantly justified? If Paul had remained silent for the sake of peace; if he had submitted his convictions to the superior authority of those who were "in Christ" before him; of those who were "reputed to be somewhat", and "to be pillars" in the Church (Gal. 2: 6, 9), then, so far as we can see, there would have been no Christianity such as we know to-day—a world religion, yielding fruit "for the healing of the nations" (Rev. 22: 2).

Other controversies which arose in the early centuries were equally natural and inevitable. It was necessary that those who valued the Gospel should guard the precious truths with which they had been entrusted, and seek to prevent that Gospel from being diluted by a great variety of pagan philosophical and mythological ideas. If paganism and Christianity had been blended in accordance with gnostic ideas then its power would have been for ever destroyed.

When we come to the later controversies, dealt with in the earlier part of this work, we find a different situation. It was the sincere conviction of the early Reformers, say from Wycliffe onwards, that the ecclesiastical authorities had, over a long period, failed to guard the deposit of truth which had been handed down by the apostles. They had allowed the precepts of God to be made void by the traditions of men. Many beliefs and practices had been introduced into the Church which were opposed to New Testament teaching. The teaching of the Church had become a vast accumulation of traditions which overlaid the essential features of the Gospel. Salvation by works—by rite and ceremony—had displaced the Gospel of salvation by faith, which Paul had so much stressed. Freedom of access into the fellowship of the Heavenly Father by the grace of the Holy Spirit, which Jesus had rendered possible, had been barred by those who claimed to hold the keys of the Kingdom of Heaven.

There is no need to exaggerate the evil situation that followed upon this perversion of Christianity. In many ways that is beyond our power. Neither do we wish to minimize the good elements that remained in the Church. There were lights that shone all the more brightly as the darkness increased. There were holy fires that were damped down but not quenched, and which, when fresh breezes of the Spirit blew, burst into mighty flame. But the story of the attempts made to put out the fire—by coercion, by the methods of the Inquisition—is the most tragic in the annals of the human race. Reformers were denounced as rebels, and unnumbered multitudes of those who breathed the very spirit of Christ were branded as heretics by the Church they loved and sought to save.

All this meant controversy, fierce and long, and those people who are inclined in these days to disparage the uses of controversy, and to blame all parties thereto without discrimination, would do well to consider how else the things we love best could have been won and handed down to us.

There are those who still look back upon the work of reformation as being mainly a destruction of good things. They see the Church of the pre-Reformation period through a golden haze. They look back with painful regret to the days when there was one Church, which could speak with one authoritative voice, and lay down laws for men and nations; one earthly head of the Church, claiming to act as the vicar of Christ; one language used in the public worship of the one God; one series of rites and ceremonies, by which the grace of God was communicated to the souls of men. Surely, they say, this uniformity was a good thing, and it ought to have been maintained at all costs.

The Reformers, however, saw things very differently; they saw things without the golden haze. They were not at first mainly concerned with the general set-up of the Church. It was what they had been used to, and they had known no other. They were concerned rather with the working-out of the system in their own parish, diocese and nation. There was no golden haze to blind them to the details of the situation. In the Church which they knew at first-hand there was corruption immeasurable; there was a terrible contrast to the teaching of the New Testament. Such uniformity as existed was largely the result of coercion; it was achieved by stamping-out anything that did not conform to the pattern laid down by the ecclesiastical authorities. The one voice they heard spoke rather in the tones of the Roman emperor than in the accents of the Man of Galilee. The more we try to see things as they were, with the eyes of those who led the early reform movements, the more justifiable does their action appear to have been. The one thing necessary above all others at that time was reform, reform even at the cost of shattering the uniformity of the Church; a uniformity which had never been of the truly Christian pattern.

Of those who regard the Reformation as a crime and a blunder we shall not speak at the moment. We wish rather to consider the attitude of those who sympathize with the aims of the Reformers, and appreciate the values gained through the painful controversies of those bygone times. We are reminded by many leaders of religious thought that a movement has now set in in the opposite direction. Everywhere, in secular as well as in religious life, there are tendencies towards unity. We are learning more and more that the universe is a unity, and that all its parts are closely linked together. They form a cosmos, not a chaos. Every part is affected for good or ill by what takes place in every other part. Since the Second World War came to an end it has been emphasized in many ways that if one member of the family of nations suffers, the others suffer with it. It is therefore to the interest of all that the hungry nation shall be fed no matter how guilty it may have been.

This trend towards unity in the political thought of our time has its counterpart in the life of the Churches. Here also the emphasis is upon unity. It is counted a reproach that the one Church is divided up into so many denominations. It is urged that the time has come when these differences in ecclesiastical organization should be, if not entirely obliterated, at least merged in a larger unity. A divided Church can never, we are told, unify the nation or the world. Such changes should therefore be made as shall make it evident, even to the unthinking "man in the street", that the Church is one. If in certain details some variety may be allowed, in the major features of the organization there should be such likeness as shall catch the eye of every wayfarer. In particular there should be one form of Church government by a threefold ministry, such as has existed in a large part of the Church for many centuries. If for some time to come this is not practical politics, it should yet be regarded as the ideal towards which there should be continual approximation. One important section of the Church of England even goes so far as to look forward to the time when once again the whole Church shall have an earthly head and centre of authority at Rome.

It is impossible not to sympathize in a large measure with these aspirations after unity among Christian people. In many ways it is so obvious that all the followers of Jesus should be united on a number of central things; that they should have fellowship with each other, and co-operate in the work of evangelizing the world.

When we examine the present situation, however, and consider the various proposals which have been made to realize Christian unity, it seems clear to the present writer that many of them are based upon false assumptions: assumptions which cannot but be challenged by a very large number of devoted Christian people who love the Lord Jesus Christ in sincerity and truth, and who wish His Body, the Church, to be all that He meant it to be.

In the judgment of the present writer one of the most untenable assumptions made by the religious authorities of England and Scotland during the past three or four centuries has been that religious unity involves a very large measure of uniformity in beliefs and ceremonies. We are not now concerned with such a central belief as that Jesus Christ is the Son of God and the Saviour of the world. But rather with such a uniformity in beliefs and ceremonies as men have, at various times, sought to enforce by Acts of Parliament. The attempts made to achieve uniformity by coercive legislation, whether in England or Scotland, whether by Romanists, Anglicans or Presbyterians, must be counted among the greatest blunders and tragedies of religious life.

A justification for these attempts has often been found in the words of Jesus, when He prayed for those who should believe on Him: "that they may all be one; even as thou, Father, art in me, and I in thee, that they also may be in us: that the world may believe that thou didst send me" (John 17: 21). Another passage frequently cited in this connection is John 10: 16: "And other sheep I have, which are not of this fold: them also I must bring, and they shall hear my voice; and they shall become one flock, one shepherd." Here the Revised Version translation, now generally accepted, relieves the false emphasis which was conveyed by the Authorized Version rendering—"one fold, one shepherd." In this passage Jesus intends to convey the idea that all His disciples everywhere shall form one flock; He says nothing about them being penned in one fold.

When we allow that Jesus had in mind a most important kind of unity, a unity which will impress the world, it still remains to consider what kind of unity He desired and anticipated. There are, in fact, many kinds of unity, and the most obvious kind is by no means the most important. The most obvious kind of unity is a unity consisting in a single organization under a single control or form of government. In political and social life the most familiar illustration is that of a totalitarian State in which all sections of society are drilled and regimented to carry out the dictates of a single will.

But there is another kind of unity with which all observant minds are familiar. On the vastest scale there is the unity which finds expression in the totality of things which we call the universe. When we think of the universe we think of the aggregate of all created things, viewed as constituting a cosmos, one system or whole. Here we have a unity which embraces an infinite variety. Indeed, except to the profoundly philosophical mind, the variety is even more impressive than the unity. Though the common man also, if he reflects, must believe that the unity is there, the more immediately impressive fact is the diversity which coexists within it. The variety is so vast that many volumes would be required to give even the most elementary account of it. There are so many kinds of trees, flowers, animals and insects. There are many different races which speak a variety of languages. There are so many different climates and seasons, etc. So great is the variety that in any given species it would probably be impossible to discover any two individuals exactly alike. Among the human species we find the most bewildering variety of all. There are no two people exactly alike, it is confidently affirmed. Men and women differ in their mentality, experience, and outlook. In a word, they are individuals.

But despite the variety there is a unity which is profoundly impressive to the reflective mind. There is such a wonderful harmony and working together of parts in the material world that the scientist is able to foretell what will happen many centuries hence. This unity is of a richer, higher type than any unity which could be achieved by a fitting together of standardized parts. So far as we can infer from a study of the universe, that is, from a study of the works of God's own hands, God is as much concerned to preserve the diversity as He is to maintain the unity.

Let us apply this striking fact to the Church, which is composed of the members of Christ's body, and intended to form a unity.

In the early centuries it was thought that when Jesus

spoke of a unity which should exist among His disciples, He meant a unity of the obvious kind: one visible organization, with an earthly head, directing the working of all its parts. Every part must be in visible connection with every other part. One writ must run throughout the whole. There must be a large measure of uniformity, even in the very thoughts of men. There must be only one language used in worship, even among the most diverse peoples. Rites and ceremonies must everywhere be alike, or nearly so. Sanction for this grandiose conception was found in the words of Paul when he spoke of the Church as the "body of Christ" (Eph. 1: 22, Col. 1: 18, etc.). Misled by this metaphor the ecclesiastical authorities did not stop to consider in how many ways the Church must inevitably differ from the human body. The members of the body, for instance, the hands, feet, and eyes, have no separate wills of their own. They are but the instruments of the central will which controls the whole body of which they form a part. It is not so in human society. God Himself has endowed individuals with freedom of will— the most characteristic feature of the life of man. Men are not merely things; they are persons, possessing wills of their own. They have certain inalienable rights. And all we know of God as revealed in Jesus Christ shows that those rights are ever respected by Him. God has resolved, if we may so speak, never to coerce the wills of men. Though He desires obedience, it is a willing, not an enforced obedience that He desires.

A recognition of this difference between men and material things, between the human body and the mystic Body of Christ, would surely have gone far to avoid some of the most terrible chapters in human history. Under the influence of the metaphor—the Church is the Body of Christ—it was argued that the Church must have an earthly head, despite the plain, and oft-repeated, assertion of the New Testament that Jesus alone is the Head of the Church (Eph. 1: 22; 4: 15; 5: 23; Col. 1: 18; 2: 19). Again, under the influence of the metaphor, it was argued that as the members of the body yield prompt and unreflecting obedience to the head (or controlling will), so must the members of the Church yield unreflecting obedience to the pope, who stands in the place of Christ. Obedience, therefore, to the earthly head of the Church, or to the priest as representing him, must be the chief mark of the followers of Jesus. Such is still the conception of religious loyalty in the Roman Church. In this principle was found a sanction for all the pitiful and tragic persecutions of the Middle Ages. Any one who knows the story of the Inquisition is aware that not only was the attempt made to govern the words and deeds of men, but more particularly their very thoughts and emotions. Men must think only after a certain pattern, the pattern being laid down by certain ecclesiastical authorities, now known to have been among the most morally and spiritually imperfect men of their time.

One could write at great length about the tragic results which followed upon the acceptance by the leaders of the Church of a false and misleading conception of Christian unity. But let us go on to consider a unity of a far nobler and richer type which can be realized without violating the fundamental rights of man, and which is in perfect harmony with the teaching and example of Jesus.

In the course of the centuries Christendom has become divided into many different parts, all claiming to be true branches of the Church of Jesus: and some making still more exalted claims than this. There are the Roman, the Eastern or Orthodox Church, the Anglican, the Presbyterian, the Baptist, the Congregational, the Methodist, and many other Churches. It is a fact beyond dispute that in all these branches of the Church there are large numbers of Christian people who sincerely desire to be followers of Jesus, and in every way to help in the extension of His Kingdom. In many ways they differ from each other—in their traditions, their ideas of Church government, their preferences as to rites and ceremonies, and so on. But despite all these differences there is a fundamental unity which springs from their belief in God as revealed in Jesus and from their experience of the gracious ministries of the Holy Spirit. They have been saved by Jesus, and are devoted to Him and seek to do the things that please Him. "By their fruits ye shall know them", said Jesus. Tried by this test it is manifest that they are vitally connected with Him and are branches of the true vine. Being so related to Him they are of necessity related to each other, though they may not fully have realized their relationship. They are members of His Body, the Church, and they cannot therefore be unchurched by any human authority. To apply the terms "heretics" and "schismatics" to such people is an un-Christian act; that is, it is contrary to the example and teaching of Jesus. Jesus said: "He who is not against us is for us" (Mark 9: 40; cf. Luke 9: 50).

Here then we have a true Christian unity, a unity which is consistent with variety. The variety is not to be lamented, much less to be forcibly repressed. It is in harmony with the variety which is to be found in every part of the universe. It is in accord with the most fundamental facts of human nature. Its elimination would result in a loss of interest and vitality. And those who desire to preserve the variety have as much scriptural warrant for their action as those who seek to emphasize the unity.

The recognition of the value of variety of form and usage in the Church of Christ is one of the most enheartening signs of the times. In the suggestions or proposals for reunion recently put forward by the Archbishop of Canterbury, and which are now being considered by the various branches of the Church, it is frankly proposed that each branch of the Church should after reunion carry on its ministries very much as it did previously. No attempt should be made to merge the various constitutions of the Churches in order to secure organic reunion as that word is usually understood. To quote Dr. Fisher's words as reported: "But now you come into it (that is, the reunited Church) with the traditions which you have grown in the period of dislocation, with your own customs, your own methods and your own style of pulpit oratory. . . . Will all these things have to disappear in a reunited Church? I should say: Heaven forbid. Should the Free Churches lose all power of direction and identity with the past? Heaven forbid. I look forward to a time when the Church of England, having been reunited, the Methodists, the Congregationalists, the Baptists and the Presbyterians will, within the reunited Church, still function with an identity of their own, much as the present orders function within the Roman Catholic Church with an identity of their own. The time might come, if reunion came about, when church notices might specify Church of England (Methodist), Church of England (Congregationalist), and even Church of England (C. of E.)."

We cannot here enter upon any full discussion of the Archbishop's proposals, or the conditions by which they are hedged around. Their supreme merit, in the view of the present writer, is that they frankly recognize the value of those differences in Church life which have for centuries prevailed in the various branches of the Church, and that they formally repudiate the idea of uniformity which has been so long cherished both in the Roman and Anglican branches of the Church, and with such tragic effects. It remains, however, still to be seen whether the proposals yet go far enough in the recognition of what to Free Churchmen seem obvious and important facts.

The main object of the proposals, it is stated, is to establish "full communion" between the various branches of the now divided Church. Among other things this is said to involve the creation or development of a type of ministry which will be acceptable in all the Churches, so that there will be no bar to intercommunion in the fullest sense, and to exchange of pulpit ministries.

In passing, it may be said that this is a difficulty almost entirely peculiar to the Anglicans among the Protestant Churches. The majority of the Free Churches have long practised both intercommunion and exchange of pulpits. The Anglicans have remained rigidly exclusive. Only on very special occasions have Free Church ministers been allowed to preach in Anglican Churches, and still more infrequently have they been permitted to share in a service of Holy Communion. And members of the Free Churches, however noted for their piety and high Christian character and service, have been refused Holy Communion on the ground that they have never been episcopally confirmed.

In proposals for reunion previously put forward an attempt has been made to solve the problem by means of some form of "supplementary ordination". This means that the ministers or clergy of each branch of the Church will receive, by some form of ordination, from the duly accredited representatives of the other Churches, an extended commission to minister in these other Churches. The chief difficulty here is the diverse meanings attached to "ordination", particularly by the members of the Anglican Church. Most of the Free Churches practise some form of ordination. Ministers are solemnly set apart for their sacred task at a special service; sometimes, as in the case of the Methodists, with "the laying on of hands". Anglicans, however, attach a very special significance to this "laying on of hands" in ordination. It must be done

by a bishop; and, further, it is contended by a large
section, perhaps by a majority, of the Anglican clergy
that the bishop must be in the "apostolical succession".
This means that the bishop must have been ordained by
another bishop who forms a link in a chain of bishops
which can be traced back to the apostles. It is this conception of an episcopal apostolical succession, and of
a peculiar grace which, it is claimed, is conveyed thereby,
which has been, and still remains, the supreme bar to
reunion.

On the side of the Free Churches, scholars, second to
none in Christendom in their knowledge of New Testament
teaching and of the history of the early Church, have
joined with leading Anglican scholars in pointing out
strong objections to this theory. It has been made clear
that there are many missing links in the supposed series
of bishops. Moreover, many of the bishops through whom
the divine grace is said to have flowed have been entirely
unworthy of such a high function. There is no evidence
of the intention of Jesus to maintain the government of
His Church in this way. Neither is there any evidence that
the grace which is supposed to have been conveyed in
this way has ever operated to produce a nobler type of
Christian living than that which is found in other Churches
without episcopal succession. The clergy episcopally
ordained have not on the average been freer from weakness
and scandal than the ministers of the other Churches.
In a word, most Free Church ministers and members are
profoundly convinced that Dr. Inge is entirely justified in
speaking of Apostolical Succession as a "fantastic and
unhistorical theory" (*Protestantism*, p. 57), a view which is
supported by Dr. T. M. Lindsay, who calls it a "gigantic
figment" (*The Church and the Ministry in the Early
Centuries*, p. 224). Moreover episcopacy has not operated
to secure the unity of the Church, since all splits from the

parent stem have been splits from episcopally-governed Churches. Prelatical episcopacy, which prevailed so long a time, was and is so offensive to the Christian sense that scarcely any one remains to do it reverence.

One of the most notable of the suggestions made by Dr. Fisher is that the Free Churches should qualify, or prepare the way, for entering into such a reunited Church as has been indicated above by "taking Episcopacy into their system", and without accepting any "theories" about Episcopacy. There is, however, a far deeper depth of meaning in this simple suggestion than appears upon the surface. It is well known to all students of the subject that it is not Episcopacy which is here in question, but rather a particular type of Episcopacy. The Free Churches have a perfect right to reply to the suggestion by saying: We already possess Episcopacy of the New Testament and primitive type. As Andrew Melville long ago contended, the New Testament bishops were simply overseers or superintendents or pastors of individual churches. And practically all the larger Free Churches have bishops in this primitive sense. They have men duly appointed to oversee the life of a church or group of churches, and who give all their time to this work. Moreover, each church possesses a group of stewards, deacons, or elders (*presbuteroi*) who assist the minister in his duties, and who correspond to the group of elders which existed in each church in the apostolic days. It is not therefore to score a mere debating point to say that the Free Churches have no objection to Episcopacy of the New Testament type. They already possess it, and have possessed it from the beginning.

We shall not here attempt to trace the causes which led to the extension of a bishop's power and authority until he became the ecclesiastical ruler of a large area or diocese. This has often been done, and the literature upon the subject is immense. Many of the causes were perfectly natural and reasonable. Some of the Free Churches have already moved in the same direction. The Methodist superintendent of a large Circuit, comprising twenty to forty churches, corresponds very closely to a bishop at one stage in the development of the office. The Chairman of a Methodist District corresponds equally closely to a further stage, and it is well known that a number of Methodist ministers have for a long time favoured the use of the name bishop rather than Chairman of a District. Objections to this change of title will probably be readily appreciated by those who have studied the previous pages. In America, however, Methodism has from its early days been developed on an episcopal basis. The other Free Churches also have moved in the same direction in that they have appointed Moderators of districts or areas, which include many churches. It is clear therefore that a number of Free Churches have both a primitive Episcopacy and an Episcopacy of a more extended type within their own borders.

What then is meant by the Archbishop's phrase when he formally invites Nonconformity to "take Episcopacy into its system"? An official answer will only be forthcoming when the results of the present discussions have been made known. In the meantime it may be said that the phrase will have different meanings according to the section of the Church to which a person belongs. Even in the Anglican Church the phrase will be variously understood. It is quite true that we have the assurance of Anglican dignitaries, for example, the Bishop of Lichfield (*British Weekly*, January 16, 1947), that the Nonconformist Churches "are not asked to accept 'theories' about Episcopacy which may be held by some Anglicans but which find no place in our Anglican formularies, and which the Anglican Church has no right (and for the most part no desire) to insist on in approaches to questions of communion or reunion with other Churches."

But, it may be asked, is not a theory implied in the call made to the Free Churches, which already have the scriptural type of Episcopacy, to take Episcopacy into their system? Surely those who issue this call must be convinced that the Episcopacy which the Free Churches lack is of a particular importance, and of such spiritual value that it is indispensable to the life of the Church, if it is to fulfil its mission in the world.

Students of the subject are well aware that two main views are held as to the virtue of Episcopacy. On the one hand are those who assert that Episcopacy belongs to the well-being (*bene esse*) of the Church. They hold that Episcopacy has proved its value in the course of the history of the Church. Of all systems of Church government which have been evolved it best secures the unity of the Church, and the most effective administration and pastoral oversight. This is a view which may be held with conviction, even by those who reject the idea that Episcopacy was a special institution established by Jesus or by His apostles, and that it was intended to be the one and only form of Church government everywhere and throughout the ages. As we have seen, this view was rejected by the Reformers, who strongly affirmed that Episcopacy, in the form in which it existed in their day, was a false development. It was, they asserted, not only without scriptural authority; it was also ineffective in the maintenance of discipline, and in the promotion of real spiritual progress of Christ's Kingdom. It was concerned with the form rather than with the substance of Christianity, and its policy of enforced uniformity was a denial of the liberty of a Christian man, and a hindrance to the free operations of the Holy Spirit.

Changes have, however, taken place in the Episcopal

Church since that time, and it remains a matter for further consideration and free discussion as to whether Episcopacy on the present model, or with some further modifications, may not be, all things considered, the best form of Church government. It needs to be said, however, that those who take the opposite view are not to be regarded as heretics and schismatics who obstinately obstruct a God-inspired movement towards unity. There are those who are profoundly convinced that the reform movements, from the time of Wycliffe onwards, were God-inspired, as tested by all the words that Jesus ever spoke, and by all the teaching of the apostles. There are also those who sincerely maintain that the unity which Jesus intended is of quite another kind than that which has found so many expressions in Anglican circles. It is not a formal unity, such as can be expressed in the government of a Church by bishops, priests and deacons. It is a spiritual unity which can and should exist among all those who love the same Lord and Saviour, and seek to carry on His work. Other things are of small concern as compared with this. If we have regard to God's method of working in every other part of His universe it would seem that variety in Church government is far more likely to be His purpose than any uniformity that has yet been proposed. We do well to give more heed to the words of the apostle: "Now there are diversities of gifts, but the same Spirit. And there are diversities of ministrations, and the same Lord. And there are diversities of workings, but the same God, who worketh all things in all" (1 Cor. 12: 4 f.).

On the other hand, there are those who take the view that Episcopacy, in its present form, does not belong merely to the well-being of the Church but to its very existence (the *esse*). Jesus, it is claimed, has ordained that His Church shall be governed in this precise way. When it is pointed out that there is no clear evidence of

Christ's intention in this respect, reference is made to the fact that we are told that Jesus, after His resurrection, spent forty days with His disciples, and instructed them in the things pertaining to the Kingdom (Acts 1: 3). It is reasonable, it is urged, to suppose that the instructions which were given at this time would embrace such an important matter as the best mode of carrying on His work.

One can scarcely conceive, however, of a slenderer basis for any important doctrine than the alleged unreported sayings of our Lord. There is, in fact, no evidence that Jesus ever ordained that His Church should have any particular form of government, whether Episcopal or Presbyterian. There is much evidence that the earliest form was Presbyterian; that is, government of individual Churches by a council of elders. Only later did one of the presbyters emerge as a president of the council, and was accorded the title of bishop or overseer.

More than sixty years ago Dr. Edwin Hatch, in his Bampton Lectures, *The Organization of the Early Christian Churches* (1882), carefully traced out the various factors which led to the supremacy of the bishop. The same work has been done many times since by both Anglican and Free Church scholars. The evidence seems clearly to show that Episcopacy, as it now exists, was not a special institution, whether by Jesus or His apostles. It developed from sub-apostolic days onwards in response to particular factors in its environment. It is of course possible to argue that everything in those days was shaped according to the leading of the Holy Spirit. But, on the other hand, there is very much ground for the contention of the Reformers that many pagan elements entered into the life of the early Church, particularly from the time of Constantine onwards; that at that time the stream of Church life was deflected from its course; and that the reform movements were born of the Holy Spirit and were absolutely essential to enable the Church to recover its vitality, and to "do the first works".

The question whether the Free Churches, after the lapse of so many years, and after being so manifestly owned and blessed by God, and producing so many fruits for the Kingdom of Jesus, and after inaugurating so many great movements for the salvation of men and the world, should now accept the present form of Episcopacy, in addition to that which they already possess, is a matter for careful consideration, and, it may be, for controversy. It is useless and foolish to pretend that the Anglican and Free Churches are at one in a number of important matters. To mention only one matter (and there are several others), the Anglo-Catholic and the evangelical conceptions of the ministry are poles apart. And even if the Free Churches were to accept the suggestion of the Archbishop it is difficult to see that the gulf would be in any sense bridged, or that there would be "full communion" between them.

It is well known that the aim of many Anglo-Catholics is to march Romewards, and to submit to the Papacy. Anglo-Catholic literature leaves no doubt upon this point. Most Free Churchmen are convinced that to move any nearer towards that goal would be wholly wrong. It would be to tread again a false way which would be attended by disastrous consequences. In the words of a former evangelical bishop of the Church of England: "It is loyalty to Christ that makes this (Roman and Anglo-Catholic) system, however successful it may claim to be in producing its own type of sanctity, impossible for the Protestant who has known the power of the Spirit in his soul, and tested the reality in daily life" (Bishop E. A. Knox, *The Tractarian Movement*, p. 374). Is it better that the controversy, which is bound to come if we are faithful to the Gospel, should be carried on inside the reunited Church, or that the Free

Churches should retain their present freedom, whilst co-operating in all possible ways with Christians belonging to every branch of the Church?

Even now one form of union is both possible and desirable. Though the Archbishop has made it clear that he does not favour Federal Union, the facts as outlined above seem to point to Federal Union as the only practical kind of union under the conditions which exist to-day. Federal Union is real union, as we see it in existence in the U.S.A., Switzerland, and elsewhere. This type of union would allow for the maintenance of that variety of life and work which is of the first importance, and which is favoured by the Archbishop. Such a union could be inaugurated, not by ordination, whether supplementary or other, which would create misunderstanding and manifold difficulties for large numbers of people, but by a Solemn Declaration in an Assembly representative of all branches of the Christian Church in this country. This Federal Union should allow for intercommunion between all the duly accredited members of the several Churches, and for such an exchange of pulpits as the local clergy and ministers may feel to be desirable. Thus the members of the Churches could "grow together" into the unity of the life of Christ, as the Archbishop suggests.

Dr. W. R. Inge, formerly Dean of St. Paul's Cathedral, has written wise words upon the subject of reunion, which members of all Churches will do well to ponder. In reviewing the Archbishop of York's volume, *The Claims of the Church of England*, he says: "The idea of a corporate reunion of Christendom has taken a strong hold on the Anglican clergy. Many of them think it a scandal that Christendom should be divided into national or denominational Churches. In reality a Universal Church is as impossible as a universal empire, and there is nothing scandalous about independent Churches, but only about the temper of exclusiveness and the spirit of hatred. Our Lord wished His disciples to be 'one flock, with one Shepherd'. He never said that they must be penned in one fold. In spite of this, foolish overtures have been made to Rome: they have been rejected with inevitable and humiliating snubs." And again, he says: "The unity of the spirit in the bond of peace is the only reunion that matters, and Christendom has never been divided in the chambers where good men and women pray."[1]

[1] *The British Weekly*, June 19, 1947.

BOOKS FOR FURTHER READING

Part One

Addison, A. G., *The Romantic Story of the Mayflower Pilgrims* (1911).

Arber, E., *The Story of the Pilgrim Fathers 1606–1623* (1897).

Bradford, W., *History of the Plymouth Plantation* (1856).

Briggs, M. S., *Homes of the Pilgrim Fathers in England and America* (1900).

Browne, R., *Treatise of Reformation without Tarrying for Anie*, ed. Crippen (1903).

Brown, J., *The Pilgrim Fathers of New England* (1920).

Carlyle, T., *Letters and Speeches of Oliver Cromwell* (1904).

Clarke, H. W., *History of the English Nonconformity: From Wyclif to the Close of the Nineteenth Century*, 2 vols. (1911–13).

Dexter, H. M., and Dexter, M., *The England and the Holland of the Pilgrims* (1906).

Foxe, J., *The Book of Martyrs.*

—— *Acts and Monuments.*

Gardiner, S. R., *The First Two Stuarts and the Puritan Revolution, 1603–1660*, new ed. (1876).

Green, J. R., *Short History of the English People*, Ch. VIII (1874).

Henson, H. H., *Puritanism in England* (1912).

Horne, C. S., *A Popular History of the Free Churches* (1903).

Hume, D., *A History of England*, Books IV and V (1875).

Knappen, M. M., *Tudor Puritanism* (1939).

Lally, A. V., *The Story of the Pilgrim Fathers.*

Mackenall, A., *Homes and Haunts of the Pilgrim Fathers* (1899).

Marsden, J. B., *History of the Early Puritans* (1850).

—— *History of the Later Puritans* (1852).

Masefield, J., *Chronicles of the Pilgrim Fathers*, Everyman ed. (1910).

Neal, D., *History of the Puritans (1732–1738)*, 4 vols.

Powicke, F. J., *Henry Barrowe, Separatist (1593–1622)* (1900).

Robinson, J., *A Justification of Separation from the Church of England* (1639).

Selbie, W. B., *Nonconformity, Its Origin and Progress* (1912).

Skeats, H. S., and Miall, C. S., *History of the Free Churches of England* (1891).

Strype, *Lives of the Archbishops (Parker, Grindal, Whitgift)* (1711–18).

—— *Annals of the Reformation*, 4 vols. new ed. (1824).

—— *Ecclesiastical Memorials*, 3 vols. (1822).

Tayler, J. J., *A Retrospect of Religious Life in England* (1853).

Tullock, J., *English Puritanism and Its Leaders* (1861).

Usher, R. G., *The Pilgrims and Their History* (1918).

Wakeman, H. O., *The Church and the Puritans*, 6th ed. (1902).

Winslow, E., *A Brief Narration* (1646).

Winthrop, J., *History of New England, 1630–1649*, ed. by James Savage, 2 vols., Boston (1853).

Wood, H. G., *Venturers for the Kingdom* (1920).

Part Two

Barr, J., *The Scottish Covenanters* (1946).

Beckett, W. H., *The English Reformation* (1890).

Beet, W. E., *A Thousand Years of Papal History* (1916).

—— *The Rise of the Papacy* (1910).

Beveridge, J., *The Covenanters* (1905).

Burnet, Bishop, *History of His Own Times*, Everyman ed. (1723).

Defoe, Daniel, *Memoirs of the Scottish Church* (1717).

Fleming, D. Hay, *The Reformation in Scotland* (1910).

Hallam, H., *Constitutional History*, Vol. I.

Haller, W., *The Rise of Puritanism* (1938).

Hewison, J. King, *The Covenanters*, 2 vols. (1908).

Knox, J., *Works*, ed. Laing. Vol. I. (1846).

Lindsay, T. M., *History of the Reformation*, Vol. II. (1907).

Macewen, A. R., *A History of the Church in Scotland*, 2 vols. (1913-18).

Books for Further Reading

Mitchell, A. F., *The Scottish Reformation* (1900).

Smellie, A., *Men of the Covenants* (1903).

Taylor, W. M., *The Scottish Pulpit* (1887).

Trevelyan, G. M., *England in the Age of Wycliffe* (1904).

Watt, Hugh, *Recalling the Scottish Covenants* (1946).

Woodrow, R., *The History of the Sufferings of the Church of Scotland*, Vol. I. (1829).

Workman, H. B., *John Wycliffe: A Study of the English Medieval Church*, 2 vols. (1926).

Index

Index